T0365641

The Last of the East Side Kids

The LAST of the EAST SIDE KIDS
Boys Don't Tell

Joseph Patrick Kenney

ARCHWAY
PUBLISHING

Archway Publishing books may be ordered through booksellers or by contacting:

Archway Publishing
1663 Liberty Drive
Bloomington, IN 47403
www.archwaypublishing.com
1 (888) 242-5904

ISBN: 978-1-4808-1759-3 (sc)
ISBN: 978-1-4808-1760-9 (e)

Library of Congress Control Number: 2015906072

Print information available on the last page.

Archway Publishing rev. date: 07/15/2015

The Last Of The East Side Kids
Boys Don't Tell

The narrative recollections of a shattered child,
and his transformation into adulthood.

Some memories are so vivid, it's as though they happened yesterday. Lucid in detail as if I could reach out touch them. And though It makes me smile to reminisce about some things, other instances stand out as nightmares. Terrible events that I experienced as a small boy and the effects they had on my psyche.

Being four years old when these events began to unfold, my world was a small place, and I was the focul point. I hadn't yet developed a history to compare against the norm. So at the time in my life when they first began, I thought these atrocities happened only to me. But by the time I reached late adolescence, I found to be true, that these things happened to an infinite number of other children, many experiencing much worse than than what I had. In fact it happened to my other siblings as well, every one of them. Though most would not admit to it openly.

I always had a feeling of being blind-sided, bushwhacked, the rug being pulled out from under me. Every time a traumatic event happened there would be a period of time in between where I would let my guard down and then, "Bang!" My whole fucking world would be turned upside down. But it wasn't always that way. There were many other times in my childhood where I felt completely content and at peace.

I

Summer days spent painlessly,
a child to be, a child so fair.
Not hesitant of love or life,
just playing games without a care.

Nursery rhymes and pleasant dreams,
a mothers love to share a kiss.
A fathers arms that hold secure,
this little boy I've come to miss.

What constitutes adulthood? What is it that molds us into the person we grow up to become? Some say we are a product of our environment. Some say our parents are the ones that mold us, either to succeed or fail. While others attribute it to any number of traumatic events both physical and or emotional that are perpetrated against us. I myself believe education is paramount in differentiating these things, either academically or through self-reflection. But they are things that come over time.

As a child not able to verbalize situations and or experiences, I have finally found the words to associate the many transgressions in my life. Not as a root cause of blame, but as an understanding that the past needs to be laid to rest, with forgiveness as a (stepping stone).

Abuse whether sexual, physical, or psychological is cause for alarm, even if it is brought to the forefront immediately. But if a child has to hold on to these things secretively, it becomes too heavy a cross to bear.

Antisocial behavior is one way to help deal with certain cases of child neglect, and I believe that to be true in my case. And though I have been afflicted by many of the above difficulties, it serves no purpose to beat the drum of my past's acrimony. So in revealing to you my story: all I would hope is that it might advocate healing.

Some people upon reading my memoir might say that I have been too profane in my narratives, but I felt it had to be written that way in order to properly denigrate the people that harmed me, and to express it in a vernacular that refuses sugar coating. I hope not to offend anyone, but if I do; my sincere apologies.

CONTENTS

CHAPTER ONE

In Retrospect of the Child

As a little boy I used to watch this television program called the *East Side Kids,* AKA *The Bowery Boys* and remember identifying and feeling a connection with its characters.

There was Slip Mahoney, the tough guy, the one you knew couldn't be pushed around or taken advantage of. Horace Debussey Jones, better known as Satch, the loveable buffoon that always bore the brunt of the joke, but didn't let it bother him. And then there was Bobby Jordan, intelligent, sensitive and suspicious of life. Bobby had a dark troubling side that always kept him at arm's length of the people he encountered. Slip and Sach represented the fellowship I always sought, but Bobby Jordan was who I most identified with, secretive of my inner workings and the anomalies of my early childhood.

I would think: how could I have identified with the other shows of my time, *Father Knows Best, Leave it to Beaver* and *The Patty Duke Show* etc. You know, the ones that had the understanding and successful parents that always seemed to be around and in a good mood. Always there with a kind perceptive word. It set the bar pretty high from where I came from. Shit! We were piss - poor, and my parents were rarely around, I surely was an East Side Kid.

I was born Joseph Patrick Kenney, son to Maggie and James Kenney, at New York Hospital in the Borough of Manhattan, New York City, on April 14th 1951. In my story I will sometimes be addressing my Father and Mother as Maggie and James, it allows me emotional seperation.

For a period of my young life I lived in an apartment on 46th Street between 1st and 2nd Avenues in a five-story walk up. It was a two- bedroom railroad apartment that held a family of five by the time I rolled around. This was long before it became a posh area.

There was a mixture of tenements and commercial buildings with a dash of exclusivity. Landmarks such as ***the United Nations*** building and ***Tudor City*** were just down the block and around the corner. Just west was ***Grand Central Station*** and the mother of all New York hotels ***The Waldorf Astoria***. Some of these became personal havens for a boy of six, a baby that truly had no one looking after him.

I played games like ***Kick The Can, Stoop*** Ball and ***I Declare War, there was Stickball, Red Light Green light, Tag*** and ***Skelzies.*** I would glide around the block on a scooter made from an old pair of roller skates, a two by four and a milk crate. I'd go sliding down the coal chutes of the tenements that saturated the area, and come up into the brightly lit street, blackened with soot, but none the worse.

TV Shows **like** ***the Mickey Mouse Club, Lassie*** and ***Superman, The Lone Ranger, The ThreeStooges and Abbot and Costello, Dennis the Menace*** and ***Rin Tin Tin***, and there were dozens more. ***The Million-Dollar Movie,*** which aired my three favorite ape flicks over and over. ***King Kong, Mighty Joe*** Young and ***Son of Kong***. ***There was Peter Pan with Mary Martin***, the many ***Shirley Temple movies*** and of course the all time family classic, ***The Wizard of OZ*** with Judy Garland.

For a meager ten cents a year a kid could join the ***Kips Bay Boys Club,*** a haven for all the boys in the neighborhood to hang out at. We were issued membership cards that were made of a material that resembled slate, and depending on your age there was a certain color and moniker attached with each card. Six and seven year olds were called tadpoles, and the color of the card issued to them was black with white lettering indicating their name and date of birth.

There was a full sized swimming pool located in the basement and everyone including the lifeguard swam naked. But first you had to take a shower. All I really ever did was run under the nozzle to wet my hair so it would look as if I showered. Then I'd run in to the pool area and dive into the water before the lifeguard could check me out. I could swim forever back then. I'd be in the pool until my skin began pruning and my eyes became so red I couldn't see clearly from the chlorine in the water. Though it never bothered me swimming naked, I connot to this day understand the reasoning behind having us swimming without anything on.

On the main floor was the front desk where you would leave your card when checking out a **board game**, **Knock Hockey** or **Ping Pong** equipment. A huge auditorium was just across from the front desk. It's where you would go to play your games. There was also a large stage at the rear of the auditoruim, a venue used for two things that I remember. A: For the movies on Saturday afternoons and B: The occasional neighborhood dance. Which was the only time females were allowed in the club.

Every Saturday afternoon a large screen would be lowered to play weekly serials like **Flash Gordon** or **Rocket Man,** which were two of my favorites. We'd also be shown an assortment of our favorite cartoons.

On the second floor was a Ceramics Shop where one could make things, like **Animals**, **Cars** and **Space Ships** from plaster molds. You could also work freestyle withj clay making **Ashtrays, Vases** etc.

Arts and Crafts was next to the Ceramics Shop, where you could draw with **Crayons** or **Chalk**. You could also make **Lanyards, Pot Holders** and other hands on stuff. A Billiard Room was just across the hall. It was where the older boys from the club would congregate.

On the roof there was a full sized **Basketball Court**, and **Skelzie**

Squares painted on the ground. There was a small gym where you learned how to *Box* or *Wrestle*. Kids sixteen and older were appointed as counselors supervising the activities. And being from the neighborhood everyone knew each other.

Camp Valhalla, as it was called was *an* affiliate of *Kips*. It sponsored the kids from the neighborhood so that they had a place to go to escape the oppressive summer heat of the city. Your family paid what your family could afford, which in my case was the dime I used to join the club.

I remember my first year going to camp and how I cried and begged my Mother not to send me. And the final day at camp where they had to send out a search party to find me because I didn't want to go home.

And when leaving for camp with a suitcase filled with clothes, how it was hard to find socks for my feet the day I was going home. I'd only have the clothes on my back, which probably belonged to someone else.

As best as I can remember there were two four-week sessions, and I went to both. The camp had of course *a Swimming Pool,* an *Arts and Crafts Center*, and daily hikes of all sorts. *BB Guns* and *Archery, Softball*, *Volleyball, Field Hockey* and *Boxing. Camp Fire Cook Outs* in front of the cabins we slept in, where we roasted hot dogs and marshmallows and listened to scary stories the counselors would tell.

The cabins we slept in were named after different *American Indian Tribes*. It was a theme that resonated throughout. We had to make our beds each morning and sweep the cabin floor. We picked up trash and raked around the cabin and it would be inspected first by our counselor, and then by any assistant camp supervisor The final week of each camp semester they would hold a sort of Olympics. It would pit one half the camp against the other in every type of game or activity mentioned above and more.

We would have to come up with a name for our team and make

up a cheer. For the cheer competition one team would be on one side of the football field one team on the other. The cheers were judged two ways, the content of the cheer and the volume. A team song would be composed and sung after dinner in the mess hall. The team that earned the most points received a trophy for each boy. It wasn't a very good trophy, but you were just as proud as any Olympian.

On the final Saturday, after dinner all of us kids would gather in front of our cabins. Then we would march single line through a trail in the woods, to an opening where an Indian Village was constructed. Once there, we would sit around the edge and have a story told about the different Indian Tribes. A genuine tepee sat along the back edge of the village. Some of the older boys would be dressed in loincloths that had tribal markings on them. They had paint on their faces and bodies and feathers in their hair. And when the campfire was lit they would dance around the fire and chant. We were taught to respect the American Indian.

When the ceremony was over, awards would be handed out to campers that showed the most improvement in areas like sportsmanship, participation, team spirit and more. I could probably write a dozen more chapters on my camp experiences, but I need to move on. Who had it better than me in those days? No one!

Everyone our family knew went to parochial school at Saint Agnes, right around the corner from Grand Central Terminal. They would shut the block down between 3rd and Lexington Avenue for lunch, and all the kids would play in the street. The nuns looking like penguins, hovered around, waiting for some venial sin to be committed so they could pounce and yank an ear or pinch an arm, even slap a face on occasion. But it was all done in the spirit of the Lord. Spare the rod and spoil the child was the spiritual malady of my particular devout persuasion. It's no wonder I started to develop an antipathy towards my religion.

I remember one instance early on when I might have been acting a little too rambunctious and Sister came over grabbed me by the ear so hard I thought it would pop off. She then threw me under her desk, and as I protested, I was given a swift kick to shut me up. Love and tolerance did not abound in this particular environment. My Catechism lessons never warned me of such transgressions.

Most people from the neighborhood attended Holy Family Church on 47th Street between 1st and 2nd Ave. The older boys playing **Stickball** used it as a pit stop for a gulp of Holy Water on a hot summer day. The church would pass out envelopes to bring home, for placing the weekly endowment, and we were assured that the priest would be looking for them after Sunday Mass. I think it was a bluff because I would open the envelope my Mom gave me and take that dime for myself. And as the donation basket went around, I would pretend to put the envelope in. I figured that with all the people at church giving money, God wouldn't miss me, or my stinking dime. I didn't consider it stealing at all. It was just going to a higher cause, the neighborhood candy store. "And didn't I always share." The rationalization of a six-year old brain that always seemed to get me into trouble."

I wouldn't have gotten caught either if my sister Katelyn hadn't told on me. Then came the spanking and being sent to bed. I never remembered seeing my Mother and Father attending church, unless there was a wedding at the hall directly across the way. My older Sisters Grace and Erin blew it off, as did my Brother Liam. So it would be just Katelyn and myself representing the family. Wasn't it only natural that we didn't want to go either?

When I was five I'd be schlepped around by my sisters and their friends, and go down to the pier behind the UN to watch the older boys swimming in the East River. I would get bored easily and my eyes would stray towards the action just behind me, the mecca of world politics, **The United Nation Headquarters**. I thought to myself, "When I get old enough, (Six) I'm going to make my way over there to see what's going on."

I always had a penchant for adventure, and was unafraid to make my way around alone. And soon I would find myself playing at the

U.N. for hours, unsupervised. It was just down the block and across 1st Ave. so it was easily accessible. I had so much fun exploring its vast venues and would always be investigating different areas of the building. And as far back as I can remember it became one of my favorite places to play.

First thing I would do was to get an adult to help me cross 1st Avenue. Then I would walk up the concrete steps and on to this huge plaza that stretched from 1st Avenue to the East River Drive, and must have been at least half a football field wide. There were always lots of people congregating and milling about. You could sit on the concrete benches strewn about the square and stare out across the East River to Long Island City, and see the large Coca Cola sign that sat perched high above one of the factories in that solely industrial area.

In the middle of the river was Roosevelt Island, a prefecture all in itself. The 59th Street and Tri- Borough bridges stood to the north, while the Brooklyn and Manhattan Bridges were to the south. It was a majestic view, breathtaking to a six year old. The East river with its swirling current and the boats traveling north and south quieted my thoughts. I felt internaly peaceful.

To the left of the plaza as you entered there was this very huge lawn. As big as anything I could have imagined. Perfectly manicured, it looked like one enormous green rug. Gargantuan statues (to me at the time) sat evenly positioned upon the grass and I would jump down and run back and forth from one end of the lawn to the other. On occasion I would climb upon one of these monolithic sculptures and pretend that I was some sort of protagonist cowboy returning from the great Indian wars. That is until the guards would come and shoo me away. And then there were times when I would enter the building itself.

I remember the first time I walked through one of the huge brass doors. The only way I might explain it was that it mesmerized me by its enormity. It might be same feeling a child today might get seeing a theme park for the first time, "It was magical".

As I entered, I first noticed that there was marble everywhere. A great winding stairway traveled up to the heavens. Massive pillars hid pathways going in every direction, each to a new adventure, and it was mine to survey as I pleased.

The General Assembly area, where I could sit upon soft plush chairs that had headphones attached to the arms. And as I sank deep into the lavish seat, I would pretend to be involved in what was transpiring on the assembly floor, where ambassadors from other countries would be discussing world policies.

There was the chapel, a place of solitude, and an area of eerie silence. It was amazing to me, thinking I was actually meditating, (Who knew?)

I'd sit by myself and let the quietness envelope me. I would stay still for long periods of time and daydream the thoughts of a little boy.

But my favorite space was at the downstairs mezzanine, where the souvenir shop was located. I would play with everything as if it was my very own private toy store. The amazing thing was, I was oblivious to every adult around me. It was great! The resources around me were there for a very happy upbringing. So what the hell happened?

It's kind of poignant that someone who at the time had four sisters, one brother and another sister on the way, felt so lonely. I always seemed to be by myself, dealing with life in my own carefree way. "It was what it was," I lived in a different time back then. I'm sorry that it sounds so cliché, but it was a fact of my being, and thus made me a target for the abusers that were lurking in and around my life. The ones never discussed at the dinner table, or at school.

Double messages ran rampant in my family, always confusing me. It was a convenience for dysfunctional parents. I remember being told, "do not talk to strangers", but if needed you may ask an adult to help you to cross the street. So any adult became a non-stranger to me, and I'd put my trust in them. Fighting was a bad thing, but it was OK to use a stick if a bigger kid was picking on you. Expressions like: What the hell are you crying for? "I'll give you something to cry for". I wouldn't even get to respond. A whack on the ass was appropriate for a child that was feeling bad, sad or just plain cranky. So subliminal became my teachings it's no wonder I've always doubted myself. And it was not just my parent's, it was also deeply rooted in my religious teachings.

The tenets they fed me spoke of a God that loved me, but that I would burn in Hell if I committed a sin, or at the very least remain in Purgatory. I never could understand the Purgatory thing. I think it's like waiting for a bus that will never come. But the idea of meeting the devil and burning in hell forever frightened the crap out of me, I wanted no part of that. Later on I was to be physicaly brutalized and and sexually molested for the third time in my young life by some of these religious zealots.

The earliest recollections of my parents might seem distorted to someone not raised in such a chaotic environment, but to me it was my reality. Dad was a Bowery drinker, an alcoholic of the hopeless kind. He was shunned by his own children for the fear of the shame it brought upon them. I myself only knew that he was my Father, and I loved him unconditionally.

I remember my Dad lifting me up in the air with his feet, on the Castro sofa my parents slept on. I would soar through the air as he pushed me up towards the ceiling, and he'd catch me in his hands as I fell back down towards the earth. Laughing uncontrollably, I'd beg him to do it again and again. Cuddling between my Father and my Mother I felt totaly secure and loved.

My first haircut, sitting on a board that crossed the arms of the Barber's chair, facing a wall to wall mirror, I saw Jim looking proudly in my direction. A dousing of hair tonic, a crisp part on the side, and the perfect mound the barber fashioned above my brow, framed the angelic face that people adored. And I always used it to my advantage.

Like when going to the Murray Hill Bar where Jim and Maggie could be frequently found. And how I would get potato chips, soda and even receive a few nickels from some of the other patrons of that extraordinary establishment.

I loved the smell of the sawdust and the stale beer emanating throughout the bar, the juke box playing songs that people would sing along to many times over, sometiomes slurring or even completely forgetting the words. And the shuffleboard table I loved so much, its top lacquered to a glossy sheen and sprinkled thoroughly with fresh sawdust. I was barely able to reach it on my tippy toes, but it was great fun. I knew the gist of the game, but was unable to play correctly due to my height. At times a fight might break out, or a drunken spouse might slap around his wife. But besides these rare anomalies, I loved the overall friendly atmosphere that emanated from that place.

I loved Easter

Colored eggs and ***Jellybeans***, ***Marshmallow Chicks*** (now called Peeps) and chocolate rabbits would be placed into a wicker basket onto a bed of green plastic grass. ***Solid Chocolate Crosses*** were given to the older children that became embarrassed to receive baskets, but still wanted candy. I remember the times when Jim was around, the ones before he hit skid row.

He would take me shopping down on Delancey Street (inappropriately nicknamed Jew Town) for new clothes to wear. A suit and fedora were the preferred look of the day. God forbid you didn't have your family dressed up for Easter. It didn't matter that most of the year we wore the tattered clothes of an older sibling, or worse, hand me downs from another family, the teasing from the other kids would be brutal.

Spiffed up, you went to church to show off the haberdashery your parents procured for you, and maybe hear the message of Jesus sacrificing his life for humanity, rising from the dead and ascending into heaven. I believe that my generation was the one that began the commercialization of Easter. And as the years went by my association with the Catholic Church abated and my cynicism of religion took hold.

I knew little of my Fathers family other than my Uncle Henny his older brother, who was a severe alcoholic and was always in and out of jail. There was a story I heard where he actually pled guilty to manslaughter, so that my Father didn't have to go to prison for a guy Jim accidently killed during a bar brawl. His reasoning was two fold. The first one being that Jim was his younger brother and he had to protect him. The other reason was that he had no children, whereas my Father had three mouths to feed. How do you pay back that kind of selflessness?

Then there was my Uncle Freddy, who was so embarrassed of his brothers that he never came around. He shielded his family from the escapades of his loser, boozer clan. I did not know my Father's parents, his mother had passed on long before I was born and his dad was some sort of recluse, never talked about. On Maggies's side was my Aunt Gloria her half sister, chubby and jovial with flaming red hair, she was always laughing and in a great mood. Unlike my Mother who was an enigma, a loving and protecting parent one moment, a violent miscreant the next;

I remember being at the local park with her and playing this game called Itsy Bitsy Spider and feeling such closeness. It was a maternal bond of love that attracted me to her. I would be at total peace, and I loved her more than anything. Another time I clearly remember was the day I was dropped on my head by my sister Katelyn. I split my head open and needed stitches. Frightened and cryng hysterically, who was there to soothe me, "My Savior, My Mom".

Another instance, when I again cut my head open, and where stitches would once again be needed. I thought back to my last experience and how it had been such a nightmare. I became hysterical. Maggie seeing how I was behaving actually took care of it herself by butterflying the wound. She could be like the lioness protecting her cub. And if she thought I was in harm's way, she would be on the attack, no matter the foe. She was my Joan of Arc and my Florence Nightingale all in one.

On the other hand, there was the time when I was five or six and one of my Mothers friend's had been sleeping over. You have to try to understand that I was an inquisitive child, not unlike any other. I noticed her friend's pocketbook lying around and became curious. So while Maggie and her friend were still asleep, I nosily went through it and spotted a wallet. I opened the wallet and saw some paper money. There were a few one - dollar bills and a five just sitting there. So I grabbed one of the bills without looking at it. It just so happened to be the five- dollar bill that I snatched. I tucked it deep into my pants pocket and proceeded to go around the corner to the candy store.

It was a wonderful establishment. It had an endless cache of penny candies, candies of all shapes, sizes, and flavors. ***Dots of colored sugar on paper,*** S*strawberry and* C*chocolate Twiz*lers, ***waxed things filled with sugary liquids, Jawbreakers, Bazooka gum and, Mary Jane's.*** There were boxes of ***Sugar Daddies, packages*** of ***Turkish Taffy and Tootsie Rolls*** and more, the list seemed endless. Willy Wonka had nothing on this place. Five bucks was like a gazillion dollars and I proceeded to try and spend it all.

I had no chance of spending so much money on myself, so I enlisted the help of every kid from the neighborhood that was available. Needless to say things got out of control fast. Word spread like wildfire and no sooner did I return home and walk through the front door, I saw Maggie standing there with fire in her eyes, and the beating began. Maggie had one of my Fathers belts in her hand and began flailing it at me. I was screaming and begging for her to stop, but she kept whacking me and yelling at me and calling me a little thief. The look on her face had me petrified. I actually thought she was going kill me. I had strap marks from head to toe and cried for what seemed like a week. I loathed this evil woman. So went my love- hate relationship with my Mom.

I understand today that She hadn't had such a wonderful life either, marrying at age sixteen to escape from her Mothers second husband. Her Step- Father was a psychotic and brutal monster. Kitty, her mom was a raging alcoholic and a mean SOB. I myself cannot once remember her being the loving type of grandmother a kid looked forward to seeing. She was a chain smoking, beer guzzling, anti-matriarch that spewed venom wherever she went. I couldn't stand her. An example of grand parenting that was better off forgotten.

Mean Kitty's

I liked the bus ride over and looking out the window,
It was never a boring sight.
Sometimes in my Sunday best, I would have an air of importance about me, an ambassador of family pride.
It only lasted until Kitty's building.

The stench of urine emanated throughout the dim lit hallways, a direct byproduct of its communal bathrooms.
Fifteen steps per landing, times four, a right turn and twelve paces.
I always liked counting things.

I would sometimes race up the stairs but the gunk on the banisters slowed me down.

There was a classic four-paneled door at the entrance to her apartment.
The top two panels were made of pitted glass.
It was installed that way to distort the interior I guess.
And when you knocked, Man! It would really sting your knuckles.

When the door opened the smell of. Reingold Beer and Chesterfields filled the air. No odor of fresh baked apple pie here.
And as we entered, she would be sitting in her place.

The ceiling above her spot was brown in color.
Gnarly yellowed fingers caed the tiny remnant of her cig.

She would plunge it deep into the ashtray already piled high, with the
mornings puffs.

We would greet her with a brown paper bag, damp from the dellies
tall icy cans. It always made her smile
When she laughed the missing teeth became prevalent, and her figure
fragile.

The pasty complexion, the raspy voice, the dingy housedress,
Her cackle's tickled my eardrums.
The use of profanity peppered the air when she spoke and like the
proverbial sailor, there was always too much candor.

Steam rising from the hissing radiators, would make me sneeze.
Linoleum laid throughout her apartment was worn and shabby.
The stove was fetid with grease and the remnants of yesterday's meals.
Cockroaches racing across the ceiling, were un-noticed by all but
myself.

Sometimes I was placed into the tub of shame, a porcelain monster.
To bathe amongst the cajoling adults, boisterous, with drunken banter.
It made me feel inadequate.
The harsh soap would burn my eyes if I let it.
A soiled and smelly towel to dry off with made me wonder why I was
being bathed in the first place.

I couldn't wait for this day to be over.
A kiss goodbye would be sloppily planted on my mouth,
so I would run in the opposite direction of her.
I hated to visit her, and cried if I had to stay over.

Thanks Grandma?

I have very few memories of my older siblings prior to the age of nine or ten. Except the few interactions with my sister Katelyn, who was two or three years my senior. My younger sisters Megan and Maeve wound up in similar situations as myself, so my memories of them are somewhat clearer.

We were poor, but the stigma of poverty did not begin to permeate my ego until later in life. Everyone my family knew was poor, or struggling at best. But as I mentioned before, things were different back then. It was shameful to collect welfare or home relief as they called it back then. As with the hand me downs, neighbors were always willing to help out in some meager way. It was the call of the times.

If you didn't't have the means, no problem, you were still able to attend the neighborhood parochial school for free. But it was at the cost of an ear being yanked or palms being slapped with a ruler. And as a rambunctious kid, I had firsthand knowledge. I was oblivious to all of the poverty in my neighborhood, it wasn't important to me.

Everyone knew each other and their families. Doors were not locked for the simple fact that no one had anything to steal anyway. People would just go into and out of each others apartments at will. "There was no privacy in our building, everyone living there knew our family business." It was at a time when people didn't get involved in each other's affairs.

There was no shame for the scenes of violence that occurred on a regular basis between Maggie and Jim. And it wasn't't my Father beating my Mother, it was Jim defending himself against Maggie's aggressions. But when the cops showed up, it was always my Father being led away in handcuffs for acting belligerent to the police. Drunk again and spending all the money he earned on booze, over and over he left us on the brink of destitution.

Even in the midst of all this chaos I remained in harmony with myself, always searching for a better environment to stretch my imagination. I loved life as a small child, I had no deep seeded fears or anxieties embedded within my mind, I was a trustful soul. But that changed too quickly for

CHAPTER TWO

The Bogeymans House

There were two major traumatic episodes that happened to me by the time I reached seven years of age. The first was my Brother In Law Singer's repeated sexual abuse of me. The second was when a stranger, a sexual deviate abducted me off the street.

Neither occurrence was shared with anyone until adulthood. I would never speak one word about it for fear of being blamed and labeled as bad. As a teenager and young adult it was even worse. I was petrified to be found out. I was sure to be labeled a Faggot by my peers, which was an express ticket to being picked on and beat up.

How was I going explain what occurred. I knew in my heart these things that happened to me were wrong, but I hadn't the vernacular to explain it, plus I'd felt somewhat responsible. I didn't understand boundaries. I didn't know much at all about what was the right and what was the wrong protocalls, I was still learning.

I was off to my Sister Graces's home in Howard Beach Queens, a major upgrade from the tenements we came from. I couldn't't tell you the reason why we were sent to Grace's. It must have been to give Maggie respite from all the kid's, because by this time Jim was on the Bowery and my Mother had become the sole provider for the family.

There were four of us going to stay over at Grace's. My older Sister Katelyn who was probably around seven or eight, my younger sisters Megan and Maeve, one a toddler one an infant at the time I guess, and myself. I was somewhere around four or five years old.

Grace had just given birth and it was our first time visiting since. It was also going to be our first time sleeping over. I remember the neighborhood being so different than mine. There were no huge buildings, no crowds of people. There seemed to be trees everywhere, "It was great". We had a good time that day playing and having fun. We had a great dinner that evening and our visit with the new baby in our family was nice. I was enjoying the day. "But then came bedtime".

Fast asleep, I was awakened by something bothering me. This something was groping me in a way that scared me tremendously. So in a semi concious state of mind I opened my eyes, to see this shadowy figure above me. It moved quickly away when I opened my eyes. So I went back to sleep, only to be woken a second time by something fumbling inside my pajamas. It was trying to put something into my rectum. It was painful and I wanted it to stop.

The room was pitch black, and at that time in my life I was very afraid of the dark. I was taught that the Bogeyman would get me if I was bad, and I was sure that this was he. I turned onto my back to try and stop the groping at my behind, petrified to open my eyes again. Because if the Bogey Man knew I was awake he would take me away to somewhere bad, to a place where I wouldn't see my family anymore.

These were Stories spun to get a child to behave in bed. So I figured if this was the Bogey Man and I pretended to be asleep, maybe, just maybe he would leave, but he didn't. I felt something again touching me in a place that seemed to be violating me. I couldn't explain it, "I was too young". With the vocabulary I possessed at the time I couldn't put it into words. I could only speak to what I was taught. My rectum was called my hiney and my penis my pee pee.

Once on my back it began with the touching of my penis and someone or some thing trying to pull my pajamas down. I was paralyzed with fear, and couldn't move. The Bogeyman began sodomizing me, and inserting his finger into my rectum. He was hurting me and I wanted him to go away. I began make making noises thinking it might stop what was happening. It seemed to work for a while, but then it would start up again moments later. I squinted into the darkness to see this shadow running away, only to come back again when things got quiet. Then it would begin doing these horrible things to me again. Eventually it stopped and I finally fell asleep. I awoke the next morning and we went home.

What happened to me was terrifying, and felt so surreal. I was afraid to talk about it for fear of having to relive it. So I blamed myself by saying " You shouldn't have been a bad boy." And so this thing that happened became a recurring nightmare for me. We spent other nights at my sister Grace's where the Bogey Man lived, and I would ask God to help keep him away, promising to be a good boy. But it didn't help.

Some years later I realized it was not the Bogeyman. It was a person doing this to me, and his name was Singer, Grace's husband, my Brother-inlaw. Later in life I was to find out that this fucking animal molested others in my family. That he had even done so to his second wife's children. But the most emotionally painful of all realities, I wouldn't learn until I was 56 years old. It happened when I was discussing these things with my sister Grace for the first time.

Grace told me that Maggie, my Mother, found out about what Singer had done to us and did nothing about it. It was so emotionally painfull I had a nervous breakdown. It would become the first of my many times being admitted to a psychiatric hospital.

They told me that I had tried to commit suicide, but I was just trying to kill the pain. I swallowed 20 200MG Seroquel pills then phoned my daughter Kirsten to let her know what I had done. She told me to open the front door and wait outside, and then she called for an ambulance. Until this day, I hold this pain inside. Not for the molestations, I've dealt with that shit. And with the help of the many psychiatrists, psychologists and councilors I understood completely, that none of what happened was my fault. The deepest pain for me today is that Singer never paid the price for hurting so many children. It still haunts me, and I have thought many times about murdering him.

I have learned to live with it and not to dwell on the past, but it's always there, lurking, waiting for something to happen in my life to conjure it up. Something as simple as an argument, someone making me feel that I have been wronged or taken advantage of in some way. It builds up inside of me and then triggers a mechanism of rage that has caused me many problems during my adulthood. I have such empathy for children of abuse.

CHAPTER THREE

The Lost Puppy Monster

I was coming home from Kips Bay Boys Club one day. I was 6 or 7 years old at the time and probably weighed 50 lbs. soaking wet. I had gone swimming in the pool that day but can't remember how I got to the club, I might have been brought there by my brother or one of my sisters, or just went by myself, but I did go home alone.

I made a detour through 47th Street Park thinking I might find my sister Katelyn hanging out. This park was a block long street that had benches and trees every 40 or 50 feet that stretched between 1st and 2nd Avenue. (It is now known as Dag Hammerskold Plaza), and all the kids from the area congregated there.

"I was approached by a stranger", and He told me he had lost a puppy. He added that he would give me a dollar if I helped him find it, and I said yes. As hard as I've tried over the years, I cannot put a face to this piece of shit. In my child's mind he is the monster, the scary thing a child imagines. Make believe things that were hiding under the bed at night or inside of a dark closet. The things ready to attack you if you so much as moved. The demons conveyed to me by teasing siblings or parents that just wanted me to go to sleep.

In reality this psycho must have seemed trustful because I went with him voluntarily, for a while anyway.

I see myself crossing First Avenue my hand in his, as I had done many times before while asking an adult to cross me. We headed towards the United Nations Park on the 48th street side of the U N building. It was the same place that my Mother would take me, that had held fond memories for me.

It was getting a little dark, and the park was officially locked for the evening. He brough tme around to the side of the entrance and told me to climb over the fence. I must have hesitated because he grabbed me by the back of my jacket and began lifting me up and over, all the while climbing over the fence himself. At this juncture I was beginning to panic, a feeling of extreme danger came over me. But before I knew it, he had me in the bushes (thick green ivy) and was on top of me.

I started crying, but remember him telling me that if I didn't shut up that I would never see my Mother again and that he would kill me. I began sobbing incessantly. I could feel him panting on the back of my neck because he was so close to me. I felt my pants being forced down around my legs, my underwear being pulled at violently, until there was nothing between me and this God damned fiend. I felt a sharp pain between my buttocks, as he was trying to force his way inside of me. I was weeping and calling for my Mother, but he just kept barking threats into my ear to shut me up.

Sudden he stopped and it got really quiet. He eased up off of me and I could tell that he was looking around. He placed a hand at the nape of my neck and pushed my head down into the ivy. Then he growled in my ear, "don't move or make a noise or "I'll kill you". "I laid very still for a time" terrified to even make a noise breathing. I turned my head slightly and saw a small light coming my way. It was the beam of a flashlight that became more prevalent by the second. It was one of the guards making his rounds and he had scared the monster away.

I saw the guard walk right past me, but couldn't move or say a word because I was so paralyzed with fear. The guard couldn't see me because I was lying down in an area that obstructed his view, plus it was pitch black by this time. I don't know how long I waited before I made a move, but the guard had already gone out of sight. I looked around and didn't see anyone. So I pulled up my underwear and pants and slowly rolled onto my back, I felt pain in my hiney. I stood up, scaled the fence and started running as fast as I could towards home, crying the whole way.

I crossed 1st Avenue by myself and walked towards 46th Street, where as soon as I turned the corner and began walking up the block, I spotted my Mother. She was walking towards me with fire in her eyes, "she screamed like a banshee, "Where have you been, I've been looking everywhere for you"

By this time I was crying so uncontrollably I couldn't catch my breath. After what just happened to me, would I be getting a beating too? Just when she was about to grab me Maggie must have seen something in my face that made her back off. She stopped and in a calm voice asked me what happened.

How was I supposed to explain what just transpired? I couldn't verbalize it. I couldn't explain it away. So I just told her that a man grabbed me and threw me over the fence at the UN Park.

Maggie grabbed me by my hand really hard and started yanking me back toward where I just escaped from (probably with my life), and wanted me to go with her to find this guy. Was she out of her fucking mind? This was the last thing I wanted to do, and I was screaming and crying for her to not make me do it. That maniac would kill us both. She let up after about fifteen minutes and took me home. I cannot remember what happened after that. I know that the police were never called, and it was never brought up again. It was a nightmare borne of happenstance.

CHAPTER FOUR

The Little Entrepreneur

I always had a knack for making money as a kid. One of the things we did was go out begging for Thanksgiving. I've asked many people over the years if they had ever heard of doing such a thing and the responses were an overwhelming "What!" It was a tradition throughout my neighborhood, or at least in my family it was,

It was pretty simple. Thanksgiving Eve, wearing our rattiest clothes and sporting Moonpie Eyes we go up to an adult, stick our hand out and say "Anything for Thanksgiving!" And hopefully that person would give us money. It was mostly some small bits of change, like a dime or quarter. But once in a while we got lucky and someone would give us a dollar. Moon Pie eyes and tattered clothes always generated more proceeds.

Then there was the gas station on the northeast corner of 47th and 1st Ave. It had road maps on a rack that were free to the public, and I'd grab a handful. I was not supposed to be taking them, it was for the customer buying gas, but I did anyway. Then with the maps in hand I would stand on the opposite corner. And when cars stopped for the light, I would try and sell them for a nickel. I also shined shoes and did other things to earn money. But nothing earned me more money that my next Capital Venture.

One day this kid named John Riley approached me about selling papers with him. I can't remember exactly how it came about, but he told me that we could make a lot of money. So he came home with me to pitch the idea to Maggie.

We asked my Mom if it would be OK. And after being assured by Riley I would be well taken care of, she hesitantly agreed. She knew him from the neighborhood and also knew his family. So off I went on my apprenticeship of hawking newspapers. I did it to help the family out financially, even though I couldn't totally comprehend the idea. By this time Grace and Erin were married and Liam was out of the house. So it was just Katelyn, the little ones who were maybe three or four at the time, and myself.

The next night we got started, it was about 7pm, just when the late editions of the Daily Mirror and Daily News would come out. We'd buy our newspapers directly from the loading docks because it was cheaper than buying them at the newsstand. In the beginning we would start by hitting the bars on 2nd and 3rd avenues.

You have to remember I was only six and a half years old. I was an adorable, tiny, blonde haired little imp. I was cute as a button and had these wonderfully sad eyes that worked like a charm. People were buying papers left and right and paying me pretty well for them too. The papers retailed for five cents back then, but I'd get 10, 15 or 25 cents for a paper. Occasionally I'd even get a dollar. But as I became more familiar with the Logistics of it all, I stopped taking a dime. The least I would take was fifteen cents.

The times I received a dollar I would usualy have to do something extra like getting patted on the head, kissed on the cheek, or given a big hug. It was mostly the ladies that felt sorry for me and would make the boyfriend give me a buck. There were also times that someone would buy all the papers from me, thinking that once out of papaers, I would go home. But we would just go and buy a few more bundles of papers and continue the route. This time we had to buy our papers at the regular News Stand price, we were too far away to circle back.

I remember that my pockets would be so full with change I could barely keep my pants up. There must have been $20 or so, and that would not be counting the dollar bills that I might have made or needed to cash. Riley and I would stop at about 9.00 PM, finishing up around 57ᵗʰ street and 8ᵗʰ Avenue. That's when he would give me my cut.

I usually made ten to fifteen bucks or so in a week, but it seemed I was earning so much more. After working with Riley for about a month some important questions began to be asked by my sister Katey. A: Is my brother being taken advantage of? B: What would happen if we decided to cut Riley out completely? C: Wasn't Joey the one doing all the work anyway? And hadn't I kicked Riley's ass once before. "OK, he's gone" Katey said. A unanimous decision was made, Riley was officially out and my sister in. Katey would go with me and be my protection. And if Riley found out and tried anything, he would have to face the wrath of my sister. And she was one of the toughest girls in the neighborhood. I knew Riley didn't want any part of her.

We did pretty well my sister and I, we were clearing forty to fifty bucks a week. We brought home 95% of all the money we made. The other 5% would be placed under the radiator in the hallway for Katey and me to split. That was my sisters idea not mine, but who was I to disagree.

I loved selling newspapers. The bars were a stage for me. I could play out the part of the waif, the little angel, the ragamuffin, and have people doting all over me. I would melt their hearts. I was sort of a Dickensian figure, this poor little cherub peddling his wares. I had the eyes of a dachshund, droopy and sad looking, it worked like a charm. There was always lots of action and excitement in the bars, and I'd meet such interesting people. It all depended on the establishment I went into.

If it was a neighborhood joint like **McGraths** on 3ʳᵈ Avenue and 44ᵗʰ Street, the people would be regular working stiffs stopping by on the way home, for a beer, a shot, or something to eat. The **Corned Beef** the **Brisket,** The **Roast Beef** and **Boiled Cabbage**. The **Mashed-Potatoes**, **Gravy** and **Corn On The Cobb.** I'd be starving by the time I walked out of there. Actually, we only went to places like that if we had a few papers left over and were heading toward home. It was because these particular clients didn't pay well.

The real money was in the side street joints and the bars on Lexington Avenue. We would hit as many as we could heading uptown. We'd go from 46th street to 56th, zigzagging occasionally along the side streets, where the high rollers drank. Joints where the clientele were regulars and well off. They didn't hesitate to tip well.

Once we hit 56th Street we would head west to 7th Avenue, where our night would finish up. Trial and error brought us the experience to find the best places to go. Places where people would feel bad for me, this little urchin that was driven to the street to help support his family. That had to do it in order to survive.

My customers would sometimes do the extraordinary. Someone might slip me a buck to make my day. It happened pretty frequently, maybe once or twice a week. That wasn't counting my three regulars a night, that left a dollar with the hat check girl so I wouldn't walk around and bother their patrons. These were the establishments with a special decor and ambiance. They were different from the neighborhood bars. They didn't have that smell of stale beer or the raucousness of the local places. The kitchens were hidden out of sight in the back, and the people dressed differently, more dignified. The mood was quieter and more laid back. These places had class, and so did the patrons.

The men were quick to show off to their significant counterparts, tossing me a buck or even a five spot, which occurred only once every few months. The women were beautiful, sophisticated and smelled great. They always had a hug to give or at the least an "Oh! What a cute a little boy," a pinch or kiss on the cheek, then a nudge for her date to take care of me. They melted in my hands and it felt great. I was the actor, the salesman supreme. I was the breadwinner, the man of the house, and my Mom seemed so proud of me. On occasion Katey and I would bring home a cake from the local bakery, or we might buy some groceries that were needed and then give Maggie the rest of the money. Things seemed like they were going Ok.

I hadn't known much about my Mom's business, where she was going or whom she was seeing. But I knew she spent many an evening at the Murray Hill Bar. During the day she worked as a waitress in one of the local luncheonettes, but that's all I knew. So I couldn't have been prepared for what was coming. It would be just one more episode of an adult harming me. But this time it was Maggie who would be the perpetrator.

CHAPTER FIVE

The Absconding Parent

I must have been coming home from school with Katey, because it was a bright mid-week afternoon. Walking down the block I noticed some people outside of my building and The closer I got, I could see that it was my sisters Erin and Grace and they had the little ones with them. It was everyone except my Brother Liam.

As we neared our building I could see my older sisters were very upset, but I couldn't understand what was going on. All I remember was Grace and Erin crying and saying things like, "I can't believe it" or "How could she do this".

By this time Grace and Erin were married with kids of their own, so it made what transpired harder to swallow. They were in shock and seemed panicked and distraught over something. I was to find out soon after my Mother ran off to Florida with some guy and abandoned us, leaving just a few dollars behind. Thus became the whirlwind that swept us up into a ball of uncertainty, just another tragic turn for my sisters and myself. We were the products of total parental dysfunction.

My Sister Katelyn was probably 9 years old, Megan four and Maeve two when Maggie took off. "Me", I had just turned seven. We had been left to fend for our physical and emotional selves under the guidance of my Sisters Grace and Erin. And as I said previously, my brother Liam was out of the picture, he hadn't been living at home for quite some time, With Jim on the Bowery and Maggie gone we were officially abandoned and homeless. "What the hell was going to happen to us?"

I remember everyone crying, so I began crying, I remember the drama distinctly. My oldest sisters having their own lives and children wondered what to do, asking themselves how could their mother do this to them. I myself had wondered over the following years, and asked myself two questions. From an adult perspective, as well as that of a confused and emotionally wounded child. The responsible adult poses the question, "How can you abandon your children? While the child asks," What terrible thing have I done to make my mother run away?"

Decisions were made, plans put into place, and off we went, on the roller coaster ride that became our lives. I don't remember what happened to my Sister Katey, but my Sisters Megan and Maeve as well as myself went to live with Erin.

CHAPTER SIX

The Short Bumpy Ride To Astoria

Erin was married just a year or so before my Mom took off. She was in her early twenties and just had a baby of her own. My Brother in law Hogan her husband, was only seventeen and was a totally immature asshole. They lived in a One Bedroom apartment in Astoria, on the first floor facing the street. So with three extra kids living there, it was extremely crowded. Erin worked as a waitress like Maggie, and to this day she is the hardest working person I ever knew. She went out to work every day while Hogan stayed home to take care of his son, along with my little sisters and I.

Hogan always had his friends coming over and hanging out. They were a bunch of bums without jobs and no place to go. These stinking cronies of his would even sneak through the kitchen window at night to crash out on the floor.

My Brother In-Law was a sadistic fuck towards my little sisters when his creep friends were around. He would place them by their little arms atop the doorjamb while telling them that if they let go they would fall and be hurt very badly. So it was natural that they were terrified of letting go. Another sicko thing he did to them was: He would take a nail and tell them he was going to stick it into their feet. Then He would place the nail in between their toes and yell and scream as if he were stabbing them. They would scream, and cry, while all the time thinking that the nail was being stuck into their foot. This scumbag bastard and his moron freinds thought it was hilarious to torture these two defenseless little children. They would be laughing, falling on the floor, as these precious little girls begged for him to stop.

If I were around I would try to stop him by swinging punches at him as hard as I could and would try to kick him in the balls. I'd be cursing at him to stop, but I was so small that I didn't stand much of a chance. But every once in a while I'd get lucky and connect, which only meant I'd get my ass beat. I'm sure I must have told Erin what was going on, but I guess she had too much on her own plate to do anything about it.

I began selling papers in the city again, because Erin didn't make enough to take care of of us all. Hogan would drop me off at 59th Street and 2nd Avenue at around 6:30 PM and pick me up somewhere around Nine. Even though I knew the neighborhood and a lot of the people there, I didn't have my sister Katey watching over me anymore, so I was naturally a little nervous. "What would I do if someone tried to jump me? Who would be there to protect me?"

When Hogan picked me up I had to give him all the money. I think he was holding out on us because Erin was always complaining about finances. I couldn't understand how, because I could make more money than the average man at the time, around fifty bucks a week. And in 1958 fifty bucks could buy quite a bit.

One night when finishing up my paper route and waiting around for Hogan, a couple of cops noticed me standing around and waved me over to their vehicle. They asked me why I out so late by myself. I told the two officers that I had been selling papers and was just waiting for my Brother In-Law to pick me up.

They placed me into the police car and waited for Hogan to show up. I was very afraid, I thought that maybe I had done something wrong. But it was my Brother In-Law that they wanted. Little did we know that there was some sort of child labor law being broken, so when Hogan showed up, the policemen put him in handcuffs and arrested him. From there we all went to the local station house where they placed a call to my sister. They let her know that Hogan was being arrested and he would be spending the night in jail. Erin got someone to watch her son and the girls and then took a cab into the City to pick me up.

That was the proverbial straw that broke the camels back. And once again it was time for the little ones and I to move on. We wouldn't be going to Grace's house because Erin knew what that fucking pervert Singer would do to us. So other plans were set in motion, we would be headed to an orphanage.

CHAPTER SEVEN

The Burning Shower

I remember being in a courtroom, my sisters and I sitting patiently on a wooden bench, waiting to hear what was to happen next. There were a couple of people speaking to my sister Erin. I could see that she was crying about something. And then I heard her say: "I'm so sorry but there's nothing I can do. I can't take care of them any longer".

It always seemed that we were surrounded by mayhem and drama, unsure of what was to happen next. It was horrible for us being separated and bouncing from place to place all the time. Running around not knowing where we would end up.

After the hearing the judge had an order written up to place us kids in the custody of the State of New York. We were deemed wards and were to be placed in a State run facility that handled children left abandoned or with parents that were deceased.

Then I was told to say goodbye to the little ones. I'd be going one place they'd be going to another, and I would not get to see them again for more than a year. They didn't have it any easier, being alone and so young. But soon after, Katey returned from wherever she had been and was placed with them. I couldn't tell you whom Katey lived with, but I'm sure it had to be someone who knew my family.

I was placed in a car along with an adult escort who was to deliver me to the next leg of my journey, and transfer me to my new surroundings, part of the New York State Department of Child Welfare. During the ride while reflecting on all that had happened that day I hadn't noticed it was getting dark.

Upon arriving at my destination, I could barely make out the dreary structure I was to be delivered to. But from there on in I emphatically remember every moment, every second I spent there. The sights and sounds, the dank odor wafting through the halls, it was haunting. The creaking sound that the front door made upon opening was eerie.

Stepping inside, I stood in this archaic, dimly lit lobby. It had hallways jutting out in every direction and I could hear sounds reverberating throughout them. One was this deep disturbing voice that had a menacing ring attached to it. I also heard the voices of children, a fearful, low tone sobbing that made me feel extremely anxious.

Out of nowhere from down one of the hallways a man appeared. He introduced himself to my temporary guardian and signed a document that released me into his care. Upon the transfer, this new person barked at me to follow him. Afraid I complied without resistance, and jumped up, hastily walking behind him.

I was brought to an area where showers were taken and was told to remove all my clothing and place them on the bench adjoining the shower stall. Then I was directed towards the nozzle closest to the entranceway.

Even though I swam naked at the Boy's Club without being shy this was far different, it felt debasing to me. This guy had a threatening way about him. I felt like that because of the way I was being spoken down to, insensitive, cold and uncaring. It was as though I had been disturbing him, creating a problem for him because he had to watch after me. I felt it in his voice that he was not a happy camper.

I stepped through the doorway and under the showerhead I was directed to, but immediately winced and jumped out from under it. The water was not only icy cold the stream of it was so powerful it stung my body. I turned around to let this man know about the problems but he was gone.

Scanning the environment around me I looked up towards the ceiling and noticed that some of the fluorescent lights were out. Even the ones that were on were flickering. Many of the floor and wall tiles were cracked or missing, giving the whole area a deep depressing atmosphere. There was rust around the drains under each showerhead. The floor tiles around them were black with mold and the drains themselves had a musty odor rising from within them.

The man returned and had a towel in one hand and a can in the other. I hung my head down most of the time, afraid to make eye contact with my custodian. I dared not complain, for fear of some sort of retribution. So with all my might I stepped under the showerhead into the cold and chafing water. After a minute or two a very stern voice ordered me to step back towards his voice and face away from him. I obeyed immediately for fearof some sort of reprisal.

Standing where I was directed to I began to notice a potent stench emanating from behind me, a very strong and pungent odor. And before I knew it I was being doused with some sort of thick liquid. Dripping down my face it instantly began burning my eyes. It wasn't like the many times I protested to my mother that she was getting soap in my eyes, while getting me to finally take a bath. This was so much more painful. I thought my eyes would be burned out of my goddamned head. I began complaining vigorously, but was told to be quiet.

My skin started to tingle and became warm and uncomfortable. My underarms and genital area began to sting and I raced back under the shower for relief. As I stood under the water trying my best to remove this caustic substance from my eyes and body I began to pray in a very solemn way to myself. Not the prayers of a child beside his bed asking for blessings to family and self, but prayers of desperation and anguish. "God what have I done to deserve this, Where's my Mommy and Daddy? Where's my family? God please help me."

As I exited the shower and started to dry myself off with the towel set on the bench, I noticed my skin had a pinkish hue, as if I had been out in the sun a little too long. It tingled all over and was sensitive to the touch. I was to find out later that it was Pine Soap, an industrial cleanser used to mop floors.

After drying off I was handed pajamas to wear that were too big for me. I had to hold them up with my hands or I'd be balls ass naked. I was ushered down a corridor to an office where I was to be formally admitted. And as I sat there quietly, I could hear the sound of people approaching, coming from down the hall. I glanced toward the doorway and saw this gargantuan black man enter the room with about half a dozen children in tow. They were making pleas for leniency and begging him to not hurt them. Not unlike my pleading as Maggie beat me with a strap.

As they entered I remember that I hadn't wanted to look directly at any of them, but out of curiosity I took a peek. There was a little Hispanic Boy at the front of the line looking directly at me, his eyes red from crying. And as hard as I wanted to, I wasn't able to look away. He stood there crying softly, his expressions giving him away. Something terrible was about to happen, and he looked around for an advocate, one that maybe, somehow could obtain him clemency. Clearly what was about to happen to these children, these little boys that looked to be between seven to ten years old was seriously frightening. These were very young children that were going to feel the wrath of this Neanderthal.

They were ushered into one of the interior offices, and the door was shut behind them. A few moments later I heard a sound that startled me. It was a sound that I was familiar with. It was the sound of a strap hitting skin, the whack of the belt. Then came the screaming, pleading and crying, begging for leniency and forgiveness. Tears began welling up in my eyes and my mind began racing again. I kept softly repeating to myself, "Please let this be a dream, God Please let this be a dream," But it wasn't. Thank goodness my paperwork was completed quickly, I wasn't going to hear any more of the heartbreaking pleas coming from behind that door.

I was ushered out of the office by my jailer-warden and taken to a dormitory that housed at least fifty beds. It was dark and unnervingly, a silence, a quiet that I wasn't used to. I was directed down the middle of the room to an empty bed. I climbed in and laid my head on the pillow. And as the man left I began going over the day in my mind, and it took all of my courage not to break down into hysterics. So lying in a fetal position I cried as quietly as I could, recounting many times the events of the day until totaly exhausted, I then cried myself to sleep.

Roused from bed the next morning I felt emotionally exhausted. An uneasy feeling filled my mind. I believe it was my first experience of an emotional hangover. And as I tried to gather my thoughts it struck me. I was in a place where no one cared about me, where I was vulnerable to abuse and there was nothing, nothing at all I could do, I was totally helpless.

I looked around at the other children in the dormitory getting out of their beds. I noticed that they were mostly boys of color. Black and Hispanic children with a few Caucasian boys like myself. This was all new to me. Though I had seen Black and Hispanic people before, because I lived directly next to a large commercial building, I had never socialized with any children outside my race. Like most of the kids in my neighborhood I had heard the derogatory remarks spoken so callously by our parents and noticed for the first time in my life, a feeling of being so very different.

There were no children of color that went to my school, none that went to the Boys Club or the church around the corner. I had never spoken to or played with any children like these, I was intrigued. And as we went to breakfast I could hear in their voices and see in their gaits an array of behaviors new to me. The accents and elocution tickled my ears. The assurance in their steps captivated me. It was my first feeling of ease since coming here. But it was not to last, as I was immediately whisked off to my next destination.

My older sisters had arranged with Father Marinachi from Holy Family Church that I be placed straightaway into a Catholic institution rather than where I had initially been dropped off. I felt relieved

> Patience my boy still your mind
> the troubled times, that weather there.
> The anxiousness that seizes hold
> does dissipate within its time,
> and with it spells your will to shine.

CHAPTER EIGHT

Saint Ritas's and the Nuns of Repentance

t was a very long ride to Saint Ritas's Home for Boys in Suffolk County, Long Island, a trip that allowed me to contemplate the last couple of days. Staring out the window of my transportation, a black sedan baring the insignia of New York State pasted on either side. I could finally breathe deep and exhale, to purge myself of the tension that had my stomach tied up in knots.

The ride was strangely quiet, and as I laid my head against the window of my transportation, I would nod in and out of consciousness, opening my eyes to notice the landscape ever changing. It was becoming much more rural, with lots of trees and minimal traffic, a very tranquil environment.

We finally arrived at my destination. A long tree lined driveway that led to the main house. A house as big as any I had ever seen outside of the commercial properties of my neighborhood. Yes I had seen buildings much larger but this was different, this was an actual house, and I had never been inside one so large before.

It was a pristine setting, like something out of a Christmas Carol. A beautiful Victorian Mansion with a forest green shingled roof and matching clapboard shutters. Six dormers sat aligned across the top of this Three Story Manor, like tall sentries standing guard. The front of the house emitted an alluring charm. The landscape was inviting. It gave me a good feeling, one that conveyed to me a relief that I was in a much better place than I had come from.

The car proceeded through a semi-circled driveway and stopped directly in front a large porch that stretched the width of the house. I exited along with my chaperone and walked up the three steps to the porch. There we passed through two magnificent oak doors and into the main lobby. And as I entered through the front doors, things became even more captivating.

There were dark wooden floors that stretched across a magnificent corridor, every step we took slightly creaking, echoing to its inhabitants that visitors had arrived. A mild scent of pine filled the air. Along it's off white walls framed beautifully in cherry wood, hung large saintly portraits, their piercing eyes seaming to follow my every step, as if to dare transgressions of any kind.

Statues of Jesus Christ and the Virgin Mary stood hallowed against the walls. Leather cushioned kneelers were placed before them. The votive brass racks with candles burning in front of them, shed a sacramental light against the walls, it was inspiring. As I sat in the drawing room on its plush upholstered seating, directly in front of me was a stairway, regal in size and stature. It was wide enough to accommodate traffic in both directions at the same time.

I stood up and walked around inquisitively, trying to gain bearings on my new surroundings. I proceeded towards the rear of the house. Once there, I gazed through the four French Doors that opened to the rear of the property. The yard had an unspoiled touch of nature. Large oaks, Pines and elm trees dotted the grounds, a large barn like structure sat about fifty yards off from the main building, blue slate pavers led the way.

There was a small pond situated perfectly, inviting to the viewer. Its tranquility comforted me. And as I stood there taking in this stunning landscape I hadn't heard the nun coming down the staircase.

She was reverend in her attire, her hands were secreted in the pockets of her flowing robe that was belted with a thick black rosary. She addressed me by my name and asked me to follow her.

I saw in her eyes compassion, her face framed by the starched habit of her customs, espoused a sanctifying tenderness that put me at ease. She was also very much younger than any of the nuns I knew from Catholic School, she had a childish air about her that made me feel comfortable.

As I followed behind, my serenity was disturbed by the sound of footsteps on the stairway, and as I looked up another nun was leading a procession of boys about my age down the stairs towards me. As they passed me by I could feel the steely gazes and hear the whispering. It made my stomach queasy. Once again I would have to try to prove myself, and to try and fit in.

Sister brought me upstairs to a room that I would be sharing with three other boys. It was to be my room throughout my tenure at St. Rita's. It was a far cry from where I had just come from. This room was spotless and neat. There were four beds with a nightstand sitting next to each one. I noticed a catechism was placed upon each nightstand, readily available. Sister pointed out to me that I would have to bring it along with me during religious instructions class. The linens on the beds were clean and fresh. A towel and washcloth were placed at the foot of each one. Sister told me to place my bag on the bed and come with her. And as she walked out of the room and down the hall I sheepishly followed in tow.

We came upon a large bathroom and shower area. There on a bench was a towel and face cloth, a bar of soap and a clean pair of pajamas and slippers. Sister kindly directed me to shower and told me to wash up well, that she would be in the hallway when I was done. And as I stood under the warm refreshing water and soaped up, I felt the stress of the day release from my body. A deep sigh of relief came over me.

When I was done and in my pajamas I exited to find Sister

standing there patiently. She asked me to place my dirty clothes, the washcloth and towel I just used, and place them into a bag she was carrying. Then she inquired if I was hungry. And as I hadn't eaten all day, I replied yes, very much so. Sister then marched me downstairs to the dining room and prepared me a plate of food with a glass of milk. As I sat there hungrily devouring my meal, I thought to myself, "Joseph you're going to like it here."

Her name was Sister Elizabeth and during my time at Saint Ritas's she became my favorite. She would also be my teacher during school hours. She noticed my potential and nurtured it. In fact I told a little white lie about the grade I was in and ended up skipping a grade. When Sister Elizabeth found out she didn't punish me, she talked to me about telling the truth. She decided to keep me where I was because I was doing so well. I never gloated about my academic achievement openly, but I basked in the attention that was given me by Sister Elizabeth. I developed such a crush on her.

My stay at St. Rita's was basically uneventful except for a few instances. There was the occasional yanking of the ears or slap to the back of the head for being too lively during school time or church services, but it wasn't so bad.

There was the time while playing outside in the cold, and not paying attention. I stood on the pond thinking it was completely frozen. All of a sudden the ice began cracking and I fell through, ending up waist deep into the freezing water. Soaking wet, I pulled myself out of the water and walked back to the house to get out of the cold. But the nuns wouldn't let me back in the house until they finished cleaning. So I waited on the side porch with my teeth chattering and my body shivering. When they finally allowed me entrance and saw my condition, they encircled me. And with warm towels in hand they shook me violently until my body stopped shaking. Ninety nine percent of the time the nuns were very loving towards us all.

Sister Elizabeth being the youngest of the nuns acted more like an older sibling to me. I was always playing little tricks on her so she would chase me around the grounds and give me a loving noogy when she caught me. She was the person I could go to when I was feeling melancholy. Thinking I was unwanted and hated by my parents, she explained to me that Moms and Dads sometimes get sick, and need to go away so they can get better. She also said that it's not because they don't love me, it's because they don't feel well, and that as soon as they get better they will come back for me.

She was the one that walked me out to the Visitors Room when Jim showed up the first time. She was the one that walked me back inside and held me as I cried the minute my Father left. She told me that God would take care of me if I prayed hard enough. I loved her so much.

The visits by my Father were extremely painful. He had stopped drinking and was taking care of himself, and beginning his journey to getting his life in order, and his children returned to him. It was always painfully sad when Jim left, the bellyache I would come to know on every occasion, was the rejection I felt. But I began to adjust and accept things more easily as time went by.

Very few things bothered me during my tenure at St. Rita's. But there were these two male workers that looked after us during parts of the day, they were very much older than us kids, but still kind of young. Gauging their ages I would say that these two mutts were probably between eighteen to twenty years old. I can see their faces if I close my eyes tight. The malevolent smirks, the vicious stares let me know that they were two people to stay far away from, and I did my best to make sure of it. Years later I discovered that it was exactly what I had suspected, they had been molesting some of the boys. I learned this when I ran into one of the kids that had been there the same time as me.

My prior experiences awarded me a certain focus to detect sexual predators (It was like radar), and so I stayed as far away from these two animals as possible. These types seem to prey upon the weak and separate them from the rest. I noticed the ones they favored, the boys that were given little extra privileges, little gifts. I could see beyond their wretched smiles, and when one of these creeps put their arms around me I'd pull myself away. The hugs and privileges were to prime you, for you to succumb to them. It was all done to make you become sexually complicit with them.

There was this kid Bruce I knew from Saint Rita's whom I would meet up with years later. He was one of the chosen kids these perverts focused on and turned out sexually. He had been abused on a regular basis and begun to act out inappropriately towards other kids. In fact when I met up with him later in my life He suggested that I might want to experiment with him, Insinuating to me, a sexual encounter. I vehemently said "No! And I told him that if he ever spoke to me about it again, I would kick his faggot ass. It's a shame that some children are targeted by these deviates, fragile enough to succumb to them without letting another adult know what was being done to them.

Around Christmas time there was a day that I called Orphans Day. The department stores Macy's and Gimbels would hold a breakfast for us and other similar agencies throughout NYC that held children whose parents had either passed away or couldn't care for them. After the breakfast a man dressed up as Santa Clause would pass out Five Dollar vouchers, to every child. It was a kind and noble gesture, but whatever we bought was confiscated and put into a communal area for all to use. We were not to buy any guns or war toys, the things boys my age wanted most, so board games became the gift of choice. And they would remind us that Christmas was not about receiving toys, but giving thanks that our savior Jesus Christ was born. I remember one time thinking to myself, wasn't it Jesus that received gifts from the three Magi, or better known in the Catholic circles as The Three Wise Men. It didn't matter; I still enjoyed the breakfast party.

When I turned eight years old I was transferred to **The Home** for Boys in Rockaway, Queens, It was where kids nine to twelve years old resided. But being I was in the fifth grade at only eight years of age, it was determined that I should be sent to **The Home**. It is here that

I would receive one of the most inhumane treatments of my young life. I believe this is the place that I lost my spirit, my belief in God.

On the day I was leaving St. Ritas's Sister Elizabeth and I sought each other out. And though she was sad to see me leaving, she knew it was best for me. There were new happenings on my horizon. I had to turn the page on this short chapter of my life and seek out bigger and better things. And though leaving St. Rita's stirred up the memories I had of being separated from my own family, it was to be an auspicious beginning for me. As I hugged Sister Elizabeth goodbye, tears welled up in my eyes, I was going to miss her more than anyone.

CHAPTER NINE

These Blasphemous Franciscan's

To the Franciscan Brothers at the orphanage: "I wonder who had taught you how to behave?" "Just who was it that explained to you what tolerance and compassion meant?" "Who told you that being mean spirited and abusive was the proper way to teach a child about God?" Because God only knows that the type of behaviors that were exhibited towards us only bred fear and resentment.

The Home for Boys was located adjacent to the boardwalk of one of the nicest beaches in New York State. It was an area bustling with the excitement of people reveling about, enjoying the summer sun and surf of the Rockaways. It was an exciting time for me.

There were the many bars and restaurants that cluttered the area. The smell of French Fries and Hotdogs permeating every corner and alcove, the banter of people enjoying the hot summer days and nights made it a haven from the doldrums of every day life. A colorful collage of rundown bungalow's dotted the neighborhood. The sound of the carousel and the roller coaster boomed from Rockaway Playland, an amusement park resting perfectly amidst this sandy oasis.

The Home was a three story brick building jutting outwards to the boardwalk, an extension attached to an older, white, clapboard dwelling. There was a large fenced, asphalt yard the size of a football field where we would play during our leisure times, which seemed few and far between. We resided in a dormitory setting, two rows of bunk beds lined from one end of the room to the other. There was a large shower room on the left front side of the dorm as you entered and the Brother in charge had his room on the right. It all reminded me of an army barracks. Once again I had to readjust to a new environment, and this one was what I can only explain as being corporal.

Lights went on at 7:00am and we would assemble in front of our bunks to recite the Our Father. Then we'd all wash up and brush our teeth, assemble in a double line at the front of the dorm and be marched downstairs to the chapel for mass.

Mass lasted at least an hour and was excruciating, my stomach growled so loud at times that the kids sitting next to me could hear it. After Mass we were brought to the Dining hall to eat breakfast, but before we actually sat down to eat we had to stand behind our designated chair and recite Grace, thanking God for our food, and our bounty. I myself only prayed that maybe my lord could suggest in a dream to whom ever created the rule of mass before breakfast, and make them come to their senses, and let us eat first.

Our breakfast was always in front of us when we arrived, most of the time consisting of hot cereal, either oatmeal or farina. But by the time we sat down it was usually cold. There was always plenty, of milk and bread, supplements I'd used regularly to bolster such a meager meal. I wasn't starving, but my choices were slim.

After breakfast we would go to school located in the old building behind the main residence. It was a rickety batch of wood and nails that squeaked with every step you took. "You couldn't sneak up on a deaf man if you tried." The place even smelled old.

Like every other aspect of this institution, our education was basic. It was the **Catholic three R's, Reading, Writing and Religious Instruction.** "And then came Mathematics!" With the limited resources they had I can honestly say I was receiving a decent education. There were extra curricular activities like **Tap Dancing** and **Choir,** and the usual physical stuff such as **Calisthenics** and **Team Sports.**

We had a lay teacher for our primary studies. She was this middle-aged matron, a stern but fair woman. We addressed her as Ms. Jean. But I wasn't one of Ms. Jeans. favorites because I had the bad habits of talking in class and not being able to sit still, a double edge sword for discipline. There was the ruler across the knuckles or possibly the flying eraser. I became her main target, the proverbial bulls eye. And if none of these penances calmed me down, she would stick me in the corner with a dunce cap on. I never lacked for negative attention, but at least it got me noticed.

One day we had a visitor to our class. A gentleman that must have been of some importance because our Ms. Jean was making this big deal about his coming, and reminded us that we must be on our best behavior.

When this person arrived I noticed that Ms. Jean immediately began doting all over him, a phoniness of the utmost proportion. As she spoke to him about our curriculum, he interrupted her. He said that he had a game to play and he would choose some of us to face him in a challenge of memory and mathematics.

There were only four of us that volunteered. We each were stationed at the large blackboard in front of the class and handed a piece of chalk. He began slowly with one single number, then gave us another to add to the previous one. After that another number, but this time we had to use this number to multiply the sum of our previous two numbers, then bam!, a number to subtract, a number to divide and add again other numbers etc. etc. etc. And as he sped up the process, one by one each volunteer fell by the wayside. After just a few computations one was gone, then two, and finally after a rat a tat barrage of questions I was the only one left. "Kudos young man, an excellent job" he told me, even though I hadn't known what kudos meant.

But the inflection in his voice conveyed to me that I had done something spectacular. Being I had sold papers only a year ago and made change for customers on many occasions, I believe it gave me a penchant for mathematics that the normal eight year old would not have developed yet. I enjoyed my mastery of the American currency, I had to think on my feet all the time when breaking a buck or a quarter or even a dime. I could bust a Five Dollar bill quicker than most adults.

So here it went. 26+42, I easily answered 68. 68-29, 39 I responded, +36, 75, x2, 150 divided by10, 15, x9, 135+12-42 105 etc., etc. As he pounded me with figures one right after the other I was even amazing myself at the accuracy of my answers. And after what seemed like twenty or so calculations I was finally tripped up, he got me. And then with me not expecting it, a cheer rang out in the classroom. I had astounded my classmates with my abilities not only in mathematics, but to be able to stay cool and collected under such pressure.

Ms. Jean stood there with her mouth wide open, shocked by what she had witnessed. Here was one of her most miscreant children. One that she thought would never shine, blowing her away. Her pride soared like the gulls over the Rockaway's. She beckoned me to her desk at the front of the class and in full view of all, hugged me like I was her own son returning after a long absence. The gentleman shook my hand vigorously and congratulated me again, Ms. Jean couldn't stop gloating, and in the future the ruler always seemed a little less harsh.

My best friend at this time was a boy named Paulie. He had an older brother Robert, but we were closer and went nowhere without each other. He slept beneath me in the bottom bunk, we sat next to each other during meals, sat in Chapel beside each other, nudging or kicking each other playfully. We even showered together, "We were inseparable". Paulie made me feel safe, un-alone and worthwhile. I was something to someone. He was like a brother to me.

At Christmas time families looking to do a good deed would

volunteer to take one of the kids into their homes for the day. They would give them a home cooked meal and maybe a small token gift to unwrap. "It was very nice of them". But at the same time it also made me feel dissimilar.

"I should be experiencing this with my own family" I thought. But the next best thing would be if Paulie and I spent the holiday with each other. So when I was chosen by this man and woman to spend the day with them, I asked if Paulie could come also, and they obliged.

For a moment at this couples home, I imagined that I was back among my own family. My Mother and Father together with us all, a happy family enjoying the yuletide season together, enjoying one anothers loving company. But that dream was short lived, and we were returned to our reality. We had enjoyed a very nice meal, and even a small token as a gift, a shirt. But they were confiscated upon our return and placed into the Community clothing bin.

At *The Home* there were certain rules that all the boys had to abide by when they first arrived. One was that you could not leave the property on your own. If you were on the beach, it had to be between 110th and 111th Streets and no further. Any straying from this rule would bring swift punishment from one of the Brothers.

Talking when lights went out. That brought on what I called the airplane. That would be where the perpetrator would have to kneel on the hard tile floor in front of their bunk and with arms stretched straight out and palms facing up, Brother would put books on your hands. God forbid you dropped them right away Slam! Bang! You were off to bed with a slapped face and crying yourself to sleep.

Or if they thought you were being too high spirited for your own good it would be the pinch of death. They would pinch you so fucking hard it would cause a blood blister. It didn't matter which punishment you received, they were all corporal and all painful. The knuckle rap to the head and the swift kick in the ass were meant to get and keep your attention, and it worked very well.

With most of the Brothers it had to be a severe breach of the rules to receive such severe types of retribution, small discretions usually meant a stern warning. It was all that was necessary most of the time. But the Brother that was in charge of my dormitory was swift in using such means to get our attention and even seemed to relish his behavior. His name was Brother Richard, and I remember him all too well.

He wasn't a very tall or a muscular man, but had an arrogance that exuded physical confidence. The thing I remember most was the eerie scorn that always accompanied him, making him seem absolutely unapproachable. A malicious resentment always seemed to follow him and he made no attempts to hide it. His mean spirited demeanor made the fear of reprisal heighten when he was around, you always walked on eggshells in his presence.

Another quirk about him was the way he would look at you when you were showering. An inexplicable stare that caused an apprehension to being naked around him. His stares at us boys showering was uncomfortable, it hinted to me an awareness that this could be yet another sexual deviant entering my life, so my fears became intensified. He was also not the only person that I felt this way about, there were a few others including one of the priests.

After about a month or so my Father came to visit me. I hadn't seen him since St. Rita's. I believe they had to do some sort of investigation to assure he wasn't drinking and that I could be safe around him when in his care. In fact after a few visits I was able to travel with Jim to visit my sisters at the St. Joseph's Home For Girls in Brooklyn. It was always a solemn trip full of aloof nuances, of hugs and kisses and missing each other etc., the kind that made me realize the predicament we truly remained in. A family estranged by addictions and abandonments that bore my sisters and I shame, and made us feel we were outcasts, only visitors to our own flesh and blood. This became a weekly sojourn for me.

But after a month of meeting Jim at the 116th Street train station, I began meeting him in Brooklyn at the Hoyt and Schimerhorn station. In retrospect it was kind of amazing. Here I was, an 8year old traveling from Rockaway, Queens to meet up with a 44 Yr. Old man in Brooklyn, to visit with his sisters for the day. It was a trip I would make on many occasions, a trip that was also an adventure.

I would walk to 116th Street to board the Subway. The old trains back then had an ambience and flavor to them. I remember the wicker seats, "I swear they smelled like hay". The overhead fans, the leather straps with white teardrop handles dangling above my head, the ones I would somersault from whenever I rode the train. The beat of the subway rattling along the tracks had a somber, relaxing effect on me. It gave me a chance to think, to prepare myself, to imagine things differently.

I usually left early on a Sunday morning when ridership was at a minimum. The straphangers that crowded each car the rest of the week were nowhere to be found. Daydreaming, I would envision families walking together, dressed appropriately for church services. The girls in their frilly dresses, the boys in their Sunday bests The Mother and Father walking hand in hand, with their children close by. Daydreaming was putting it lightly, my reality was that I, this 8 Yr. Old Child, had to travel into Brooklyn, to meet up with his Dad and continue on to Saint Joe's, to visit with his siblings.

There was always a little something special during these trips, besides being able to see my sisters. Jim would usually allow me a small treat at the store down at the bottom of the stairs from the train station. Maybe an egg cream perhaps, or some other type of confectionery treat. We did this after our visit with the girls, right before we were to embark on our separate ways. Dad to wherever in Manhattan he lived, myself back to *The Home.*

It was always a very sobering moment when we were packing up to leave. The little ones crying, my sister Katey overwhelmed with the task of looking out for her younger siblings. You could see the sadness in her eyes. I would embrace her with vigor in hopes of instilling the strength for her not to cry in front of the little ones, because she was their only protector, and like myself, had to stay strong. To Flatbush

Ave., a kiss by my Dad. Hoyt and Schimmerhorn and back to the Rockaways once again. It became a weekly sojourne for us all.

There came the day Paulie and I earned the privilege of being able to leave the campus property on our own, it was supposed to be a special time. We immediately ran towards the sounds and flavors of Rockaway Playland, a place of legendary proportion. It was an oasis of pleasure affordable to the common man. **Cracker Jacks**, **Cotton Candy**, the smell of **Hot Dogs** and **Hamburgers** wafting through the air, **French Fries** and the fragrant sea breeze, all together a tantalizing allure for any kid. The booths with their games of chance to win some type of stuffed animal, the screams from the Rollercoaster and the other rides would excite any kid, any kid that had family looking after them.

With the brakes of reality steadily applied I return to reason, this shit takes money. So as not to continually tease ourselves, we wandered regularly in the opposite direction towards 116th Street, which was the main thoroughfare in the area.

116th was a small strip about ten blocks long, that stretched from the boardwalk and beach, past the subway station to the bay. There were nattily colored rooming houses that people would flock to during the summer if a bungalow had not been available. There were many local eateries, ones that sold **Burgers**, **Hot Dogs Fries** and some other sorts of seafood fare. There was a **Drugstore**, an **A&P** and a **Five and Dime**. It was not an A list resort area, but it was always bustling with people and the sights and sounds of the seaside.

The beaches were always crowded with families. Enjoying the sand, the surf, the summer breezes off the Atlantic Ocean and the relief it brought from the unbearable heat of the city.

Paulie and I became regulars to the area on the weekends, trying to tag along with some of the kids visiting with their families and maybe, just maybe, get invited to a barbeque, a picnic or some other function that these kids would be attending, anything to break the monotony of our life at **The Home**.

I knew how to work a crowd from my days of selling papers. We became chameleons, able to adapt and fit into whatever situation was presented us. Not in a bad way, but just to feel like normal kids, kids with a family that loved them, that quenched the thirst all children have for attention and the need to be acknowledged and loved.

We were hanging out with some kids from the area one day and decided to go to the **Five and Dime** to buy some candy. One of the kids had a quarter on him and was going to share in his good fortune. As we didn't have an opportunity like this on a regular basis, Paulie and I jumped at the chance and sheepishly tagged along.

Once in the store we immediately headed towards the candy counter, our eyes scouring the shelves for any items we could afford with this meager remuneration. There were six of us and we had to be ever vigilant of our budget. **Bazooka Gum** was always a good way to go, as was the many other items that could be shared among such an eager bunch. **Good and Plenty, Mary Jane's, Turkish Taffy,** It didn'tmatter the fare, it was candy and we craved it.

Being one of the have not's, we would agree with our benefactor immediately upon his choice. On this particular day it was gum, and with **Bazooka** in hand Paulie and I set our sights in another direction, the toy area. Packages of **Army Soldiers,** a **Slinky,** a **Kite, Balloons** etc., tidbits of toy land that inundated the area and appeased its younger population. We were only browsing this day. But even when delving in such fanciful delights sometimes the thoughts of coveting these things sprung up. And in the minds of young boys that have no means to buy such things, or parents to solicit, before you know it, self will concocts an absurd reasoning to obtain these items in a fashion inappropriate to society.

While browsing through a **Super Man** Comic, I noticed out of the corner of my eye Paulie shoplifting some of them from the rack they were on. My heart started racing immediately, my throat and mouth dried up to where I was not able to swallow or speak. I was sweating profusely and my face felt hot. My eyes met his and he gave me the wink, the wink of "be quiet!" act natural, and " let's get the fuck out of here". I was thinking,"Man, has Paulie has got some balls," way to go Paulie!

Walking towards the exit thinking it was nonchalant, I had completely forgotten that I was never very good at deception. I probably should have worn a sign that read thief leaving the store. It would probably have been less conspicuous. Just a few steps from the door, a stern voice bellowed, "Hold it!" I looked over my shoulder with my best quizzical glance, the one that read, "What's going on, are you addressing me?

It was the manager of the store walking after us. "Hey you two, get over here", the voice commanded. And as the words left his lips, the heads of every patron in the store turned to see what was going on. "What do you have under your shirt?" the voice roared, seeming louder with every word he spoke."Nothing", we both answered, our voices cracking our bodies beginning to shake and sweat. "Lift up your shirt so I can see". And before he spoke another word, I bolted for the door yelling for Paulie to follow me. But it was too late it was not going to happen. The guy grabbed Paulie by the arm, lifting his shirt, exposing the comics. "I gotcha!" the guy told him, "you have to come with me to the back office", and as he was led away he looked back at me with eyes that begged me to do something. But there was nothing I could do, so I ran from the store. Guilt by association is a lesson I would soon come to learn.

CHAPTER TEN

Richard With The Black Heart
And the day I lost God

I left the store in a total panic. What were they going to do to Paulie? Maybe they would just give him a warning and let him go. Maybe if they find out he was an orphan, they might even let him leave with the comic books, after all the poor waif was just trying to possess the mere rudiments of a normal childhood. Self-serving answers were the call of the day. So I waited about a block away for Paulie to be released on his own recognizance.

Soon a cop car pulled up to the store and I thought to myself, " There must be some sort of mistake, this was no stickup, there was no murder committed, what the hell were the cops doing there?" I was to learn later that the people of this fine community did not enjoy having the type of institution we resided at in their own backyard. So any case they could make for their prejudices would be made loud and clear.

I was waiting around for about ten minutes when Paulie appeared in police custody. And as they placed him in the police car, I slowly made my way back towards *The Home*, all the time thinking what might happen to Paulie. What type punishment would Brother

Richard mete out? Would he make him kneel on the floor for hours while hammering it into his brain, the transgressions placed upon his soul by committing such a mortal sin as stealing. Or would he have him beg forgiveness and seek penance with his maker by reciting the rosary, say maybe ten times?

Leniency. The virtue of an adolescents pleas for mercy, were resounding in my mind. "Please don't let Brother Richard be too harsh on Paulie God, he is my best friend and his poor judgment was just the sin of coveting, please forgive him!

Ok, here I was standing outside the fenced in area of the yard, a lot of the boys were milling about, some huddled in groups, some playing basketball, some tossing a baseball around, all seemed normal to me. But once I was spotted, a group came running up to me and said in voices reeking in doom, Bother Richard wants you upstairs right away, and he is pissed. My heart sunk, my face grew pale and I began to shake. "What does he want me for? I didn't do anything." "What did Paulie say?" "Did he somehow try and involve me in this situation?" "What the fuck!"

I went upstairs to the dormitory and there was Brother Richard, the look of hostility, a bloodcurdling stare. He was an angry person to begin with, but this was different. He screamed at me to change into my pajamas, and as I started towards my bunk I began to protest on my behalf. I was beginning to get emotional, tears welling up in my eyes and I was trying to tell him that I didn't do anything. But he wasn't hearing it and said that if I didn't get into my pajamas immediately things would be worse.

As I started towards my bunk I could see Paulie lying in his bed, and as I grew closer I could hear him sobbing uncontrollably. I whispered to him, "Paulie what's going on?" Just then I got a hard smack to the back of my head, It was Richard and he barked at me to not talk to him. Now I was beginning to become frightened. "What was going to happen to me?" This was one mean bastard, and I was not sure just what he had in store for me.

Richard stood at the front of the dorm, in that robed garment with the big rosary hanging by his side like some sort of six-gun ready to be fired. He was carrying this long paddle in front of him, grasping it with both his hands, a look as sinister as can be imagined by a little kid. He never hid his agenda of spare the rod and spoil the child. In fact there seemed to be a joy he received by meting out harsh punishments. He was always the quickest to respond in a corporal manner, never once had I seen him sit down with a boy to talk to him. His responses were always aggressive and now I was to experience his complete wrath.

After about ten minutes Brother Richard yelled for Paulie and Me to come to the front of the dorm. I sheepishly made my way there and noticed all the other boys from our floor standing nearby. They were assembled to witness what happens to someone if they commit such sins as stealing and lying. There were no judicious explanations to be heard, I was guilty and would be served my punishment in full view of my peers.

I was trying to muster up all my strength not to cry in front of all the other boys, but I had seen Brother Richard come out of his cubby with his paddle and knew I was in for something really bad. I had never before really examined it as I had at that moment. It was actually a baseball bat that had been shaved down on two sides to craft a paddle.

This was a weapon that was going to be used on me. Here I was, a nine year old that couldn't have weighed more than 70 lbs. and this animal was going to beat me with it? I was screaming in my head, "Please God" This can't be happening, I'm so sorry, and if I can get out of this trouble, this would never happen again." At that same moment my prayers were interrupted, it was Richard barking at me to pull down my pajama pants and lay across the nearest bottom bunk.

This is when the pleas for leniency blurted from the deepest part of my stomach. I became nauseous and faint from fear and was also feeling the shame of such a public humility. He yelled, "Lay down

across that bed or I'll give you worse than what you are going to get."
So I layed across the bed and squeezed my eyes shut as hard as I could
then tightened up my buttocks to hopefully absorb some of the shock.

All was quiet, when all of a sudden "wham!" the paddle struck
my buttocks, and the most excruciating pain I had ever experienced
shot from my behind up to my head and I let out a scream. I jumped
up and down and began running in circles all the time rubbing my
buttocks and crying out in pain. I couldn't have prepared myself for
such barbarism. The pain emanating from my behind was unrelenting
and I was yowling uncontrollably. Then he yelled, "Get back down
there! You're not done."

I began begging him to not hit me again, that I was sorry for what
I had done. Please! Please don't hit me again I pled. But this man, this
God damned sorry ass excuse for a human being grabbed me by my
arm and yanked me back down.

As I laid upon the bed, this time I had my head turned towards
him, pleading with all my might for some sort of compassion, but
this fiend was unable to muster any sort of humanity, it wasn't in his
soul. He was a hateful and bitter human being and he was going to
take it out on me.

As he reared back with his bat, I began to move away from its
trajectory, which seemed to make him even angrier. When he swung
the next time I flinched towards the side and bang! This one caught
me across my legs and sent me writhing to the floor in pain and terror.
As I rolled about unable to even standup I heard him say, "Get back
up there, that didn't count." "That didn't count, what do you mean
that didn't count", that shot just about paralyzed me. "Please Brother
Richard" I reiterated, "please don't hurt me any more." But his fury
was not about to be cut short. And his retort to me was. "Get back
onto that bed or else there will be even more coming to you."

As I hesitantly headed back to the bed I made eye contact with
some of the other boys that were forced to view this archaic, barbaric
behavior. Sheer terror loomed in their eyes, but there was also a look of

concern on their faces, a realization that this was going way beyond the bounds of punishment, to sheer torture. As my eyes strayed backwards I saw the next one coming, my body began to go limp, and the next shot hit me across my lower back. I believe that after that one I must have gone into shock because I barely felt what would normally send a grown man to the ground. There was one more to come and by this time I could just about kneel next to the bed. Barely able to move, the last whack sent me into a temporary loss of consciousness. I had a ringing in my ears, I felt dizzy and sick to my stomach.

As I was marched to bed that afternoon I remember the hate that began to brew in me. I lay there sobbing quietly, my small body burning, in pain. And I told God right then and there that I hated him and would never, ever pray to him again. I also remember wishing that Brother Richard would die a most horrible death. And as these petitions of resentment began to overcome me, somehow I drifted off into a painful slumber.

I tossed and turned during the evening and through the night, I constantly had to move to my stomach or side because lying on my back would cause me too much pain and awaken me. Each time I stirred I remember awakening, then crying myself back to sleep.

When I rose the next day I could barely walk, every step I took begged me to stop. The skin on my legs, back and rear felt as if it were tearing with each stride I took. Then upon reaching the bathroom to relieve myself and wash up there he was, the sick bastard who did this to me with that fucking smirk on his face, that diabolical half smile.

As I was just about to walk by him, he forcefully grabbed my arm and told me that I was not allowed to speak for the rest of the day. I turned and looked directly into his eyes. I stared at him emitting an aura of complete derision. I had no fear of reprisal, for my mind told me that if he ever laid a hand on me again I would fight to the death to repel him. This son of a bitch would never subject me to such a beating as Paulie and I received without consequences. I would kill this MotherFucker in his sleep if he ever touched me again.

   And I believe that when he looked into my eyes he saw pure hate emanating from within me. He noticed my hands balled in a fist, my jaw clenched, my face red with rage. All of a sudden for one short moment I felt no pain, only total hatred. After washing up as best I could, I changed into my clothes, gingerly lifting my legs and sliding into my pants. It was just as difficult to put on my shirt, because when I extended my arms, the pain in my back made me cringe. And as I slowly walked to the front and joined the line, to go to breakfast, some of the boys whispered soft words of encouragement. I could only nod my approval.

Richard the Dark Heart

>   Pious in robes that bare the teeth
>   of Satan's work amongst the meek
>   Paining children within his care
>   The Dark Heart roams to ply his wares.
>
>   On bended knees sincere the words
>   The pleas denied to halt the scourge
>   Bring loss of faith in all it means
>   And bury deep resentment's seeds.

CHAPTER ELEVEN

The Erogenous Priest

As usual we went to mass prior to breakfast, and as I genuflected before entering the pew, the lower back pain was excruciating. The skin on my legs and buttocks made it difficult.to sit. It only aggravated my injuries. So I leaned over to put my head upon the back of the pew in front of me, alleviating the motions of sitting to kneeling. I would have to rise when it came time to do so, but could fake the other movements.

During Mass, I deposed any thoughts of God as my savior. For if he was truly my savior, where had he been during this latest debacle. Why would he allow a man of the cloth to commit such a heinous crime upon me? I was through with him. The deity of my religion was dead to me.

There were a handful of priests residing at the rectory of **The Home**, and beyond their vocational obligations some took care of the administrative duties, and some were strictly there to council the boys in their religious upbringing. One of the latter was Father Frank, a quiet but respected elder.

Breakfast that morning was a struggle. It was so was uncomfortable when I sat, it made the food unpalatable and my appetite to diminish.

During grace I cursed my maker, I cursed Brother Richard, my Mother and Father, and any other person that was responsible for my dilemma. The resentments helped to veil my fears and anguish, and alleviated some of the physical pain.

As we left the dining room and headed up to our dorm I was pulled out of line and escorted to Father Frank's office. Evidently he had heard from someone about the vicious behavior of Brother Richard and wanted to discuss the matter with me. As I entered Father's room he was sitting in a large wing chair reading a book. He looked up and gestured for me to come over. I gingerly walked over and stood directly in front of him. He reached out and clasped my hands and drew me into a gentle embrace and whispered something like this: "You have sinned my boy. And though your punishment was harsh you must understand that God does give us lessons for our sins."

I began to cry softly, and Father drew me closer to him gently rubbing my back. One of his hands then slid down my back and touched my rear end, gently stroking it. I was startled and withdrew from him. He then asked how much it hurt and I responded, "Father it hurts so much. It hurts when I walk or sit, or do anything." He again beckoned me towards him, and as I once again stood in front of him he turned me around and told me he wanted to see my injuries. Father gently pulled down my pants and underwear, and as I stood naked, he bent me over his lap and began gently rubbing my buttocks.

I can remember feeling ashamed and helpless, self- loathing flooded over me. I blamed myself for being put in such a vulnerable position. A sense of being violated permeated throughout my mind, it was happening again. So I jumped up, lifted my clothing back on, and asked Father to excuse me and allow me to return to my dorm. And as he discharged me I sensed a look of embarrassment on his face, as well as a stutter in his voice. He told me that I may visit with him any time I pleased, and that he would be there for me. I thanked him, and as I left his office I reminded myself to not be alone with him, ever.

CHAPTER TWELVE

Guilt Makes For Poor Decisions

T wo weeks after the despicable acts perpetrated against me by Brother Richard and Father Frank, Maggie just happened to show up on the scene. She had taken off to St. Petersburg, Florida with her boyfriend Lenny to escape the pressures and responsibilities of raising the children she bore with my Father. Riddled with guilt, she must have believed visiting her offspring would alleviate some of her culpability.

Sunday afternoons were set asside for visits. Sometimes it would be from the extended family of one of the boys, sometimes from the parents themselves. Paulie and I would look out of the windows to see who had company, and watch intently for any signs of swag being delivered. We'd then nonchalantly saunter by and introduce ourselves. Every once in a while we would be invited to partake of some special provisions.

I had my off campus visits with my Father and Sisters and nothing more. So I was surprised at being informed that a visitor was awaiting me.

The visits were held in the yard, weather permitting. It just happened to be a beautiful spring day when Maggie came to see me.

After being informed by the administrative office that I had a visitor, Brother Richard escorted me downstairs and into the yard. But on the way down he grasped my hand in a forceful manner, an attention getter to remind me of who was in charge. I knew what he meant, "Do not cause me any problems by telling your Mother about what happened, the consequences would be harsh".

As I stepped out of the door and into the yard my heart began pounding, the anticipation of seeing Maggie after what seemed a lifetime poured over me. The surge of emotions I held inside for such a long time revealed the pain of my separation from her. And as our eyes made contact, we both began to cry.

The initial physical contact was tenuous for both of us there was a nervous feel about it. Clumsily we both reached out to hug each other, and once again began to sob uncontrollably. My mother then pulled me toward her tighter for a long awaited embrace. And as she did, a pain radiated from my back to my rear and legs and I forcefully withdrew from her, I was still recuperating from my injuries and still very, very sore.

Once my mother realized that it was not a rejection of her, she instinctively knew there was something amiss. She turned me around and gently lifted my shirt. She let out a gasp of horror upon seeing the large black and blue welt displayed across my frail back. She proceeded to lower my pants revealing similar markings on my rear and legs. As she did, I fumbled to hurriedly pull my pants up. There were other people watching this exhibition unfolding and I felt embarrassed by the fuss she was making.

I cannot say for sure what actions were taken or what channels followed, but by this coming out into the open, within a week I learned I was to be placed into Maggie's custody. Brother Richard would not have any direct contact with me anymore. It was a bittersweet time, and though I was happy to be leaving, it also meant losing my very best friend Paulie. I would miss him dearly, In fact I petitioned my mother to adopt him, to no avail.

CHAPTER THIRTEEN

The Greyhound Bust

The whirlwind that had become my life continued, incessantly spiraling along. There was the subway ride to to Mean Kitty's apartment for the night. A short taxi ride to the Port Authority Bus Terminal the following morning, and I was on my way, off to the Sunshine State. There were no farewells by me to any of my siblings, no indications given to my Father that I was being whisked away. We never even said goodbye to each other. Maggie was always a spur of the moment type. Her compulsive behaviors became embedded in my mind. It was another one of the gifts bestowed upon me by parents without any discipline.

As we boarded the bus for Florida, I felt an uneasiness come over me. I was unsure of what was to happen next. The situation I had been in had some dreadful instances, but it also provided a basic structure that every child needs. In all my years (nine to be exact) I had only felt the terra firma of good old New York under my feet. And now I was to travel twelve hundred miles, pass through eight states as well as the District of Columbia to a part of the country that was as foreign to me as if I was being brought to Siberia.

Of the many stops we made, one in particular caused me to look at a situation and question its significance. It was when we stopped for breakfast in Alabama. I told Maggie I had to relieve myself and would be right back. She reminded me that I needed to hurry because the bus would be leaving shortly.

Upon reaching the Men's bathroom I noticed that there were two entrances. One was marked Whites, the other Colored. I became quite perplexed, and upon finishing using the toilet, I raced back to tell Maggie what I saw. I have to admit, as much as she shirked the issue, her explanation made some sense. She said: "It is a terrible thing, and I do not condone the behavior, but it had been acceptable in this region of the country". From that day on this incident would remain indelibly planted within my mind.

I became very ill towards the end of the trip, feverish and vomiting. The excitement of the long journey, the climate changes, the poor diet during our rest stops, and the constant odor of fuel emanating throughout the stations we pulled into. It was always hurry up. Eat quickly. We have to go. These things contributed to my feeling nauseous all the time.

CHAPTER FOURTEEN

Everything's Coming Up Rosie

Finally we arrived at our destination, St. Petersburg, Florida. A sanctuary erected for the SnowBirds of New York and it's surrounding territories. Away from the places north, where the winters are bitterly cold and unforgiving. There was just too much snow and ice and it became a hindrance living there. Shoveling in such harsh conditions was too much a burden. And with their children long gone from the nest to live their own lives. They could quietly live out their days in the sun.

Hundreds of rest homes and hospices, the population of this community with an average median age that seemed well over 65 was not what I had expected. Upon exiting the bus we were greeted by a tall, tanned gentleman. And as he grabbed the suitcase from Maggie, he leaned over to give her a kiss on the cheek. I looked at this scenario unfolding and became suspiciously curious. I thought to myself. "Who is this person kissing my Mother?" Then no sooner did that thought pop up, Maggie turned to me and said, "Honey this is Lenny! Lenny this is my son Joseph! Lenny, Joseph, Joseph Lenny," "Who gave a shit", I just wanted to know what was going on. "Who was the bald headed asshole with the hearing aid, that was kissing my Mother".

All during my visits to my sisters, Jim would pound into my head week after week that whenever I got the chance I should whisper into Maggies's ear: "I wish You and Daddy could get back together so that we could all live happily as a family." I always felt uncomfortable when we discussed it and let my Father know that I didn't like talking about it.

Lenny was the guy my Mother met at a bar she worked at in New York. He was there on business and I guess they hit it off pretty well, because he's the one Maggie took off with. He was the one she abandoned her children for. Mom was around 39 when she left and Lenny was about five years her junior. He was an engineer of some sort, an educated man that seemed nice enough. He would go on and to try to make friends with me, try and acclimate me to the fact that he was in my Mother's life, but I would hear none of it. His bribes and favors towards me over the next year would be accepted, but with rancor.

Lenny drove us to a place where I would be staying at for the next month while Maggie secured a job and an apartment. It was her friend Rosie's house, and she and my Mom had become close friends over the last couple of years. I would imagine that their similar situations created a bond, as she was also separated from her husband. But she never abandoned her children. Kudos Rosie!

Rosie had three girls. Mary a Fifteen Year Old Boy chasing vixen, who wasn't very attractive, but had a great body. Linda her second oldest was twelve years old and a boy bashing Tomboy. She became a tyrant towards me. I didn't mind too much because she was the prettiest of the three, and I developed a crush on her. Alice was the youngest she was about 8. She had blonde hair, was a little on the chubby side and wore thick glasses that always seemed too big for her face. Mary always pushed Alice at me like she wanted me to be her boyfriend, but I would have none of that crap.

My time at Rosie's was filled with exuberance. School was not in session so there was a lot of time spent with the girls playing, going to the beach, boy hunting with Mary, dodging Linda's cruel jokes and keeping Alice at arms length. All in all it was OK.

My mother would come over every day after work, down a few beers with Rosie and compare war stories about their lives. Then she would leave to be with Lenny. A month later Maggie and I had moved into our ownplace, but we would frequently visit Rosie and the girls. They became sort of a surrogate family to me and I grew to have deep affection towards them all.

CHAPTER FIFTEEN

The perpetual motion of pre-pubescence

S o here we were, at our own place, the new start. It was a relatively small rundown house reduced to two apartments. We had the apartment on the first floor, a small one bedroom flat that barely gave us room enough for the pull out sofa that would be my bed. It was a suffocating environment in the stifling heat of Florida.

The only house on the street, it was isolated from the similar homes in the neighborhood. Directly across the road was a large lot cluttered with debris and overgrown weeds, it was surely a dumping ground for the area. But it could also be a treasure trove of fun for an explorer like myself. The tossed out mattress became a trampoline, the large appliance carton a fortress of solitude. The dangers of broken glass and rusty nails, the nuisances of the brier patches and mosquito's nests never bothered me, I it turned into my very own private playground.

As I became more comfortable and my mode of transportation improved (Lenny brought me a bicycle that he had owned Not much to look at, but the purpose was served well), I began to expand my horizons. There was a Sears and Roebuck about half a mile away, and on Saturday Mornings it became a tradition of mine to go to the appliance section, open the door to one of the new style refrigerator freezer's, where they had kept cut up pieces of fruit stuck on to toothpicks. I'd grab a handful and then go sit myself down in front of the most up-to-date televisions to watch the Saturday Morning Cartoons. Never once was I harassed about this weekly routine.

And there were the many trips to the local motels, where I would spend many a hot afternoon swimming in their pools, most of the time in the shorts I was wearing. Then it was McCrory's, a large department store that reminded me of the Korvette's Department Store from my old neighborhood, but with more of an old time elegance and charm.

I went there strictly for the toys, and their toy department had everything. The **Cars** and **Guns**, the **Kites** and **Planes** the endless cache of **Plastic Army Men**, **Cowboys** and **Indians**. I would sit in the aisles and open the many **Board Games** just to see what was inside, and to get the gist on how to play. I could write a jingle about my escapades there. I was never hindered by my Geographics and never allowed myself the feelings of boredom, never needing a suggestion on what to do. I was my own man and did as I pleased.

So this one particular day while playing in my usual area a boy came up to me and said hello. He was different from any other boy I had met up to this point in my life. He had dark brown skin and a different type of hair than I did. And when he said hello to me the twang in his voice made me chuckle. So I said hello back, and as I did, I couldn't help but reach out and touch his hair. It felt very soft to the touch. So with introduction's concluded, we went on to play for hours.

After a while I began to get hungry and said to myself "I hope Maggie is home by dinner time, so I can eat right away." Maybe we could go to the McDonald's Restaurant, the one with the delicious hamburgers, fries and shakes. The one with the sign that posted the amount of people that they served. Incessantly moving, ever flashing the placards: over and over 1,100,095-1,100,096--097 etc. It was my first sampling of a McDonalds hamburger. The year was 1959.

But during this daydream of delight I was interrupted by my

newfound friend and asked, "Do you want to come over to my house to play?" And without one bit of hesitation I agreed, and off we went. Over the years I would hear the figure of speech, the other side of the tracks. But as I traveled to my new companion's home, we actually had to cross over the railroad tracks. It was a semi-secluded area, a cross section of factories and run down houses. This was what I would come to learn later as Negro Town. Even upon hearing this discriminatory verbiage, it was not in my make up to truly understand it's vile meaning.

My friend and I played for a while then sat down to eat dinner. I was glad because my stomach had been grumbling from hunger and from the exotic aroma in the air.

It was an extraordinary cuisine consisting of fried chicken, grits, collard greens and Black Eyed Peas. It was absolutely delicious. It was a friendly atmosphere filled with respect and love, and I felt very secure amongst these nice people.

After dinner we went back out to play some more and before I knew it, the sun was setting and it was beginning to get pretty dark. My friend then asked if I would like to stay over, and once again my immediate response was yes. I don't remember the circumstances surrounding this decision, whether we asked his parents or even if I was asked if it would be all right with my Mother, it just happened. So we played the night away, washed up and then turned in.

I awoke very early the next morning and and the instant I rubbed my eyes to clear the cobwebs, I had the eerie feeling that even though I had a great time, there was the chance I might have made a mistake in judgment. That dear old Mom could be wondering where I was. And so this pang of guilt began to turn to worry.

Could I be in some sort of trouble for this indiscretion? And if so, how bad was it. I thought to myself, "Was it the yelling and screaming deep shit, or the beating with the strap deep shit." I began to feel very anxious as the thought of repercussions flooded my little mind, so I began to trigger the lying machine.

What possible story could be made up to convince Maggie that it was a good idea that I stayed out all night long, what sorry tale of doom and gloom could induce a positive response. I walked out of my new friends house without even a goodbye.

All of a sudden my gait went from a nonchalant walk to a worried trot. My brain was trying to conjure up the perfect excuse, but it wasn't going very well. Any story I came up with would have to be of the life or death nature, but I was drawing nothing but blanks.

I was being interrupted, by the constant sounding of a car horn. It was trying to get my attention. And as I turned to see who so rudely distracted me from concocting the perfect alibi, I became frozen in my tracks. It was a police car, and there was a policeman waving me over towards him. As I got closer, he asked, "Son, are you Joseph Kenney?" I replied in a very somber manner, "Yes Sir, I am". And in a very calm tone the policeman said, "Get in the car boy." And so I tentatively complied.

As I sat there trying my best to come up with anything that could possibly redeem my actions, the police officer said the worst possible thing I could imagine. He said, "Don't you know that your Mother has been worried sick about you?" "And that she had the police out looking for you all night."

"No Shit!" I was in some serious trouble now. What the hell was I going to do? So I reached very deep into my bag of misguided reasoning and pulled out the line, the big lie. It would be the line guaranteed to provoke empathy for the perpetrator of such an unforgivable decision. A decision, though definitely in the top ten of stupid was not done with malice, thereby deserves absolution.

The words also needed clout, and tears always gave the line clout. So in my best tearful display for sympathy, I began to spin my tale of woe. I began with whining to the cops, telling them, "My Mother's going to kill me. She beats me all the time I said." I was trying to drum up as much ammunition as possible, hoping to form allies to my predicament.

Once home, we were greeted by Maggie, with her own Crocodile Tears. A narrative constructed to relay the message of the perfect parental distress for a child gone missing. Wasn't it her that had caused an all points bulletin to be set into place? It was all an act to set the officers minds at ease. But not without a final retort to her, a warning by the officers not to use corporal punishment against me.

Maggie was told in not so many words that if she were to retaliate against me, that there would be consequences. There was the threat of having me removed from her care, or the possibility of having charges filed against her for child neglect. With all that said, I had a sense of relief that I had escaped the maelstrom of her wrath, my stretching of the truth had surely earned me an Academy Award.

Upon assuring the officers that her only concerns were of my safety, she replied that there would be no forthcoming punishment. But no sooner had the officers departed the screaming began, "Do you know how worried I've been?" "That maybe you were lying dead in some ditch. Or that someone had abducted and killed you."

I sat there apathetic, unable to respond, not understanding that what I had done was very wrong. It was just an impulsive act without reason. "Do you have anything to say for yourself, she roared." And as I sat there with my best perplexing gaze, her hand came flying across the side of my face.

I placed my arms over my head to protect myself, but it only seemed to make her more furious. She began flailing at me with her fists, and as she did the only words I could utter was "I'm sorry Ma."

Once her assault on me ceased, a calm came over her. She told me that she was sorry that she lost her temper with me, which was always the norm for my parents. And no sooner were those words spoken, she also admitted that she could not take care of me by herself, that she would have to find someone to look after me, that she did not want me to be alone as much as I'd been. So off again I would go.

CHAPTER SIXTEEN

The Naked Truth

Within the week I was placed with a couple that lived about an hour away from us. It was in the city of Tampa, across the bay from St. Pete's, a much more rural area with rows of small one story houses aligned perfectly up and down its streets. And if it weren't for the addresses flawlessly placed on the mailboxes you could not tell them apart.

Bob and Carol were considerably younger than my Mother. They were a handsome couple that seemed pleasant enough upon my meeting them. Their home was immaculate, in that everything seemed to be new and in perfect order. Everything seemed to have its place. Even the room that I was to call my own was meticulous.

My room had a single bed made up perfectly, with hospital corners on a blanket that was so taut you could bounce a quarter off of it. A nightstand was on one side of the bed with a lamp placed within arms reach. A dresser sat exactly in the middle of the room towards the foot of the bed, it all made its simple decor pleasing to the eyes. So my Mother and myself felt quite at ease in the fact that I would be living in a safe environment. Everything looked well enough, but looks can be deceiving.

It was around the time for school to begin and once again I would be placed into an environment that was alien to me. There was the prospect of meeting new kids. Of trying to fit in and of making new friends, which seemed so difficult. I felt so unique, so less than most of my peers. For as far as I could tell, all these other kids had lived a stable life with a loving Mother and Father to encourage them, that would booster their self esteem, to insure their safety, and present them the skills to succeed in life. Myself, I would put on the facade that all was well with me and wear the mask of indifference to hide the shame I felt about my own life.

As always, the explorer in me ventured out into the neighborhood, to stake my claim and blend in as much as possible. To try and make friends and hoping the incessant and tiring questions of whom I was, and where I came from would not last too long. My fictitious accounts of my perfect life usually caught up with me. The frustrations of trying to keep my stories straight caused aggressive behaviors that kept me at arms length of getting too close to someone.

I met this kid next door that fit the mold perfectly. He didn't ask shit and only cared about making a new buddy. His name was Johnny and he was the same age as myself. He even had the same physical characteristics as me, medium height and lanky, with blonde crew cut hair that extenuated the size of his ears to the point of embarrassment. An Alfred E. Newman look that the other children tended to tease him about.

Johnny and I hit it off pretty well and we would spend a lot of afternoons playing together in the neighborhood or at his house. He became my best friend, the hostage I usually took to deflect my own feelings of insecurity.

Within two weeks I began school and prepared myself for the stares that would ubiquitously come my way. The new kid in town, the kid from New York with the funny accent that was kind of puny for the sixth grade. The big eared, gangly, four eyed doofus that was going to try and fit in, with assets that left much to be desired.

Would I be the withdrawn preteen punk that bared the scornful look, that might relay something like, "Hey I'm a crazy Mother Fucker and you better not mess with me." Or would it be the jester, the kid that everyone kept around and dared to be the card in social situations. Flinging the brunt of a joke at some other poor kid, in lieu of them raining down on himself. To act out in class regardless of the consequences. I wanted to be neither I just wanted to be left alone.

Back at Bob and Carol's things started to change fast. I was told not touch anything outside of the room I slept in. And without a TV things became boring very quickly. They began to go out on a daily basis leaving me alone for long periods of time. I was allowed to play after school until dinner, but as soon as dinner was through I was bannished to my room and told to put on my pajamas. The twiddling of my thumbs to fall asleep became very old fast and I began to broaden my horizons upon their leaving to go out.

At first it was to turn the TV on with the volume very low. It was nerve wracking, because every slight noise made me jump out of my skin, to shut off the TV and scurry into bed. Every five minutes I would be making a mad dash to my room, my heart pounding and the fear of being caught tightening my throat. And the trepidation of the consequences that would befall me would cause my mouth to dry up so badly I wouldn't be able to swallow. But each time that it was a false alarm I became more and more brazen, more comfortable, until that fateful night that my luck ran out.

Bob and Carol left around 6:30 PM and as I peeked through the blinds to make sure their car had left, I immediately ran and turned on the TV. By now the volume had been raised so as to not have to struggle to hear the words being spoken on the tube. I was becoming increasingly more comfortable in this endeavor, but had become more and more careless also.

As I sat watching one of my favorite TV westerns the **Rifleman,** I became somewhat hungry and went into the kitchen to prepare myself a bowl of cereal. I returned to the sofa and continued to view my program, when I must have dozed off. All of a sudden a noise awoke me. It was Bob and Carol returning home. They were opening the door and I was about to be found out. A sudden burst of fear encompassed my body. I jumped up to begin a mad dash to my room, when all of a sudden "Bang, Crash." I had forgotten the bowl of cereal that was on my lap. It was still half full and when I jumped up the bowl and all of its contents flew into the air and came crashing down onto the coffee table shattering the bowl and whatever bric-a-brac that it landed on, causing a mess of gigantic proportions. I stood there in shock thinking "Oh Boy am I in for it now."

Upon setting their eyes on the disaster I created, a double-barreled burst of profanity rained down on me. "You Son of a Bitch! You little Son of a Bitch! what the hell have you done." It was coming at me so fast I wasn't able to determine who was saying what. "Get into that fucking room you little bastard" Bob screamed, as he grabbed the back of my neck to force me in the right direction. "Get into your fucking pajamas and get to sleep you ungrateful little Brat." And as I went to bed I could hear a heated argument on the other side of the door. For the next few days the daggers of contemptibility rained down on me from both of them.

Maggie would come to visit me about every two weeks and it just so happened that her weekend came on the heels of this latest fiasco. Upon her arrival Bob brought her to the side and discussed with her what had happened. Later in the visit Maggie pleaded with me. She said, "You have to behave yourself, it's costing me enough money just to have you here, I don't need the extra expense of you damaging things." As I apologized to her I said, "Ma I hate it here, these people don't like me and they treat me bad. I'm not allowed to do anything, touch anything I can't even watch television. All I do is stay in my room."

"They leave me alone all the time, I don't like what they eat, I just hate it here." She said, "I can't take you back with me, I haven't anyone to watch you, so you have to be on your best behavior." And

I remember upon her leaving that day, the love I had for her, once again faded a little bit more.

During the next week when it was time for Bob and Carol to go out, Bob said to me, "I want you to get undressed, no pajamas, everything off." Complying without objection, I stood in my underwear facing him. He barked at me again, "Everything, underwear also and hurry up." I began to protest but was cut off in mid-sentence, so I did as I was told. He took all of my clothes, even the clean ones in the dresser, told me to shut the door and get to bed.

As I laid there under the covers, just staring at the ceiling I heard them leaving. After a few minutes I decided to get up and just take a peek outside the door to check if they had gone. As I reached for the doorknob I noticed it would not turn. I kept trying to turn it with all my might, but it wouldn't budge. I was locked in the room.

All of a sudden I had to go pee. I thought to myself, what am I going to do? I started to panic, I began looking around the room to find somewhere I could relieve myself, but there was nothing. I finally looked at the window. It was facing the back yard and if I could reach it, I would be able to piss outside. . There was a desk chair opposite the bed, so I pulled it toward the window stood on top of it and peed right through the screen. I went back to bed, and as I lay there ashamed of my predicament, I made a petition to God. It was "God please get me away from here." Then I remembered it was useless, it hadn't worked in the past, and nothing changed. So once again I cried myself to sleep.

The locking me up in the room continued every time they went out, which seemed to be more frequently. If I learned one important lesson from this all, it was to piss before they leave.

The next time Maggie came, I told her what they were doing, but she didn't believe me. She told me to stop lying and accept having to stay there. She also surprised me with accusations by Bob and Carol that I had broken something else in the house. And as I began to profess my innocence, Maggie began to get angry with me and cut me off. I told her that if she didn't believe me, I didn't want to see her anymore, and I stormed off, back into this place I hated so much.

My attitude in school began to get worse and worse, and my outbursts of bad behavior escalated. I withdrew within myself Even Johnny noticed it during the bus ride to school and when we played outside his house. When I couldn't hold it in anymore, I confided to him what was happening. He told me he believed me and that he felt bad. Johnny was the only person that seemed concerned for me. But nothing happened to change the situation. Johnny even said that he spoke to his Mom about it, but that she kind of brushed it off as if she didn't want to get involved.

Finally I had had it and decided that the next time I was going to do something. Running away didn't seem to be a viable option because I had no idea where the hell I was. What was I going to do?

The next time I was left alone I waited in bed for about half an hour after Bob and Carrol left. I just wanted to make sure they were long gone. Then I jumped up out of bed naked as a jaybird and walked over to the window. I stood there for a moment pondering what I was about to do.

I pulled the desk chair to the front of the window, kneeled upon it and opened it as much as I could. Then I attempted the same with the screen. I had forged my plan. I would go to Johnny's house and when his Mom saw me naked, she would call my Mother. Then Maggie would have to believe me. But as I tried to lift the screen it wouldn't budge. I couldn't figure how to open it. Facing the window and standing on the chair I kicked as hard as I could with the bottom of my foot, and the screen popped out.

Bare ass naked I climbed out the window into the back yard. I ran as fast as I could through the back yards (thank God there were no fences) and came to Johnny's back door. I knocked and Johnny's Mother answered. And as I stood there with both my hands covering my privates I began to cry,

I had made it to freedom. Johnny's Mother whisked me inside and got a blanket to put around me. As she questioned me about what happened, I proceeded to explain to her that this is what they did to me any time they went out, and that my Mother didn't believe me when I told her.

She brought me a pair of pajamas to put on and put me into Johnny's room to stay with him, and then she walked out. Johnny turned to face me and said, "Boy you sure have some nerve, I don't know if I could have done that." And in my best bravado I came back with, "No big deal." Trying my best not to show how scared I was.

The police were called to the scene, my Mother was notified to come and get me, and then back to Rosie's I went. Within the next few months my Mother and I were on our way once again, back to New York. Leaving the sunshine state behind for what was to be just another time we would do so.

CHAPTER SEVENTEEN

The Whack-Whack Attack

B ack to mean Kitty's, the place of the embarrassing baths, and the doing your business in the smelly, dirty, hallway toilet. The bitter drunken witch who never shed a tear for her grandchildren, only complain about how we were such a burden, and how much we were imposing on her.

The only good memories I have from Kitty's, was when the Good Humor Man would come around. All the kids would be yelling up to their apartment windows and, begging for a dime to be thrown down. This was just another rite of passage for the kids living in the tenements of New York. So as not to have the dime bounce sky high after hitting the ground, and going under a car, or God forbid roll into the sewer, the parents or guardian would wrap it up in paper before tossing it out the window. The paper would fall slowly and gently down like a helicopter to the ground.

We stayed at Kitties house for a few months. Maggie enrolled me at The Sacred Heart Of Jesus Catholic School on 52nd Street between Ninth and Tenth Avenues. In the short time I was there, my rebelliousness towards the Catholic hierarchy would always cause me to recieve some sort of corporal punishment. There was the **Knuckle**

Wrap to the top of the head to gain your attention, as was the ***Burning Noogie***, or if called for by some severe offense, like talking back to Brother or even just talking in class while you were not supposed to, there was the trip to the Dean of Brother's office where in his infinite wisdom he would justly distribute a few whacks on the palms of your hands with a thick leather strap, and man did it sting.

I honestly believe that Corporal punishment was part of the curriculum to becoming a Nun, a Brother, or a Priest. This was the 1950's-early 60's and I can only imagine what they did to children just twenty years before.

While at Sacred Heart I heard the tale of a punk who actually put his dukes up to one of the brothers, and after doing so was brought to the basement and brutally beaten to death. With his own arm no less. The culprit was supposedly the Dean of Brothers. I would guess that this rumor was started to keep boys in check, the ones that had any ideas of retaliation.

If you acted out, you would be sent down to the Deans office to explain yourself, and depending on what egregious sin you committed, (like talking during class, or the infamous speaking back to brother, or even the occasional scuffle) it would determine the punishment that needed to be meted out.

Whack! Whack! Whack!, three to each hand with the leather strap was the norm. You would return to class, show brother your reddened palms then sit down. There would always be the muffled chuckles from the rest of the class. It usually made you laugh also, even though the sting wouldn't wear off for about an hour. Kids living during that era couldn't run home to complain to their parents or else a beating might ensue for your bad behaviors. Mostly it was "You got what you deserved, and that's it," so bringing it home made no sense.

One time I was at school without a pencil to write with so I leaned over to ask the kid next to me if I could borrow one of his. I whispered ever so gently so as not to disturb Brother Maclain laying out our studies for the day. But it was not quiet enough. Brother Mac spun around and yelled, " Kenney! Go down to the Deans office for talking in class, and take your friend with you. I said, " Brother Mac, I was just borrowing a pencil, I wasn't fooling around." And before I could get out the last word, he said, "Also tell brother you were talking back to me." As my classmate and I sulked out of the room you could hear the snickers.

We were headed for the Deans office, when I came up with a great idea. I grabbed my accomplice by his arm and yanked him into the Boys Bathroom room with me. I began to explain to him this fantastic plan I had concocted. We would stay in the bathroom for a while, rub our hands continuously on our maroon corduroy pants and then head back up to class to show Brother Mac that we were meted out our punishment. The honor system would be the means of our escape from the unjust punishment we were to receive.

The plan was hatched, and we vigorously began rubbing as hard as we could against our pants, almost to the point of rubbing right through the skin of our palms. We were comparing each other palms waiting for the nod of agreement that our hands were red enough to be shown to Brother Mac. When we reached the point of agreement, that our hands had seemed to reveal a swift and just punishment for our crimes, we began rubbing at our eyes also, efficiently enough to seem that we had been crying. The perfect plan had been devised.

We knocked to enter our classroom and immediately walked up to Brother to show him our palms. With the appropriate punishment being meted out, he told us to return to our seats. Once again the smirks and chuckles accompanied us on our trek back to our desks, only this time the smile of triumph encompassed our faces. It would be fodder for our tale during recess.

Only one problem, no sooner did we sit down, the Dean of Brothers walked in into class. "No fucking way!" I said to myself as I slumped down deep into my seat. My profanities through most of my life danced through my thoughts only, but every once in a while one might slip out and cause me to have to eat a bar of soap. "What were these people thinking?" Oh yeah! "Put lye in their mouths, that should teach them not to swear like us." The do as I say crap not as I do rhetoric always confused the shit out of me.

There must have been some discussion between Brother Mac and the Dean because as I sat there slumped in my seat, their heads would turn to look towards me, and my partner in crime. They were eyes that spoke, GOTCHA! Then the Dean yelled "Mr. Kenney! Get up here." And as I tentatively walked to the front of the room and stood in front of Brother, I was given the noogie from hell. And then the Dean escorted my crime partner and I back down to his office for our just due. I could swear a lump was developing from where Brother nuckle bopped me on the head.

Needless to say the next two weeks the palms of my hands looked as if I had left them on a hot stove for an hour. Thinking back, it seemed I was never able to get away with anything. But it never stopped me from trying.

I had finished the year at Sacred Heart and was heading for the seventh grade when Maggie informed me that we would be going back to Florida, as she had saved enough money to return.

CHAPTER EIGHTEEN

Katey's Return

It was towards the end of my Fathers Bowery Run and he was beginning to stay sober for longer periods of time. The little ones, Megan and Maeve were still at St Joseph's, and I had learned that Katey had been living with a family friend named Frank for a while, it was her second time going to live with him. The first time was when the Little Ones and I went to live with Erin.

Frank was a man handicapped by Cerebral Palsy, but didn't let his affliction stop him from being a successful businessman. He owned some sort of company that had him in the city most of the time, and besides his house in Connecticut, he also had an apartment that was just up the block from where we had lived on Forty Sixth Street. We used to call him Uncle Frank, but back then anyone we knew by first name automatically became an Aunt or an Uncle. I remember Frank always having some change for us whenever we bumped into him. If not some change, a piece of gum or candy was always on hand. He was a very upstanding and gentle soul, and everyone admired him a great deal.

Somehow my Sister Katey became a ward of his and lived in a style that we were surely not accustomed to. She lived in a beautiful home in the country, attended a very good school, and had a loving benefactor that took wonderful care of her. But that was all about to change very shortly.

Maggie was working very hard as a waitress and bartender. Her plan was to make as much money as she could and return with me to Florida. Little was I to know, she had allready accrued enough for bus fare and a couple of months rent, so we would be off posthaste. She did not want my Father to know she was in town because it might spoil her plans. I was sitting in Shitty Kitty's kitchen when Maggie rang the bell, letting us know she was coming up the stairs. She yelled out for some help, so I raced out the door and down the hallway.

I peeked over the banister below and could see her walking up, (her hand sliding up the banister each half a flight, one direction then the next. "Wait a minute," sliding its way up the stairs was a second hand. Who could this be with Maggie? And as I met my Mother on the floor below I noticed someone standing directly behind her. She was a young girl about thirteen years of age or so, and as I took a closer look I realized that it was my sister Katelyn. It had been about a year and a half since I saw her last, but I didn't hesitate to run to her. I immediately gave her a hug and a kiss and helped her and my Mom upstairs.

Over dinner Maggie explained to me that Katey would be coming with us to Florida. We would be living together as a family in our own place, and that meant I would not be left alone anymore. It seemed so long since I had seen any of my sisters, and though I felt aloof, I had nothing but warm feelings upon seeing Katey. But I couldn't help thinking of Megan and Maeve who were still at the orphanage. It bothered me quite a bit. What was to happen to them? Who would be checking in on them? They were so little.

"Wouldn't it be nice if we were all together" I'd think, living like one big happy family. I heard that spoken many times by Jim, and it sounded good. But that wouldn't be the case, because before long my Father would gain custody of Megan and Maeve. While looking back as a teenager, I came to the conclusion that we would have all been better off where we were. It's a sad truth, but an honest assessment. Jim and Maggie didn't know how to be parent's, they didn't know how to raise children. And they should have left us where we were. At least in the orphanage we would have received a good education and most assurably been more successful.

The Greyhound bus ride and a short stay at Rosie's became my Mother's mantra. And within a month we had our own place, our own home.

In the beginning things were idyllic, Katey and I got along like perfectly loving siblings. I had shown her around St. Pete's, shown her where all the good Motels were, where we could swim at without being bothered. We watched TV and ate frozen fruit at Sears and Roebuck and played almost every day at McRory's. But slowly and subtly we began to get on each other's nerves.

I would get bored, so I would antagonize her to the point of her kicking the crap out of me. It never stopped me though. I needed the attention, and like my whole life up till then even negative attention was better than none at all. But isnt that really the way Big Sisters and Little Brothers act? Little Brother goes, Nyah -Nyah!-Nyah! Nyah! Nyah! And Big Sister goes, Bing! Bang-Boom!-Bam!-Bam!. But even through all the ass whippings, it was still better than being alone. And in reality, just like when we were younger, she would always be there to protect me, and I loved her for it.

CHAPTER NINETEEN

The Mistake at the Mirror Lake

I t was the end of August, time to go back to school, and even though I had missed a lot of school days the year before, my time at Sacred Heart and my test grades allowed me to proceed on to the seventh grade. I was only ten at the time and Katey and I would be going to the same school, Mirror Lake Junior High.

Mirror lake itself was a man made pool of water, a perfectly excavated oval. It was glass like, a dark and shimmering perfect mirror. And besides the occasional duck swimming about, it was perfectly still. It had a walkway that encircled completely around the lake, it would allow two people to walk side by side comfortably. Beautiful palm trees were planted so evenly, that they blocked out the sweltering afternoon sun no matter where you stood, giving respite from the heat and humidity that was St. Petersburg. Every few yards there were park benches, and in the morning scores of students hung out together, sitting and socializing.

Mirror Lake Junior High School was massive, and accommodated a multitude of students. It was at times overwhelming to me. Up to this point in my life the schools I attended were puny in comparison. Even the largest school I attended had but a few hundred pupils attending. I'm sure Mirror Lake had at the least two thousand kids going there, maybe more.

To get there I would take the Main Street bus downtown, get off at my stop and head south for a couple of blocks. This is where it all became daunting to me. Crowds of kids came from every direction. They came by the hundreds, every one of them bigger than me. I was ten years old and entering the seventh grade, I wouldn't turn eleven until the following April. Though she protected me in the past, my sister didn't want us to be seen together, I embarrassed her, so she would take an earlier bus.

The school itself was captivating, its campus picturesque. The building was a massive four-story structure built in a Mission Revival style. Its stucco walls were imbedded with Chattanooga stones, which gave it a unique hue,

The outside campus had a baseball field, a football/soccer/lacrosse field and a dozen outside basketball courts. The indoor gymnasium had a full size basketball court with bleachers on both sides. There was also an indoor, Olympic Sized pool.

The entrance to this magnificent structure had three very large arched double doorways that allowed the foot traffic to enter and exit easily. Once inside the noise from the crowded hallways was deafening. Kids were bustling in every direction like mobs of scurrying rats. I think I had a panic attack every time I had to enter the hallway between classes. It was a feeling that I might be trampled upon, and once the dust had settled they would find me crushed to death.

The classes were not only big they were overcrowded. When I entered I would race to the back of the classroom trying to blend in with the furniture like I always had.

This was also the first time in my life that I had to go from room to room for classes, it was excruciating and I couldn't wait for the day to be over. It was all, so beyond my imagination. The only sports complex we had were schoolyards made of concrete with maybe a half dozen backboards and a few handball courts. We played stickball in the streets, frequently interrupted by an automobile maneuvering down the block. Impatient, the drivers would push heavily upon their horns.

I wasn't the only one distinctly different, there was only one black student in the whole school, and it happened to be a girl. I imagine she must have felt as intimidated as I did, maybe more.

Entering my assigned Home Room I did as I'd always done, I kept my head down so as not to look anyone in the eye and walked to the back of the class. The apprehension that I experienced immobilized me. Peeking up I could see all the other kids staring at me, checking me out. I'd imagine them thinking, "Who was this puny little runt, and what the hell was he doing here?"

I had made my way into the back corner desk closest to the door. I always felt the most comfortable there no matter what school I was going to. It allowed me to be able to escape quickly, to run away if for some reason I felt too much anxiety. Like being called upon by the teacher, fearful that I would be singled out and become the brunt of teasing because of how small in stature I was.

As our Homeroom Teacher entered the classroom things began to settle down and everyone returned to their desks. He began by writing his name on the board and pronouncing it. It was one of those names that were difficult for most to enunciate, you know with a lot of K's W's I's and Z's.

After introducing himself, he started to take attendance. He asked that when your name was called out that you stand up, give your name and announce "Here!" One by one kids were standing up to say who they were, and occasionally would have to correct the pronunciation of their names to the teacher.

As the names were being read aloud I remembered how much I hated to hear my last name spoken, it sounded so Irish, and I felt ashamed by it. Having been teased about it in the past, that all Irish were Drunks and Lowlives, it influenced my disdain for my moniker. Some kids would tease me and call me a filthy Mick, "Why? I don't know."

Finally my name was announced. Why did it always seem more audible than the rest of the names, so stern and boisterous with a tinge of, "I'm better than you." I never felt that way or wanted to be perceived in that manner.

As I rose to say my name I could feel everyone's eyes being transfixed upon me. I could feel the blood in my body rush to my face and I began to sweat profusely. My hands began to tremble, my mouth became cotton dry, and I could swear that when this happened, it made my ears stickout even more. Joseph Kenney "Here" I blurted out. And when I did it sounded like the yelp of a puppy. Immediately all 35 kids began laughing at me. Even the teacher had an amused look about him.

"Why does this shit have to happen to me" I thought? "As hard as thing's are why can't I even say my own damned name right." And when I started to sit down, the tears began to well up in my eyes, and it became difficult to breathe. Feeling frantic, it all began to get the best of me and I grabbed my notebook and ran as fast as I could out the door, down the hall, and out of the school.

Racing down the outer steps of school I could feel a cool breeze come over me. My breathing became less labored and the sweat on my body began to dry up. I ran around the lake to the other side and sat down on one of the benches. I thought to myself, "Whats wrong with me me? I just want to be a normal kid." Struggling to stop the voice in my head, I put my hands up to my face and began to sob. Because of many similar experiences, I would find that over the next few years, I was unable to sit in class without this overpowering urge to get up and run. So I began to cut classes and play hooky a lot more often.

It seemed that I was in detention all the time at Mirror Lake. I think that I even preferred detention because at least I was amongst what I deduced were my true peers, the Doofusses, Retards, and Misfits. But detention also afforded me a platform to be noticed. For one little moment, I could to feel good about myself. Besides the badge of courage I donned for being the outcast and rebel, I was also able to show off my above average intelligence.

Detention at Mirror Lake was a contest of solving basic mathematical problems. It consisted of apiece of paper with twenty math problems on it. There were five addition problems, five subtraction problems, five multiplication problems and five division problems. The problems kind of looked like this.

addition
537993178265626282889
+83765445370387252457
+98348784847456474747
+77673559047003673489
+72430786342346378834=

subtraction
69585656542368540958577758856909696 8995959599
-5352367673475337663 42376785006040484653
-6475968632453774747
-653208532=

multiplication
06958576383i9399393910 8635432322336758887
x95756565788588587566=

division
838346558858969969967 89895853240472433323 57005857555
564547
divided by 7464580900 =

Detention was supposed to keep you busy for about two hours and many of the kids were not even able to solve half of those problems in that time. But if for some reason you turned in a paper completed, it was checked against a master sheet. If anything was wrong it was handed back to you to figure where you made the mistake. It drove most of the kid's nuts. I was very good at figuring out basic math problems, but most of these kids hadn't even memorized their multiplication table yet. That was over two years ago for me.

I took on the juggernaut of this challenge with great fervor. I tackled each problem with a steadiness and consistency of someone much older than myself. And within forty-five minutes, I would hand in my paper to the teacher, who upon checking for mistakes became amazed at the accuracy. I would goad the teacher and arrogantly prance out the door.

These moments few and far between became some of the only times that my pride matched or bettered my low self-esteem. Even so, it did not deter my acting out antisocially. I continued to miss school on a consistent basis. Going back and forth from New York to Florida so many times I got lost in a system of red tape, and languished in the seventh grade for the next four years. Being left back three straight times, without one word from Maggie or Jim.

CHAPTER TWENTY

The Pains Of Owning A Bike

And Other Stuff In Between

The St. Petersburg P.A.L. had a program for the kid's less fortunate. You could get a bicycle for free under two conditions. A: You have to build your own bike, with the help from one of the adults that worked there and B: You would have to pay Twenty-Five cents to purchase a bicycle license.

"Yes" all bicycles were to be licensed by the Police Department. I thought it was dumb, even my Mother agreed, as she put the quarter in to my hand. This was my first bicycle, my very own not borrowed like the one from Lenny. It gave me a sense of empowerment that I had never felt before. I could get places faster, I could go longer distances, and my boundaries could become endless. The freedom and happiness it provided made me feel grateful. My bike became my best friend.

There are three occasions that stick out regarding my first couple of bikes. Two were extremely painful, as well as somewhat comical. I was riding my bike along side of this kid I met, the first time I went to live in Florida. He was of one of the few friends I had made and we were just out for a leisurely drive. We were jabbering back and forth, just goofing around and occasionally I would peer over my right shoulder to look at him. We were riding on the sidewalk when I turned again to look towards him and relay some stupid joke, when all of a sudden he yelled, "Watch out!"

I turned to see what the problem was and BAM! I hit a lamppost dead center with my front wheel and was thrust head first into it. The sound it made reverberated like a Chinese Gong for about ten seconds. I was sitting on the ground rubbing my forehead and noticed it had begun swell up almost immediately. It was numb to the touch and hadn't begun to hurt yet, but the bump itself was growing quickly. Within five minutes it was like I had a horn in the middle of my head. Being it didn't hurt I just laughed it off so I wouldn't feel so stupid in front of my friend. I picked up my bike and told my buddy that I would see him later I wanted to go home to lay down for a while.

When I got home no one was there so I proceeded to go into the bathroom to check my head. "Holy Shit!" I blurted out, knowing no one was home to hear my use of profanity. But this bump on my head had deservedly earned such use of the English language. I looked like a fucking Rhinoceros, or at least a Unicorn. I had this huge purplish and blue protrusion directly in the middle of my forehead. It couldn't have been placed more centered if you used a ruler and a pen to mark it. Man! It was ugly.

All of a sudden I got a splitting headache, and went to my bed to lie down. I fell asleep for a while, but was woken up by the sound of someone entering the apartment. It was Maggie coming home from work. And when I got up to go outside to greet her, the sound of her scream upon seeing me sent chills through my body. I must have looked like a monster.

After explaining to her what happened she applied ice to my injury and just shook her head. A look that spoke to something like, "So, What am I going to do with you? You're going to be the death of me." I'm sure I must have sustained a concussion, but nothing came of it, it was just Joey being Joey.

The second chapter in this bicycle saga was not painful. It happened one day as I was setting out to ride to the beach. When I rode off on my bike I would take a shortcut down one of the alleyways, then I'd cut through a neighbor's back yard and go down a hill towards the Elks Club parking lot. This is where I hit Main Street and ride west towards the beach.

It was late morning and getting pretty hot out. I had my bathing suit on already and was raring to go. I had a habit of taking the hill very fast and speeding through the parking lot. It was fun to see just how fast I could go. I had come out of the Elks Club lot like a bat out of hell and hit Main Street in full stride when all of a sudden a police car came up behind me and put on his lights. I slowed down a bit and was waiting for him to go around me, but that was not the case. He was signaling for me to stop.

I thought, "What did I do" So I stopped and pulled over to the curb. The officer exited the car, came over to me and asked where I was going. I told him that I was headed for the beach and was going to meet a friend. He told me that I was speeding, going forty miles per hour. I looked at him quizzically like, "Ok I was going fast, it won't happen again," but before those words could leave my lips he told me that he would be impounding my bike and that one of my parents would have to go to the police station for me to get it back. "What the hell! He's impounding my bike? This is pure BS."

I began protesting vehemently, even begging him to not take my bike, but it was to no avail. And as I sat watching my prized possession being thrown into his trunk, I thought to myself: "How am I going to explain this one to my Mother"

When Maggie returned from work that day, I proceeded to tell her my tale of woe. The story needed no embellishment the truth was enough. It was so utterly preposterous that she did not believe me at first, which was normal. She was sure that I committed some sort of egregious offense, otherwise why would my bike have been confiscated. I swore up and down that I was telling the truth and if she came down with me to the police station she would see for herself.

My mother accompanied me down to the Police station. She was sure that there was more to this story than I was letting on to be. That I must have done something terrible, or else why would they confiscate my bike?

Entering the Station House we walked up to the desk sergeant and asked whom we were to speak to regarding this matter. When all of a sudden I spotted him, pointed and I said "Ma! That's the guy."

We walked over to him and my Mother asked, "excuse me sir, did you take my son's bicycle from him." He answered, " yes ma'am, he was doing forty mph in a twenty five mph zone and I confiscated the bike. He needs to be more careful."

Well! My Mother launched into such a profanity-laden tirade, it made my face turned red. She ridiculed him beyond ridiculousness saying things like, "Don't you have anything better to do than harass my kid because he was going too fast: YOU FUCKING ASSHOLE! How is it possible for a child to reach 40 MPH on a plain bicycle? It isn't even a ten speed bike you moron. There's no possible way."

And as he backed off from this barrage of insults, you could hear his colleagues behind him roaring with laughter. My Mom, all four foot ten inches of her had succeeded in belittling this big guy to the point of him actually apologizing to her. Maggie had come through she had saved the day. And so I left with great satisfaction, knowing this guy wasn't going to take my bike from me ever again.

My second painful bicycle memory was when Katey was living with us in Florida. She had also gotten a bike from the P.A.L. and we would ride together some times. One day as I went to get my bike to go for a ride, I noticed I had a flat front tire. I'd need to purchase a patch kit to repair it. The Sears and Roebuck was the only place I knew to purchase one and I wanted it done as fast as I could. So I asked Katey if I could borrow her bike, but she wouldn't let me. She didn't trust me with it. She knew I drove mine with complete abandon and had quite a few small mishaps causing numerous dents, dings and unaccustomed impressions. If my bike were a car, it would have been relegated to the junkyard. But it was mine and I loved it. What did she expect? It was a boy's bike and it was supposed to look that way.

My sister adamantly refused to let me use her bike, but said that she would give me a ride. I dejectedly agreed, I needed my bike back ASAP. I couldn't ride sidesaddle because it was a girl's bike, so I had to sit on the handlebars. I remember feeling awkward-when we first took off, the bike was wobbling and out of control. I wasn't sure that she could handle it because we had to attempt it a few times before she gained some sort of ballance. The third time was the charm and we took off to the store.

About five blocks away I began to feel uncomfortable and began fidgeting around, every bump we hit would hurt my bony little ass to the point I wanted to jump off. The next bump I shifted a little too much and began sliding forward. We were traveling at a pretty good rate of speed and I became frightened to jump off for fear that she would run me over. And as I struggled to shift back on the bike my feet went inward and were sucked into the spokes.

The wheels suddenly froze and I was flung forward off the handlebars slamming full force into the ground, BAM! Thank God I had put up my arms to cushion my head, because I went face down at warp speed. I lay there dazed for a few minutes and then tried to get up. When all of a sudden the pain began to set in. "Shit!" I couldn't tell what hurt more, my arms, my head or my feet.

My hands and arms were pretty scraped up, the sting of hitting the funny bone on my elbows felt like my arms had separated from my body. My hands had the skin on the palms torn back with gravel embedded in both of them. Though my hands cushioned my head it was still ringing as if I had slammed it full force into a wall. My nose was bleeding and I had a small cut on my forehead. "But MAN! My feet, my poor feet," they were screaming in agony. I thought I broke every bone in them.

I gingerly untied my sneakers and removed them. I noticed that my socks were bloody so I removed them also to survey the damage. I could see an indentation in the skin exactly where my feet had met the spokes. The skin on my feet, like the palms of my hands, had been lifted, and around the indentations it began to show a purplish hue. I was too dazed to even cry, as I sat there stunned, and with my head ringing. I began to hear something in the background. It was muffled laughter. "Son of a Bitch! Katey was laughing at me". I'm here in semi critical condition and my sister who just flew to the top of my most hated persons list is fucking laughing at me.

I became so enraged that I began to cry. My crying surely would extract the compassion this accident deserved. But no! She was laughing hysterically and rolling around the ground. I knew then that if I could only muster up enough strength to get up and reach her, I'd grab her by the neck and choke her to death.

Suddenly, a police car pulled up to the curb that I was sitting near and this big cop got out to see what was going on. When we explained the situation he began to scold us for riding the bike with someone on the handlebars. He said it was against regulations because you could get hurt doing so. That definitely was not what I wanted to hear. I wanted him to arrest my sister for feloniously laughing at me.

The police officer threw my sisters bike into his trunk, helped me get to my feet and gave us both a ride home. Sitting in the back of the car, I gave Katey a brisk elbow to the ribs and said, "There!" For the next few days I walked around like a duck, waddling in pain.

CHAPTER TWENTY ONE

Miscellaneous Mayhems and Mishaps

I t was about a year before Katey came to live with Maggie and me, and around three months removed from the Rhinoceros incident. We'd been living in this small 2 Bedroom home. It was a pink monstrosity with a huge back yard. The property stretched from the front of the house, on 1st Avenue and 46th Street all the way behind the house to 2nd Avenue. It had the exact address as the place I was born at, 313 on 46th Street. The only difference was that instead of it being 313 East, it was 313 North.

One day while I was playing with a friend of mine, I came up with what I thought was a great idea. I said: "let's go play up on the roof, it'l be fun, we can use the ladder behind my house to get up there." My friend agreed, and so up we went. We grabbed the ladder, leaned it up against the side of the house and scaled our way up onto the roof.

The pitch on the roof made it somewhat difficult to walk around, so we slowly surveyed our surroundings. I noticed the tree closest to the house, and how near it's limbs were to eave of the roof. One was actually at eye level when I stood near the edge. I turned to my comrade and said: "lets jump out onto the tree limb and climb down, it's close enough."

Being the mastermind of this folly, I knew that I would have to go first. No matter how many dares, doubled or tripled, whoever came up with the idea had to go first. So I gingerly made my way as close to the edge as I could. I slowly swayed back and forth to give myself the utmost propulsion forward. I stared intently at the branch trying to gauge my leap, when I became distracted. My stupid friend began saying, "What's the matter, scared"? And even though my inner self had alerted me to the possible danger, my childhood ego took over and I jumped.

As I flew through the air, my belly began to flip. It was the nauseous feeling my body would exhibit when I suddenly felt in Jeopardy. My breath immediately left me, my mouth dried up and I felt a weakness blanket my body."Oh Shit!" was all I could think of.

As the gravity started to tug at me, I noticed that the target was going to be met. I would reach my goal, but Oh! the things I did not take into account. I did not take into consideration the thickness of the limb, that it would be too wide to grasp securely. And I also didn't take into effect that a tree limb is knotted, and not a smooth object.

Upon hitting the target, everything I supposed would happen went out the window. I made it to the limb okay but I was barely able to hang on. My body's weight caused me to swing outward. And as I did I could feel a burning in the palm of my hands as they raked across knots of the tree limb. And as soon I became parallel to the limb I lost the battle to hang on.

Like the trapeze artist when he releases the bar to perform a somersault, I began to fly up into the air. The only problems were, A: There would be no one to catch me, and B: There was no net underneath to break my fall. It was almost as if time stood still for a minute, It seemed surreal.

I could see my surroundings, but they were all upside down, and things were moving fast. Then whoosh! I began plummeting down towards the earth. My natural instincts were to outstretch my arms to break my fall and somehow I was able to carry this out while dizzily tumbling upside down and backwards. As I reached terra firma, the ground proved too much for my skinny little arms. They buckled like a can of soda stepped on by a gorilla.

Finishing that remarkable handstand I rolled a little bit and came to a stop at the trees trunk. I shook the cobwebs out of my head and thought, "Holy Shit! I survived without breaking my neck. Whew!"

I was stunned pretty bad and sat there for a minute to gain my composure. My arms were numb from landing full force the way I did, so I began to rub them vigorously. But all of a sudden I began to feel pain. It started in my wrists, a throbbing ache surrounding the joints just above my hands. Then every beat of my pulse sent a shooting, stabbing feeling directly into the bone. I tried to get up but was unable to put any pressure on my hands, so I rolled onto my stomach, bent my body at the waist and used my head to get to a position where I could lift myself up. As I stood there for a moment I noticed my friend. His mouth was agape with a look of wonder and awe in his eyes. They told the story of the most wonderful accomplishment he had ever experienced. But what came out of his mouth seemed so anticlimactic. "Wow! That was cool!" Wow that was cool! Wow that was cool! "Shit, that's the best he could come up with".

My wrists were not the only joints to sustain damage. I tried to lift my left arm but it wouldn't cooperate. My right shoulder felt locked in place and every movement felt as if I was shot with a gun. Upon bringing my arm up towards my chest to cradle it in a protective position my elbow hurt like it was hit with a two by four. "Now it was time to cry. I was fucked."

My Mother had been working the lunch counter at the local Five and Dime so it was the logical place to go. I'd stop in once in a while for a Banana Split. They had balloons lined up and down the counter and you would choose one and whatever price tag was in the ballon is what you paid for it. It was one penny up to 39 cents and Maggie allways knew where the penny and nickel balloons were. I asked my friend to come with me, but much to my dismay, out of the blue he remembered that he had to get home right away. So I ran as fast as my battered body would take me. Every pounding of my legs to the ground, exacerbated the pain in my arms. And along the way all I could think of was,"Crap! Maggie's going to be pissed at me."

As I reached the doorway to the Five and Dime I had to time things perfectly. The doors swung open towards the outside and I was unable to grasp the handle to open it. So I waited for someone to exit then jumped at the door to put pressure on it with my back. Upon entering I ran directly towards the lunch counter. I spotted my Mother serving something to eat to a customer and yelled out to her. "Ma! I blurted out, cryin, I hurt myself bad, I fell out of a tree."

Maggie could tell that something was terribly wrong right away. By this time both my wrists and my right elbow had begun to swell badly. My elbow began to show terrible bruising and she could see in my face the excruciating pain I was in, so she told one of her colleagues that she had to leave right away. She then took me by taxi to the hospital.

When we arrived at the hospital the triage nurse took me at once into the emergency room area, and a doctor was at my bedside within five minutes to examine me. He knew right away by looking at my arms and hands that there were fractures. So I was placed in a wheelchair and immediately brought to be X-Ray'd. Every time they moved my right arm to place it into position to be shot I would let out a scream, every movement was agonizing.

When the results of the x-rays came back, it was worse than we imagined. I had sustained breaks in both my wrists, a fracture of the left elbow and a dislocated right shoulder. My Mother upon hearing the results could only shake her head. Within a couple of hours I had a cast on my left arm that extended past the elbow about six inches, a perfect L-shape. The right arm was cast just below the elbow and both arms were in a sling. It must have looked pretty comical at that moment, but the next six weeks were murder. For the first few weeks not only did I need Mother feed me, she also had to bathe me.

The
BRANCH and
END TIME

After a couple of weeks I was able to feed myself with my right hand, my four fingers protruding from the cast were no longer hurting when I moved them. Thank God Maggie would no longer have to help me bathe.

Within the next month I would have to have my right arm recast because I tried to use it as a hammer and destroyed it completely. Six weeks after the accident my left arm was cast free and the right arm was re cast cast just above the wrist. Three weeks after that, done.

Things were pretty much going well for Katey and I, we had settled in and had formed the typical sibling bond, a love-hate relationship between a brother and sister. There were the times when she was with her friends that she would totally ignore me. But on the other side of the coin, there were the times when we would forge alliances for the common purpose.

One commonality that we shared was our disdain for our Mothers boyfriend Lenny. Not that Lenny was a bad guy. In fact he actually tried hard to adapt himself to our family. He would take us places and buy us things to endear us towards him. But the brats we were would have none of it. As far as we were concerned, Lenny wasn't our Father and he took time away from us being with our Mother. He was an outsider that didn't belong, and he had to go.

There were the times he would stay over and we would act out in ways that were not conducive to making someone feel welcome into the family circle. We became boisterous and argumentative any time he chastised us.

Lenny was totally deaf, and wore hearing aids in both ears. Evidently he didn't wear them to bed because the nights he stayed at our house he would emerge from the bedroom the next morning without his hearing devises, and Katey and myself would put our hands in front of our mouths and would utter some stupid profanity that made us laugh. Unless Lenny could see our lips moving he hadn't a clue we were making fun of him. Whenever his back was turned we would give him the finger.

He knew most of the time what we were doing, because in our callous manners we never hid it very well. We constantly verbalized our discontent towards Lenny whenever my Mother was around. The relentless harassment and rudeness towards him caused his visits to become less and less frequent, until after a while he didn't come around at all.

It wasn't until I was much oldert that I had a better understanding of the situation. I realized that my self-centered behavior probably denied Maggie the satisfaction of having a loving relationship of her own. Her relationship with Lenny couldn't sustain the negativity and eventually they both came to realize it couldn't work out.

It was getting harder and harder for my Mother to make enough money to support us in Florida.The minimum wage was one of the lowest in the nation for waitresses, and the tips were terrible. Most of the people in St.Pete were retirees. They were living on fixed-incomes and tipped miserably. Lenny was not in the picture anymore and there was really nothing holding her back, so she decided to return to New York. It would be for the final time.

It was 1963, the Beach Boys and Four Seasons were topping the charts, and the Twist, the Locomotion and the Watussi were the dance craze. Motown was starting to gel' My Mom's favorite's songs were Hello Dolly by Louie Armstrong and Red Rose for a Blue Lady by Bobby Vinton. Life was good and we were heading back home to New York.

The day we were leaving we had things packed up and we were carrying them downstairs to be loaded into a friend's pickup truck. My Mother had placed the birdcage on the top of the outside staircase. We were going to take it onto the bus with us.

Inside this cage was a parakeet, loved by my Mother more than any of her possessions. I sometimes thought she loved that bird more than her children. It was not only a pet he was a drinking buddy. "Yeah! a drinking buddy!" Maggie would let it out of the cage while she was home. It had free reign of the apartment and used to fly all over the place.

When Maggie was sitting at the kitchen table she would feed him tiny scraps of food. But the funniest thing was when my Mom was drinking beer from a glass. This little creature would fly over, sit on the edge of her glass, and dip It's beak into her beer. I'm sure it was alcoholic because it would fly from the table, and bump into the walls on the way back to it's cage.

So what do I do? Like many times before, when not paying attention I became the stupid klutz, only this time it wasn't my fault. I was carrying a box down to the truck when I bumped something, and when I looked to see what it was I noticed that I had accidentally knocked the birdcage off the ledge of the stairs.

I knew there was going to be big trouble because the cage plummeted about fifteen feet and crashed onto the ground just about demolishing it. I saw the bird sitting outside the cage. Somehow the parakeet survived the fall.

All of a sudden it takes off. My terror filled scream signaled to my Mother that something terrible had happened, and when she came out and looked down from the second floor to see the cage crumpled to bits and her bird missing, she came running down after me, cursing up a storm and promising that when she caught me that she would kill me.

She was chasing me in circles, trying to get her hands on me, but I would just keep running around the truck staying just out of her reach, all thetime pleading with her: "Mom!, It was an accident, I didn't mean it! Please don't hit me!" And as she tired, she came to her senses and realized that I didn't mean to do it. I actually liked that bird a lot because he would also come over to me when I called, and sit on my hand.

We had a half hour before we had to leave and spent the whole time trying find the parakeet, but it had flown off. Maggie took it very hard and cried all the way to the bus station. I felt so terrible.

CHAPTER TWENTY TWO

Stories from Astoria

B ack to New York we went, with a short stay at Kitty's until Maggie could find an apartment for us. My sister Erin was still living in Astoria and now had two children of her own. She found an apartment for us on 38th Street and 23rd Avenue, and once Mom furnished it we moved in.

The apartment itself was a small one bedroom on the second floor of a brownstone that stood directly across from a factory, and adjacent to an apartment building. On one corner of 38th Street and 23rd Ave., was an Italian deli and on the other side a Knights of Columbus Hall. One block west was Steinway Street the main thoroughfare of the community and all its regional points of interest. I'm sure it was given that name because at the northern most end and the last stop on the bus line was the Steinway Piano Factory, a huge brick building that sat between, the Con Edison Power complex, and a colossal dump site.

Just across 23rd Avenue and Steinway was a tavern called Short's Bar. It became a favorite haunt of Maggie's. Many an evenings you could find her sitting at the bar acting like some sort of starlet, situated amongst her many admirer's and possibly a potential beau.

During the week, the clientele was less to be desired, usualy consisting of the of the neighborhood beer boys with nothing better to do or the occasional working stiff having a beer or a shot before heading home. Occasionaly one of the old drunks would buy Maggie a drink, and she would bask in the attention. She was the Queen of Sheba to these derelict old men. She was the atypical Bar Fly.

On the weekends a younger crowd would congregate and lend credibility to this neighborhood beer garden. If I was ever looking for Maggie all I had to do was walk across the street. She would be sitting at the bar, closest to the door, her stool quick to spin around and greet the next patron coming in, maybe her next free drink. Don't get me wrong, my Mother was no beggar, but she had two kids to take care of. So once in a while she accepted a drink.

School was about to begin and I had to be registered. I was placed in the seventh grade once again. I had been put there because my records from Florida did not attest to the fact that I had completed enough of the curriculum necessary to advance to grade eight. School began to be too bothersome, and so I continued on the path of playing hooky, or cutting classes.

On the first day of school at PS 141 I noticed I wasn't the smallest kid anymore. I had caught up to my peers. And in order to find and fit in to the crowd I desired to hang out with, I had begun to smoke cigarettes out in the open, in front of the school, as regularly as I could. I'd access them by stealing a couple from my Mother's purse or bumming them off my Sister. On rare occasions, if I had enough money I might even get someone to purchase a pack for me. Smoking made me feel a little tougher, a little older, to fit the mold of deception I wanted to portray.

There were a few occasions that stoood out during my short time at J.H.S. 141. One was the time during lunch break I had the chance to get even with this bigger kid that was constantly harassing me. He had noticed that I was new to the area and that I had no friends to speak of. He would as often as possible bully me in front of the other kids, making my time at this school difficult.

I was in the lunchroom one day when they were serving the meal that was the least appetizing to me, Chicken Chow Mein. It looked like a giant glob of snot and I wasn't about to put that crap in my mouth. I would rather go hungry than eat that pile of shit. And just as I was about to toss it into the trash bin I noticed my nemesis sitting at one of the lunch tables. I had this great idea just pop into my head that would get even with this asshole.

I walked over to the table he was sitting at and addressed him by his name. Then putting on my best perplexing look, I laid my tray in front of him and asked: "Do you see that goddamned bug in my lunch?" He replied quizzically, "No!" "I said: look closer it's right there." Pointing to the center of the plate. And as he bent over to look, I slammed his face into this mass of gook with such force the food splattered all over the table. And when he raised his head the Chow Mein dripped from his face all over his clothes.

The place went nuts. Kids were falling off their chairs and rolling on the floor with laughter. Here was this kid that would constantly intimidate me, my oppressor, beginning to cry like a baby, and run to the nearest teacher to tell on me. I saw at that moment, that this dick I had just humiliated in front of the whole school didn't have many friends, he wasn't as well liked as he might have thought, because many of the kids came up to me afterward and told me that they admired what I had done. This was to be the first of my many suspensions from Junior High School 141.

My next encounter happened to be with my English teacher, a real pompous jerk that had many of the teenyboppers falling all over him. This Piss Pot thought he was the Romeo of J.H.S. 141, and played the role to a T. I wouldn't be surprised if at sometime in his self absorbed illustrious career that he had been caught screwing one of these star-crossed schoolgirls. I didn't like him and I knew the feelings were mutual. I always played the clown during this particular class and would aim most of my jokes towards him.

One day after the numerous times being sent to the principal's office for my outbursts, he told me to stay behind after class was dismissed. With everyone gone he approached my desk, and out of nowhere he began this tirade of profanity-laden threats to fail me. It wasn't long before I fired back my own salvos of "I don't give a shits and fuck you's." I wasn't going to let this jerk off push me around. I was becoming accutely angry and thought, "Don't this Cocksucker know who he's Fucking with?"

I was getting to a point in my life where I decided to take a stand in certain situations. To not be pushed around and taken advantage of. To stand up for what I believed was right. The only problem was with all the mixed and fucked up messages I received, how in the hell could I possibly determine what was right or wrong? So I only went with the feeling in my gut, and that usually led to many bad decisions. Like exploding in a blind rage. So here we were face to face trying to best each other, screaming profanities and insults as fast as they could leave our mouths.

I must have struck a chord when I called him a Faggot because he grabbed me by the throat, kneed me in the stomach and raised his hand to punch me in the face. I tried my best to grab him back but he had me pretty good by the Adams Apple. I remember that when I tried to speak the words were barely audible, they sounded as if I was gurgling. I began to feel like I might pass out and so I began punching at his arm as hard as I could to get him to let go of my throat.

He punched me once in the chest, and as always when I became frustrated and full of rage I began to cry. I began flailing my fists trying to punch him in the face and then tried to kick him in the balls. But he grabbed hold of my shirt and kept me at a distance. Then seeing how out of control I was becoming he began letting up on his grip around my neck, all the while trying to calm me down, telling me to be cool, stop yelling and relax.

I'm sure that he realized this incident had escalated way beyond what was intended. That he might get into trouble for hitting a student like he did. And once I calmed down a little, he assured me that this was not what he meant, and he wanted to apologize for his actions. But he also explained to me that my behavior's needed to change, that it wasn't fair to him and the other kids disrupting the class like I did. So I agreed that in the future I would behave myself accordingly. My truancy continued to escalate, and my times attending classes diminished. But when I did attend English, this teacher and I developed an amicable relationship.

I was no angel, but I was suffering. I had been bouncing around my whole fucking life never feeling stable, never feeling like I fit in. I was always the new kid, the one that was looked upon with suspicion. I didn't want to make friends, what was the point? I was probably going to be moving somewhere else soon enough. It was very emotionaly painful when I left St. John's, simply for the reason I had been so close to my friend Paulie. I hadn't found a person since then that I cared very much about. We dreamed dreams of importance, where we would one day be rich and famous. We would live together in mansions with our families, and would be friends forever. But I found out it's not that way in real life, in real life people always go away.

My next memory was the time I was at school for the mid-term exam in Mathematics. I figured that I wouldn't do well because I had missed so much actual class work. I would never have gone to school that day if I had known about the test. But here I was sitting at my desk in the back row waiting for the test booklet, The one with the hundred problems to solve, and the correct reply staring you in the face somewhere enmeshed between three wrong answers. And the answer sheet, the one that had an immeasurable cache of ovals to be darkened even before the actual test was to begin. The test the teacher had to go over step by step to insure that your name and class number were marked in its proper place. It was the beginning of the computer age, and no one explained that to us.

In his final instructions the teacher informed us that we could receive extra credit on our test score. If we were able to finish the test before the time limit was up, we could receive extra credit. For every completed tTimes Table we wrote on the blank piece of paper handed to us we would be given an extra point. Example: the One times table, one point, the Two times table one point, and so on etc.

Students were beginning to get excited, thoughts of nineties and hundreds on the test drifted throughout the room. This was going to be a breeze! Though it really didn't matter to me because I was probably going to get left back anyway, as a goof I decided to do as well as I could, to finish as fast as I could and to do as much extra credit as I could. I was looking to make a statement, to remind myself that I was just as good as anyone else in the class, that I wasn't stupid.

The teacher gave us the go ahead to proceed and I opened up to the first page and there in front of me were the most mundane math problems you would want to see. It contained the most basic of arithmetic questions, Additions, Subtraction, Multiplication and Division. I breezed through the first fifty questions like I had the answers in front of me. I hadn't even taken a minute to actually study. The fifty questions that followed consisted of Fractions, Decimals, Percentages, and Mathematic Comprehension.

I was going through the test so fast it was scary; For sure I had made numerous mistakes. But I kept pushing myself, "Come on! go faster, you can do it". Even with my double-checking certain answers I was the first one done, which was my primary objective. I immediately began writing down the times tables.

One through Twelve was simple; I had memorized them two years ago. It was a breeze. I hadn't memorized the Thirteen times table, but it was easy enough, as were the rest. I had just completed the Twenty Third times table when we were informed that it was time to stop. I felt exhilarated in the fact that I had done so well. There would be no reason for me not to score 100%. I was sure that no one had matched or exceeded what I had accomplished, due to the fact that the braggarts in the class were telling everyone that would listen how far they had gone. None of them were even close to what I had done. It was one of the few times I walked out of class with my head up.

It wasn't until about a month later when I learned my midterm mark in Math. The teacher had spotted me in the lunchroom and ran up to me to let me know that not only did I get a mark of 94 on the test itself. I had actually been given a mark of one hundred and seventeen. On my report card I received 100% and thought to myself that the mark looked kind of funny sitting between all the F's that I received from every other class.

One day, not much later I was coming home from playing hooky all day I noticed the mailman had just made his rounds to my building. Not having access to the mailbox key, I peered through the slot to see if I might detect a truancy letter. I knew what one looked like, Maggie had shoved them in my face enough times, while reminding me that I was wasting my life, that I would grow up to be a bum. "Yeah, so frigging what."

By this time I was becoming much more rebellious and disrespectful. I would always have a smart-ass remark that would incite her. It usually led to being whipped with the belt, Maggies's favorite form of retribution. But on this occasion I beat her to the punch, because as I stared through the slot I could make out the form a postcard. It had typewritten markings on it and fit the description of the postcard of notice my school would send to the parents of a truant.

I decided that I was going to intercept this correspondence and defer the usual sermon and punishment. I tried to stick my little pinky into the slot hoping to somehow grab hold of it and slide it up along the front and out into my waiting hands, but I was barely able to touch the top of the postcard. I couldn't muster enough of a grip on it to slide it up and out. It was teasing the shit out of me, and like the proverbial carrot on the stick, it was always just out of reach.

So I asked myself. "What would happen if I put a lit match inside? Wouldn't it completely destroy the evidence?" Thinking this might be one of the most brilliant ideas I ever concocted I proceeded to take out a book of matches, (I had been smoking a couple years by now and I always carried them). I lit a match and tossed it into the mailbox,

Poof! It went out. I tried another and another, each time failing in my mission.

So I ran outside into the street looking for something to stick into the mailbox alongside the postcard to aid in my destroying the evidence. I spotted a piece of gum wrapper on the ground; it was exactly what I needed. So I picked it up and brought it back to the mailbox. I lit the wrapper and then slid it inside; this time it worked.

"Hallelujah!" I exclaimed to myself, my determination had finally paid off, the postcard had caught on fire. "But wait a minute" I thought, it looks a little too bright in there and there's more smoke than I had anticipated". "Holy shit! This is beginning to become a small blaze, what the hell am I going to do."

Frantically I began to blow air into the slot to try and put the fireout, but succeeded only in burning my lip. As the flames started to spill out of the slot I began to panic. What did I do? "God please don't let the fucking building burn down, I made a big mistake" (The foxhole prayer of a devout atheist.)

Then all of a sudden just as if I had a direct line to my maker (You Know, the one that I had completely disavowed in the past.) the fire died down and extinguished all byitself. An immense feeling of relief came over me. I had averted a complete catastrophe.

But I wasn't out of the woods as of yet,. There was still a lot of smoke that I hadn't taken into consideration, so I opened the vestibule door to air it out. Only problem was, it blew the smoke directly into the hallway causing some of the other tenants to open their doors to see what was burning. As soon as I began to hear the sound of voices, I let go of the door and ran out into the street before anyone could see me. I had been given a reprieve of the greatest magnitude. I hadn't burned down the building and had accomplished what I had set out to do, which was to destroy all evidence of my truancy, so I had thought. I went out to play for a while, it would be an hour or so before Maggie got home, dinner wouldn't be ready until about Six, so I figured I'd stay outside until then.

When I returned home, and as I opened the door to our apartment, Maggie was standing there waiting for me. She was standing with her hands at her side, my sister Katey was directly behind her. Something didn't feel right; there was a tension in the air. So I tried to break the ice with a cordial salutation, "Hey Mom, how was your day." But before another word came out of my mouth, Maggie raised her right hand and between two of her fingers were the remains of a postcard, it's blackened edges revealing a story of intrigue.

"What the hell is this"? She screamed. And as I tried to reply my throat immediately began to constrict and any moisture that I had in my mouth disappeared. "What are you talking about Ma, I don't know what that is." "Don't lie to me you son of a bitch or you're really going to get it." But what I learned during my short period here on God's green earth was, no matter what, "deny, deny, deny, lie, lie, lie."

I had stopped believing that bullshit about being honest long ago, I was going to get my ass handed to me whether I told the truth or not. So as soon as I denied my culpability, Maggie commenced to wail on me with a belt. As she did I raised my hands to block some of the lashing, so much so, that she began to punch me. She was acting her normal frustrated self, the frenzied lunatic that would stop at nothing to mete out punishment.

But I was starting to notice something. I was beginning to be able to defend myself a little more now. Instead of cowering and retreating I found myself advancing toward her, grabbing the belt, and deflecting most of her punches. She wasn't hurting me as much anymore. A sense of freedom came over me.

After Maggie's tirade when things calmed down, I found out that the card burned in the mailbox happened to be from my sister Katelyn's school not mine. Boy did I feel like an ass.

CHAPTER TWENTY TWO ½

The Turning Point-The Roundabout

Maggie's outbursts were legendary. To people outside the family she was a barbarian that didn't take shit from anyone. That's why in our home, it wasn't the Husband and Father that was the batterer it was the Wife and Mother. Take in point the following two examples given.

Jim was a pathetically serene drunk until the cop's would come to take him away. Then his belligerence would rear its ugly head, and he would challenge them to a fight. Things were different back then, the Cops didn't give a shit, they'd crack your head open in a second. That's why there was usually a brawl where Jim would wind up being thrown down the stairs, have a few teeth knocked out, then handcuffed and taken away. It was a lovely sight for small children to see.

Here's how it usually went. A) My Father comes home drunk and broke. B) My Mother curses, screams and punches the shit out of my Father. C) My Mother's fists begin to hurt from the barrage to my Father's's skull. D) My Mother calls the cops and my Father is arrested and locked up. It went this way almost every time. Don't get me wrong, Jim"s alcoholic drinking and degenerate gambling would infuriate anyone. I just wanted to make a point of how violent Maggie could be.

There was a time one Thanksgiving day when I was being my typical bratty self, I upset Maggie so much, she wound up dropping the turkey on the floor. She became so furious, she threw the carving knife at me, barely missing my head. I looked directly at her with a scowl on my face and decided right then and there something had to be done. I just didn't know exactly what that was, yet.

CHAPTER TWENTY THREE

Stories Continued

Outside of school I was starting to adapt to the area and began making some friends. We would hang out at Steinway Park, a small area about half a block long and half a block deep and covered by cement and blacktop. It was a small park even for Astoria. It consisted of a half dozen swings, and see-saws, some benches, and two handball courts. There were six backboards and rims for playing basketball. And some stone chess board tables. There were also two Bocce courts in the center of the park, it's where the elder Italian men of the neighborhood would congregate. The Bocce competition was fierce, the gambling out in the open. You actually had to leave the park to get to the other side because of the crowds.

The neighborhood was multi-ethnic, A Greek influence took shape along Ditmars Boulevard, with the rest of the area a combination of people of Eastern European descent It was a bustling community filled with mostly working class people. Quiet and safe, it seemed the ideal place to live.

One day while out playing, this kid Charlie asked me if I wanted to do something cool. Being the new guy and wanting to fit in, I enthusiastically agreed. He told me that I would have to ride on the handlebars of his bike because what he wanted to show me was a distance away. "Whoa, wait a minute! I said to myself," I'm not liking this scenario. Hadn't I learned my lesson about riding on the handlebars of someone's bike? Hadn't my past experience with my Sisters bike been enough to deter me"?

I didn't want to seem like a punk, a Faerie, a Sissy, things you never wanted to a labeled as. So I jumped up on his handlebars and we took off. I questioned him about where we were going, but his response was, "Wait you'll see."

We were flying down Steinway Street towards the Con Ed Plant. It was mostly factories and commercial businesses. Right before the Piano Factory was the Tri-Borough Bus Depot, the final stop on the bus line that linked Astoria to Manhattan. It was huge. There were always scores of buses parked there that needed maintenance done on them. Also on the lot was a large brick building that was used as a garage to perform many of the mechanical repairs. It also contained an office where bus drivers would receive their schedules. This was our destination.

Charlie drove to an opening in the fence where buses would pull into alongside the brick building. As we made the turn along the front of the building I noticed one of the bay doors to the garage was open. This was the area where buses would pull into to be serviced. As we passed by, this large German Shepard came out of nowhere, barking and chasing us, snapping at our feet. This dog was mean and I wanted to get the hell out of there.

Charlie peddled as fast as he could and we flew through the exit on the other side of the property. Once the dog reached the exit it just stopped, turned around, and walked back into the garage. My heart was beating very fast, I was sure that we were going to be mauled by this animal and I was relieved we had escaped with our feet intact.

Charlie began laughing hysterically at me because he saw how I had reacted. I was screaming like a sissy for him to go faster. There was this squeaky sound of desperation in my voice. Big fucking joke: I told him as we slowed down to a crawl, "What the hell was that?"

He said: I do it all the time, its funny how the dog just stops at the gate and returns to where it came from. Charlie said, "You should've seen your face, it turned pale white," and after calming down I realized that it was pretty funny. A couple of weeks later during a boring point in the day I said to Charlie, "Let's go down to the bus garage and tease the dog again." He didn't too need much coercion, so I jumped on his handlebars and we peddled off down Steinway Street.

Charlie did his usual drive by to incite the dog and then headed towards the exit. The dog immediately began chasing us, barking and snapping at our feet. But this time as we sped through the exit gate a car had just begun turning into the driveway. Everything after that was secondhand information, with Charlie the only person that really knew what went down.

Evidently he swerved enough as not to meet the auto head on, but was clipped on the backwheel, sending me flying into the air and slamming my head into a parked car. Charlie said I layed there not moving, he tried to talk to me but I was unresponsive. He said the guy that clipped us got out of his car and raced over to see how I was. Seeing that I was unconscious he ran into the bus terminal yelling, "I need an ambulance, there's been an accident and someone's hurt."

An ambulance was called and I was transported to Astoria General Hospital. I was in a coma for ten hours, and had suffered a severe concussion. I also had dislocated the Clavicle on my right shoulder. When I came out of the coma, by my bedside was my Mother. She had been there just about the whole time I was unconscious. She leaned over, kissed me and said, "There you are. It's good to see you, Mommy was very worried." But as I looked into her eyes, I could see that things were wearing on her, she looked tired.

The next morning I left the hospital with my right shoulder wrapped in Ace bandages and my arm in a sling. I was to be in this condition for the next six weeks, less the headache I had the following few days.

CHAPTER TWENTY THREE ½

The Continuation of Maggie's Consternation

About three months after the accident, and fully recovered, I had been playing outside with my friends when a bunch of us decided to climb up to the train trestle and walk over towards the Hells Gate Bridge. The Hell Gate overlooked Astoria Park and the East River and gave a bird's eye view to everything around us. You could watch people walking around the park, some lounging around on the grass, some with a picnic lunch placed on a blanket. You could see right into Astoria Pool, the epicenter of the park it's sparkling cool water would bring respite on a hot summer day. You could see and hear the laughter of children playing, splashing around and having fun.

There were the many cars lined up along the street adjacent to the parks edge closest the water. They'd be stopping to look out across the East River towards Manhattan. The City skyline from that view was picturesque. You could see from the bottom of Manhattan all the way up to Harlem and the Bronx, every main bridge to the outer boroughs, except Staten Island. And Roosevelt and Governors islands as well. It was almost Zen like, a serene and relaxing view.

There was a spot up on the bridge overlooking the park that had a thick rope dangling down from under the railroad track. We'd shimmy down the rope to a concrete ledge, and from there, drop down into the park. You would think that it might be easier to just walk the dozen or so blocks to the park, but what was the fun in that?

I remember that almost every time we were up there one of us would place a penny on the track and watch it get flattened like a piece of paper when a freight train passed over it, or sometimes we would walk out onto the Hells Gate and throw rocks into the East River. It would become a contest of who could throw thier rock the farthest. It was easy to judge by the splash your rock made.

About ten of us were hanging out one day looking for something to do. So when the consensus was that we would go to Astoria Park. We headed towards the train trestle. It was the most fun way to go.

In order to reach the trestle we had to cross Astoria Boulevard at 41st Street. It was two lanes of traffic going west separated by a walkway overlooking the Grand Central Parkway, and then another two lanes of Astoria Blvd heading east. There was also a roadway for cars to cross the Parkway also.

We were doing our usual horse playing, not paying attention to anything around us and anticipating the fun we were about to have. The poking and jabbing, the slaps to the back of the head were the usual forms of banter. As we approached Astoria Boulevard, I smacked one of the kids on his head and he playfully began chasing after me to reciprocate the deed. Like in the game of tag, I wanted to avoid him touching me and ran out onto the Astoria Boulevard without looking.

All I remembered was someone yelling, "Watch It," then the sound of a horn followed by the screeching of tires...and then Bang! I was struck by a car traveling along the west side service road. I went flying high into the air, (an almost surreal feeling of floating and somersaulting in slow motion) and then. Splat! I hit the ground.

I had been violently thrown completely over the car and onto the street. "Thank goodness there were no other cars behind, or I might have been hit by another car." As I lay there dazed, I could hear a voice in the distance, and as it got closer I heard a man's say "Oh my God! Oh my God, I'm sorry, are you OK?" I heard this a few more times while focusing my eyes towards the voice. I saw this man running towards me. Once again he spoke: "Are you OK?"

Wanting to get up on my feet I raised myself to a kneeling position and tried to stand. As I rose up my left leg buckled and gave out, and I fell back down to the ground. The man told me to just stay there. Trying again to stand, I yelled out him, "I'm alright, I'm alright! If my Mother finds out I was hit by a car again, she'll kill me."

That's all I could think about, all the other accidents I had and the stresses that it put on Maggie. It caused her to age well beyond her time. So there was no way I was going to a hospital. Once again I started to get up, but this time the driver of the vehicle helped me. I was able to stand while leaning into him. He asked me again if I would like to go to the hospital, but once again I stood firm, I did not.

I had severe pain where the impact of the car struck me. It felt like getting the worst Charlie horse you could imagine. I had a few other scrapes and contusions, but was basically OK. The man offered me a lift home and I obliged him. After saying goodbye to my friends, I got into the automobile and headed home. When we reached my house he asked if I needed help going upstairs and I replied: "No thanks! I'm OK." And while I was exiting his car, he reached over and placed something in my hand. It was a Five Dollar Bill. He said here, this is for you. I said thank you, got out of the car and limped into my hallway.

Now I had to come up with a story to tell my Mother. I had to be on top of my game, because if I wasn't Maggie would see right through it. Thinking real hard, one popped into my head almost immediately. I would explain to her in great detail that I was at the dumps, and while I was playing I lost my balanced and stumbled down the side onto some rocks and other debris. Yes that was it! I stuck to my story and closed the book on that encounter.

The Steinway Dumps as we called it, was a large landfill down towards the river that also became a dumping ground for almost every business, every household, anybody that might need to clear out their unwanted garbage. There were **Old mattresses, Broken Baby Carriage**s and all sorts of **Discarded Furniture**, not tomention the commercial waste that was strewn along streets surrounding this urban mesa.

The dump might have been an eyesore to the community, but if you were a young kid it was literally a mountain of fun. We would **Scavenger Hunt, Play Tag** and have **Rock Fights**. We'd **Smoke Cigarettes** and **Curse** at will. There were times when we would spend the whole day up there. So the excuse I gave Maggie about my injuries fit the scenario. The scrapes and bruises healed soon enough, but my thigh had such a large black and blue mark, it took a month to fully go away.

CHAPTER TWENTY FOUR

Go West Young Man

Somewhere around this time I began visiting Jim on the weekends, just for the day in the beginning, but eventually spending the entire weekend there. He was living on the West Side of Manhattan on 49th Street between Ninth and Tenth Avenues, right in the middle of Hell's Kitchen. How appropriate a moniker, it was well known for its rat-infested tenements, its raucous saloons that drunken brawls. The brutal assaults on wives, and children, that were always kept secret from outsiders. So they thought.

Everyone knew where the black eyes and bruises came from. It was the alcoholic that despised his life so much, he'd spend too much money drinking and gambling, leaving his family destitute and beaten.

The murders in the area were legendary, only whispered about between friends. Tales of the Irish gang known as the Westies, whose stories of brutality were so heinous, it would scare the shit out of most men. We were told as kids that they cut up bodies, and spread the parts around the neighborhood, sometimes keeping the hands or head in a Freezer just for the fun of it. They were feared by anyone not affiliated with them.

Then there was the story of the Cape Man Salvador Agron, a Puerto Rican kid who was a member of a gang called The Vampires. His moniker was given to him because he wore a long black cape with a red underside.

The story goes, the Cape Man and his cohorts came downtown for a rumble with a local streetgang, but when they arrived and the others didn't show, he cold heartedly stabbed three local kids with a twelve inch dagger that he kept for such occasions, killing two of them. When he was arrested he told the cops and reporters, "I don't care if I burn," (meaning the electric chair). These were just a couple of the stories from Hell's Kitchen that were told to me.

My first visit to Jim's was Deja vu all over again. It was just like Mean Kitty's house, except with an infestation of bed bugs. Sure Kitty had cockroaches, so did everyone in the area, but this was nasty to the extreme. My little sisters, who Jim had supervision of by now would continually get head lice and be bitten all over their bodies by bed bugs. It was so bad, that you would wake up feeling as if you danced through poison ivy.

They had welts all over their little arms and legs. Even when Jim had an exterminator come by, within a week or so they would be back, because the apartments below and above them were infested also. In one apartment below there lived a woman called Mary. She was helping My Father with the girls, making sure they got home from school OK and fed supper.

Jim and my little sisters were living on the fourth floor of this Five Story Walkup, a semi-dilapidated brick shithouse. The stairways were lopsided and creaky, the banisters shaky to the touch. Its hallways were dimly lit and filthy, a single dirty low voltage bulb the only light. One of the only good things about this place was that the bathroom was inside the apartment and the tub was in the bathroom.

The typical railroad flat, it opened into the kitchen whose only two windows faced a garbage-strewn backyard, with clotheslines stretching from every window in the courtyard. In the summer time if you concentrated hard enough, you were able to hear just about every conversation, taking place in the whole sector.

I could see that my Father had been struggling financially, otherwise why would he choose to live under such squalid conditions. The appliances in the kitchen were old and worn. In fact when I first saw the stove, I could swear that it must have used wooden logs to cook with. It wasn't so much it being old, but it looked as if no one cleaned it since it was new. The bathroom was so small that when you took a crap you couldn't wipe your ass without your arm hitting the back wall. Not to mention that if you stood up too quickly you would hit your head on the water tank above. The tub was squeezed into an area so small that on three sides there was not one inch of room. You had to enter and exit at the foot of the tub, and if you weren't careful your foot would bang against the faucet. "Man! That hurt."

The floors of the kitchen were covered in grimy cracked linoleum. Broken off in spots, you were able to see the previous tenants choice of flooring. The two bedrooms were extremely small. The paint on the ceiling and walls was peeling. The floors of the bedrooms were bare to the wood, and had dirt embedded into every crevice. The living room floor was covered in a similar fashion as the kitchen, worn, shoddy, and filthy linoleum.

There were two windows in the living room leading out onto a fire escape facing the street. This room is where my Father slept on an old pull out couch, covered with holes. It looked as if Jim might have plucked it from the street, a discarded piece of junk.

The place was so infested with cockroaches that you couldn't eat a meal without shooing one away. This was definitely not the way I was accustomed to living. There were many things wrong with Maggie, but cleanliness and her living conditions were not one of them.

My younger sisters Megan and Maeve (seven and eight respectively) were with my Father now. In retrospect, I felt that like myself, they would probably have been better off in the orphanage. This environment was no place for them to live.

The little ones were being looked after by Mary while Jim worked. Mary was separated from a brutally abusive, alcoholic husband, and left with two children with no means of support. Her only resource of assistance was to latch on to someone that could supplement what little income was available.

I had developed an immediate connection with my little sisters. I was the big brother and fell madly in love with them. Megan was the older one, who had a Buster Brown hairdo and frail little frame. Maeve was the one with the big doe eyes. It broke my heart to see them living this way. "Why in hell did Jim take them out of St. Joe's where they were safe and being taken care of properly?" "Was it because Maggie had custody of Katey and I? Did he feel that if he had the little ones, he would have a better chance to get back with Maggie? Whatever it was, it definitely should not have been allowed.

Whenever I visited I would take the little ones to the park and play with them for hours, we became almost inseparable. It was always a sad moment when I had to return to Astoria. They would begin to cry and ask me why I had to leave. But I would assure them that I would return the following week to be with them.

Things at home seemed to be getting worse. Maggie and I were arguing every day. I had continued to be truant from school, becoming more and more rebellious. I was also getting bigger, and Marggies corporal punishment did not carry the weight it once did. She tried grounding me, but I just dismissed her and went out anyway. I was spending the whole weekend at Jim's by now, and was feeling more and more comfortable in my surroundings. I was making friends with some of the kids on the block and familiarizing myself with the area.

The neighborhood surroundings were a myriad of excitement. Just one block east was **Madison Square Garden**, home to the NBA's **New York Knick's** and the NHL's **New York Rangers** sports teams. It was also the venue for some of the greatest boxing matches of its time. They were but a few of the venues presented there.

Two blocks east was ***Midtown Broadway, The Great White Way*** the heart of the ***Theatre District***.

Just seven blocks south was the ***Port Authority Bus Terminal***, a gateway for travel throughout the entire continental United States. It became a personal playground for my friends and I. Sliding down the handrails of the escalators or playing hide and seek within this cavernous facility. We would have fun for hours.

Times Square once the paramount of entertainment, by this time had become the seedy underbelly of urban neglect. It's theatres that once staged the best of Vaudeville and big time movie premiers had been reduced to a shambles. It had become more renowned now for ***B Grade Movies, Prostitution*** and ***Child Predators***.

North was ***Central Park***, an oasis from the crowds and noise of the inner city. It's expansive lawns and abundance of foliage, were relief from the urban sprawl. ***The Zoo***, was an extraordinary attraction that drew hundreds of thousands of people a year, it always amazed me. ***The Seal Pond***, its center of attraction became my favorite haunt. I spent many hours within the confines of this magnificent park.

The Museum of Natural Hhistory, The Planetarium, Lincoln Center, landmarks so numerous and exciting it could take up a complete volume. To the west were the ***Shipyards***, the docking place for all the famous ocean liners. There has been much written in literature about this area of New York.

All I have mentioned and more layed at my feet, I fell in love once more with the city. And once again I began plying my wares, selling newspapers. I recalled the confidence earning money gave me, and the financial security it afforded me. I became the kid that always sported a dollar in his pocket. Within three hours on a Friday night I'd make enough to splurge the weekend and still have money leftover for the following week. It reassured me of my own self-sufficiency.

CHAPTER TWENTY FIVE

Fury's regrets

My relationship with Maggie was at a breaking point and was rapidly deteriorating. I was becoming more belligerent and disrespectful every day. I didn't know at the time how deep my resentment went, and how it surfaced in the form of defiance. There were very few times of civility between us anymore.

One day during one of our many arguments, (at this point she had given up on using the strap on me. It was futile because I would just yank it out of her hand) one bad word led to another and I blurted out, "I hate you! And I want to go live with my father!"

It became so silent I could hear myself breathe. Maggie had heard me say many things to her out of anger, but this was spoken with such conviction I think it shocked both of us. We stood at a turning point. Would she say to me, "Why don't you just calm down so we can discuss this?" Would I respond with an apology for what I had said? No, neither of us would budge. The pain of this relationship had taken its toll. And after a phone call to my Father it was decided I would be leaving for good come the following weekend.

For the first time in my life, I honestly knew that I was making a very bad decision. And while lying in bed that night I began to cry.

I had hoped Maggie would open the door to atonement, to sit down with me and iron out our differences. But both our stubbornness toward each other disallowed any reconciliation.

The day I left was the last time I saw Maggie cry for me. Our bittersweet relationship had finally ended and we said our goodbyes. It's not that I wasn't ever going to see her anymore, but my departure drove a wedge between us that would never again be removed. We looked at each other differently after that day.

Jim picked me up so he could help me with my personal belongings. The subway ride to my new home was filled with the voice of reason. Jim said, "Don't be mad at your Mother she tried her best to make you happy, she loves you very much." I just stayed quiet, my mind racing,

I was pondering the situation of once again having to find my niche in a new area. It wouldn't be so bad I told myself, but my gut felt totally opposite. The little ones would be ecstatic and welcome me with open arms. They had missed out on the attention of a big brother and the security that it brought. They would finally begin to feel the sibling attachment that was so lacking in their own lives. And I myself would reciprocate.

CHAPTER TWENTY SIX

Whats in A Name

I was officially a ward of James Kenney and an official Hell's Kitchen resident. I would now be formaly living in a dilapidated, run down, bug infested tenement. I had arrived! Ugh!

One of the first things I noticed within the first few days was that Mary from downstairs spent a lot more time in our house than I had thought. It wasn't just to mind the kids, clean up a little, cook and go home. She stayed very late in the evenings hanging out with my Father and watching TV. I was to learn shortly the extent to which this relationship had turned. She was more than just the housekeeper.

My Father didn't want it to get out that he had a girlfriend, a paramour, or as Maggie would call her once she found out, "a fucking whore". Once, when Maggie came over to see the little ones, Mary happened to be there. My Mother had consumed a tad too much alcohol and a full-fledged riot broke out. Maggie had been berating Jim for the deplorable conditions he had his children living in, and when Mary butted in to defend my Father, Maggie's eyes lit up like a roman candle. She began spewing profanities that would embarrass a longshoreman.

When Mary reciprocated the favor, Maggie leapt up off her chair and connected with her fist to the side of Mary's head. And before you could blink an eye, each woman had a full grasp of the others hair and were flailing blindly at their respective faces.

My Mother was all of 4ft 10 inches, and mayber 100 lbs. soaking wet, while Mary was 5-foot, 8-inches and a bruising 160. And even though Maggie had shown a lot of heart, she was no match against this amazonian creature. Kitty had been with my Mom, seemingly for moral support. But if I knew Kitty, it was more for a night out of drinking. But what was she to do? She was smaller and skinnier than Maggie. So it was left up to my Father to put a halt to this catfight.

As they were being separated, my Mother spit at Mary and let it be known, that she had not seen the last of her. And so off she went with Kitty, bruised and battered and probably on her way to the local gin mill in order to lick her wounds. Maggie was right, there would be other times.

After this incident Mary laid down the law with my Fathert. Either he lays claim to the fact that they were indeed a couple, or she would be moving on. Jim had a big decision to make. He still held deep feelings for Maggie and hopes of reconciliation, (which was the furthest thing from my Mothers's mind). Or he could keep the proverbial bird in hand.

Mary was not a local beauty she was a slovenly looking woman with long oily brown hair that was always tied back in a ponytail with a rubber band. A big boned woman, she walked like a truck driver and swore like a sailor. She wore a housecoat all the time, and moccasins that were filthy looked a hundred years old. She wore no makeup to speak of and her face seemed to bare the battle scars of abuse. The people in the neighborhood called her Dirty Mary, but never to her face.

A week later Jim didn't have to make the decision for himself, Mary told him she was pregnant. He must of thought, "Holy Shit! What have I done."

Mary had two children, a girl Diane and a son named John, that people called Johnny Boy. Her daughter Diane was big for her age, a stocky young girl, clumsy in manner that bore the brunt of her mother's unbridled rage. She was always being smacked, even for the most trivial things. Her son Johnny Boy looked okay. From outer appearances you might have even called him a handsome young boy, slender and well proportioned. He had a winning smile and curly golden blonde hair, and he took on the appearance of a well- adjusted child. But once Johnny Boy spoke you noticed a facial distortion around his mouth, and he stuttered and slurred his words to the point of frustrating himself. Neither child did well in school and were both diagnosed with learning disabilities.

These two kids were definitely the byproduct of parental neglect. They were watched after by their Grandmother Alice, a gnome like creature with long gray hairs protruding from her chin. She always seemed to be sipping from a can of beer. And like her daughter, her wardrobe consisted solely of shabby housecoats and flipflops. They were a fashion nightmare that spoke of deep poverty.

Their apartment was even more inelegant than ours and constantly reeked of urine and feces. They owned a bulldog that pissed and shit all over the place. It wasn't the dog's fault it was never walked. No one was ever invited to their house, because as poor as most of the people in the area were, few families allowed their environments to deteriorate in the manner as it had in Mary's house, it was a dump, it was totally shameful.

Most of the kids I made friends with came from some sort of maladjusted familily. Whether it was from alcohol abuse, or physical cruelty, it caused shame in all of us. There were some exceptions, but the children of those relationships were usually kept on a short leash. Sure they could play with us in the schoolyard across the street, but they would never be allowed off the block. They were the lucky ones.

CHAPTER TWENTY SEVEN

The Games We Played-The Fun We Had

I was settling in quite well and began running with some of the local kids in the neighborhood. Directly across the street from my home was the New York School of Printing. I had heard that kids from Manhattan and the Outer Boroughs of New York City that did not quite show an aptitude for academics.went there

It had a very large concrete yard on the 49th street side, slightly smaller than a football field. There were large concrete steps on the far side of the yard that were erected for the student body to congregate and socialize during breaks in class. There were two handball courts separated by a fence in what we considered the outfield when playing baseball. A couple of backboards and hoops were situated so that a few games of Half Court Basketball could be played at the same time.

The yard might have stimulated physical activity amongst the schools populace, but it served my friends and I even more. It was the epicenter of my existence, the place I could be found every day after school, and every moment during the summer.

I wasn't very good at hand ball at the time and my basketball skills left a lot to be desired. I was mostly interested in the street games we played. When we met up in the yard, If the girls were playing hopscotch or jumping rope, we would chase them away, relegating them to the sidewalks in front of their homes. It wasn't very nice of us, but it was a necessary evil. We needed lots of room for the games we enjoyed playing. Across the Border was my favorite because I loved rollerskating so much.

The game went like this: It started with one kid being chosen to stand in the middle of the yard, he was known as the border guard. The rest of us got together on one side of the yard, waiting for the three words to be yelled. Sometimes there would be twenty or so of us kids playing the game. The gist of the game went like this. The kid in the middle would yell, "across the border" and all of a sudden there would be a mad dash to get to the other side, and to not get tagged. If the Border guard tagged you before you reached to the other side, you became a border guard also

When I was chosen to start the game as a guard I would focus on the boy I knew I could catch easily, and the moment I yelled across the border, I sprinted right after him. Sometimes I'd be too aggressive, lunging at a kid and missing him completely, and I'd go crashing to the ground. I was as competitive as anyone and I had the battle scars to prove it.

I always had fresh scrapes on my elbows and knees that never seemed to completely heal. The scabs would be ripped off as I tumbled to the ground, reopening my wounds, and bloodying my clothes. The knees of my jeans were always torn and blood stained. I played the games with complete abandon, and I played to win whether I was the guard or a border jumper. When I tagged an opponent before he reached the other side, he was on my team. It went that way, back and forth until there was just one person left. That last person would be declared the winner. I could tell the kids that played like me, because like myself, they were bloodied and their clothing was torn. In the words of many of the boys from my era: "It Was Fun as Hell!"

During winter, huge snow forts were built, sides were chosen from the hordes of neighborhood kids, and a snowball war would break out. Hundreds of these missiles could be seen arching across the snow-covered terrain, raining down on kids from both sides. I played until my sneaker clad feet had no more feeling, until my lips turned blue and I shivered uncontrollably. Then I'd go across the street, put myfeet under the hallway radiator until they thawed, and back outside I went.

Ring-allevio or ring-allerio (Its name depended on the block you came from) was the most popular game in the neighborhood. It was a two-team sport whith parameters that were distinguished by how many kids showed up. It began with two captains (usually favorites) who then picked the sides to play. Going first in picking sides was established by a game we called Choozies, where each captain would make a call of odds or evens and then at the count of three, both would flash one or two fingers. Though the mathematics favored choosing evens, It didn't matter to me. I enjoyed the machismo of looking straight into my opponents eyes and thinking, "I know exactly what combination he's going throw."

I'd square up to my adversary, circle around him like a wrestler ready to pounce, then I'd rear back my arm, and at the count of three, I would propel my body forward stomping my foot just in front of his and yell out my call. Odds or evens, it didn't matter, as long as I'd shot my finger forward as hard as I could. Though in this scenario, it was to see who picked first (a game within a game), Choozies settled many an argument in my neighborhood.

After this melodrama unfolded came the part of actually choosing sides. The kids that were in high demand always stepped forward, they were usually the biggest and fastest, though sometimes cronyism played a big part. But if you wanted to win, those thoughts went out the window.

Then there were the kids chosen only to fill out the roster, the Runts, the Retards and the Mommas Boys. Labels applied to fuel the ego of the taunting bullies of the neighborhood. Though I didn't care for this particular means of prejudice, my main concern was not to be equated into the category of a loser. The politics of growing up in this area could be as despicable as any on Capitol Hill today, so you toughened up, or you were labeled a little fairy.

Once the teams were chosen, boundaries had to be decided. The one block rule usually did the trick. Then an area would be settled on to become the imaginary jail, where the prisoners captured would be held. Then it was Choozies all over again. It was to determine if you would be on offense (the hunted), or defense, (the hunter). The defensive team would have to count to one hundred before they were allowed to begin the hunt. The offensive players would scatter in all sorts of directions to elude their captors, running up and across the block, ducking into hallways and down cellar stairs They'd be bent down and hiding behind the garbage cans, leaping over fences and hiding in the darkness of the back yards. Some even shimmied up onto fire escapes, but the roofs were usually considered out of bounds.

Once the counting reached one hundred the defensive team went out to capture the other team. If an opponent had been spotted one or two of the hunters would chase after him. When caught the hunter held his prey and yelled ring-aleevio three times. Once that was accomplished he was walked back to the jail. At this point someone was appointed to guard the jail, usually one of the bigger kids. This was because any time during the game an opposing player was able to free the captors by getting by the jailer and tagging his teammates. Once there was more than one person in jail, the defense would appoint two or more jailers.

The way I helped to prevent an offensive opponent from breaking through to free his teammates. I'd form a clothesline around the jail with mine, and when someone tried to get by us, we'd raise our arms about chest high to our opponent and, wham! His ass would slam to the ground.

We played until every one of the hunted, were caught, then we switched sides. One time when I was out on the offensive and sneakily making my way back to emancipate my teammates. Little by little and without being seen, ducking in and out of hallways and behind cars I slowly crept towards my objective and when I thought I was close enough I made my break. I noticed ther keepers of the jail were looking the other way, I'd be able free my teammates and force the other team to start anew. About thirty feet before reaching my target they turned and spotted me. But I was too close. They joined arms quickly to set up a barrier, but nothing was going to stop me. I built up more speed and right before attaining my goal I leapt full force up into the air to break their grip and crashed right into their arms with my legs.

"Shit! I had leapt too high" and upon hitting this human chain I did a complete summersault. "Bam! I hit the ground like a rock," directly onto my tailbone. They counted me out and I joined my cohorts in the jail. "But Man, I had a ball!"

I could write for hours about the games we played in the street, there was **Johnny Ride ThePony**, **Yo Yo's** and **Crack Top. Flipping Cards**, **Water Balloon Fights** and **Stick Ball**. There was **Hand Ball**, **Punch Ball**, **Roller Hockey. Touch Football** and **Softball**. The list of the games we played seemed endless. And it kept us out of the house from early morning until late at night. Who wanted to go home anyhow? I know I didn't. And a lot of the kid's I knew felt the same way. Who wanted to go home to the dysfunction, the poverty or the violence of an alcoholic household? Being outside playing was surely the better place to be.

CHAPTER TWENTY EIGHT

Before Wilding Was Wilding

Like many Cty Kids we traveled in packs. It afforded a kinship, a bond, a feeling of security. A freedom to wander about the town and see what excitement we might conjure up. I had returned to selling papers and was more familiar than most of the kids about what was happening outside of the neighborhood. The route I had mapped out not only brought me to the best bars to make a buck. It also led me the best places to get free samples of candy. Like the restaurants that displayed huge bowls of mint's or jelly beans that were easily accessible from the street.

First I would set our mark. Then I'd make sure there was no heavy traffic leaving or entering therestaurant, you didn't want anyone to get hurt. Then when I gave the signal, one kid would hold the door open and we would stream in like a freight train grabbing fistfuls of booty, without breaking stride.

We'd have to run for a few blocks to make sure that no one was following us. The Green Berets could not have orchestrated a better plan of attack. I pointed out to my friends the water fountains that were strategically placed outside many of the office building's, throughout the city, that added an aesthetic appeal to the buildings facade. Most of these urban springs had money in them. All different denominations of coins were tossed into the water. It was mostly by the many tourists walking around the city.

Coins tossed aimlessly over a shoulder, accompanied by the traditional wish for prosperity, health, or maybe even the love of another human being were things that didn't matter much to us, we were there only to reap the benefits.

One of the fountains we often went to was on 52nd Street and 6th Avenue. On any given hot and humid day, you might find us swimming in its shallow waters. Frolicking about in this refuge from the city's insufferable heat. There would be times that pedestrians passing by would stop to watch us cavorting within this inner-city oasis. Maybe even reminiscing themselves about thier own youthful days. Some would toss money in just to watch us scramble to retrieve it. I spent many happy hours there.

Running with my friends through the labyrinth of Rockefeller Center, playing tag or just running and sliding upon its lustrous marble floors were not an uncommon sight. Just like we did at the Port Authority Terminal we would slide down it's many escalators and run rampant through the vast corridors.

What I remember most though about Rockefeller Center was the entranceway on 6th avenue, and how beautiful its painted ceilings were. I would imagine that the Sistine Chapel might have been painted that way. It was as awe inspiring and very spiritual.

I would visit the Money Museum with its peculiar array of currency from around the world. It's where I saw a $100,000 Dollar Bill for the first time. I would daydream about having a pocketful and using one, to pay off some meager tab. as if I were this bigshot Wall Street Tycoon. And I'd bask in the astonishment it might invoke, braggart that I was.

The golden statue of Atlas holding up the world upon his massive shoulders stood ceremoniously within its grand piazza on the 5th Avenue side, directly across the street from St. Patricks Cathedral.

The NBC Studios, where on occasion I might be spotted within the audience of the Jeopardy Game Show was plainly situated on the 49th Street entrance, along with that elegant restaurant The Rainbow Room.

While playing hooky with my friends we found many ways to bide our time, foolishly and often without thought of any consequences. Some of these activities have led to tragic results. But we stupid kids,were not cognizant of the outcomes from our often rambunctious behaviors.

One day about eight of us were horsing around on Seventh Avenue when we decided that we would head over to the Americana Hotel, a fifty story building that served the bustling district of Midtown Manhattan. Its posh lobby was the focal point for the many visitors that passed through its doors. The tourists, some of them crane-necked with excitement, from seeing such a large metropolis, would be seen exiting with maps in hand.

But the many organized events such as trade shows and conventions brought most of the clientele to this posh establishment. But we were here for other reasons.

On any particular day we would enter two by two so as not to be too conspicuous. Then we would get on an empty elevator, press the button for the top floor and then Whoosh! We would be thrusted upward expeditiously. The elevator ran at such a high rate of speed that it would clog your ears, a feeling similar to being on a jet plane that was preparing to land.

Once on top we would head for the stairwell, assemble all together, and then at the count of three a race to the bottom would begin. There'd be a mad dash for the handrails, first to be used for balance and again to gather more speed for the rapid descent. Once you took off running it was every man for his self. The pulling and jostling at each turn was cut throat. Tripping up your adversary was acceptable. Anything went except punching, shoving and kicking.

The thing I remember most besides the competition was the

dizzying effect it had on you. The further down you got, the dizzier you felt. It was as if we were spinning in place. If you reached the bottom first, you would collapse on the floor, and be declared the victor. It gave the person bragging rights for the day.

This one particular time we decided to head over to do our thing. But there was one major problem. Butch's little brother was hanging around with us and refused to leave. As fast as we would run away from him his determination prevailed, we couldn't shake him no matter how hard we tried. It didn't matter that Butch kept smacking him and giving him the occasional boot in the ass, he was resolute on staying with the big brother that he idolized. He should have heeded our advice and went home.

He lagged a good ten feet behind us, knowing well that getting too close would cause him a host of problems. There could be the **Head Lock Noogies,** the **Indian Wrist Burn**, or maybe even the classic **Pink Belly**, which was the punishment specified for the little runt who overstepped his bounds. Most of us had the experience of having these things done to us on occasion when we were younger. It was a rite of passage for us all.

Butch's brother was given one last warning, "Go home and leave us alone," but he wouldn't listen. As we entered the Americana Hotel we all headed to different elevators. And just as I was about to get in the elevator I stopped and noticed across the way the little runt getting in the elevator behind his brother. I held the door on my ride and I waited another couple of seconds, when all of a sudden this kid was jettisoned back out of the elevator, on to the floor, sliding on his ass. When the doors closed on my elevator, there were three of us inside, and as we sped upward towards our destination, I couldn't help but to laugh at what I had just witnessed.

Looking above at the directional light it showed us passing the tenth, then the twentieth and the thirtieth floors. It was amazing how fast this elevator rose. At the fiftieth floor the bell rang to alert us to the fact we had reached our destination.

Immediately upon exiting I raced towards the stairway, knowing full well I needed to jockey for pole position, because if you were on the inside you had the shorter distance racing down as well as the handrail to propel you faster. We had all assembled at the staircase and were ready to go, when we heard the cry of a small kid, "Wait for me!" he said. And when the doorway to the stairwell opened up, sure enough it was Butch's little brother.

We started goofing on Butch, teasing him unmercifully about not being able to ditch his little brother. But I think we might have gone a little too far, because all of a sudden Butch lost it.

"You little bastard! I'll show you." And he grabbed him by the collar and walked over towards the window facing Seventh Avenue. The window had three sections, a small stationary pane on the top and bottom, then a separate center pane that swung open by pulling a chain. The window was about three feet wide and in three sections about 18 inches high. The bottom section was approximately two feet off the ground.

Butch walked over to the window, his brother in tow and signaled us to come over. "Let's throw this little shit out the window!" He bellowed. We all just turned and looked at each other in amazement, I said, "Is this fucking guy nuts or what?" I couldn't believe my ears. And as we turned back towards Butch, we got the signal, the winking eye the sign that let us all know there would be a prank going on.

Butch's little brother was going to bear the brunt of one of the most stupid things we ever did. Butch whispered to us that we should hang him out the window and threaten to drop him if he didn't go home.

As one of the kids held open the window by the chain, five of us grabbed all different parts of his clothing. We were like a lynch mob. This poor kid didn't stand a chance. Everyone was getting caught up in the moment. And even when he began kicking, screaming and swearing to go home, it was too late.

Head first he was leaned on the windows ledge and then grabbed at the belt by two of us, while the others grabbed hold of his pant legs and shirt. I had his leg in a death grip and was not going to let go no matter what. I was feeling that this thing had already gone too far, and was becoming very dangerous. Butch had his brother by the collar and was slowly easing him out the window. In the next second, this little kid was dangling completely out the window up to his waist.

I had one hand on his belt, holding it as tight as I could as I stuck my head out the window to try and see his face. "Holy shit!" I said to myself, that's far down far down, everything looks so small. Right then I began to feel anxious about the situation and I said to everyone, "Hey! That's enough. Pull him in."

The kid was crying uncontrollably. He began to punch and kick at his brother and anyone else close enough to reach. "I'm telling Ma! I'm telling Ma!" he repeated over and over. And as those words echoed through the hallway an uneasiness, overcame all of us, a feeling of deep remorse. If his parents found out about this dangerous prank the beatings that we were sure to get would be tantamount to murder.

Immediately we all began to apologize, we said; "We're sorry that we scared you," and begged that he not tell his Mother. All of a sudden out of my mouth flowed the words of reason, I said: "It was your initiation into the club, we all had to do it. Now you can hang out with us."

Everyone including Butch's brother fell silent for a moment. The statement just made had to be processed and computed. All of a sudden thunderous laughter filled the hallway, the brush with death (Ours, not Butch's little brother) had been averted.

We headed towards the hallway again for our usual race, but this time the winner was to be assured, prearranged. Butch's little brother would be the victor.

The consequences of actions are never considered when a bunch of unsupervised thirteen year olds are looking for ways to amuse themselves. We were just having fun, there was no direct malice intended. It was like the time the winter before, when the bunch of us wandered up to watch the Christmas tree at Rockefeller Center. We decided to each make three or four snowballs, and then bombard the people down on the ice, skating and having fun. We rained about thirty or so snowballs down on these poor unsuspecting people, not thinking we could hurt someone. But one snowball wound up striking a little girl in the face.

Within minutes we had a group of adult men chasing after us. The guy that was chasing me was relentless. He must have run after me for a good half hour, though it seemed much longer. He kept yelling at me that we had hurt this little girl and that he was going to see that I was arrested. Eventually I lost him, and met up with my friends on the block. All we could do was laugh about getting away, not once did we think of the little girl. Shame on us!

Another time we rolled this large boulder-like snowball off one of the rooftops, attempting to strike some unsuspecting pedestrian. We'd toss snowballs or eggs at open bus windows. These were all idiotic pranks, mischief that could have hurt someone seriously. But this stupid thing we did with Butch's brother was much worse than all of them It was Fucking Dumb! We were unable to see the big picture, and it got us in trouble often.

Children that are not supervised are a danger not only to themselves but to the unsuspecting persons around them. We'd enter buildings that were being razed and would play among the debris, traipsing up and down the stairs of these dilapidated tenements with no regard for the danger. We would throw bricks against it's the façade in an attempt to collapse a wall and watch as part of the building fell.

We played tag where areas of the floors and stairs were missing, not once considering that someone could be seriously injured or even killed. Anything would be done on a dare, and I'd always be one of the first to step up. It was my insatiable appetite for attention, to fit in and to be looked up to.

Not all of my time was spent intentionally getting into mischief, though trouble did seem to follow me. My dilemma was always to distinguish one from the other. But because of my impulsivity it was rarely considered.

As I got older some of the games we played changed. The crowd we hung out with had been scaled down. Some of the kids who we considered to be Mammas Boys had left because of the severe criticism they constantly endured. The games we were playing were more macho, more physical.

Some evenings my friends and I would play Johnny Ride the Pony. We liked playing it up against one of the exit doors to Madison Square Garden. The doors were made of thick metal and painted black. And because of the way the game was played, the metal doors wwere better than playing against a brick wall, they had some give to them, some bounce.

The gist of this game was based on teams of about ten per side, a dozen the most. We would play against other kids from different neighborhoods, challenges performed for bragging rights. This time it wasn't choozies that determined offense from defense, it was now Paper, Rock, Scissors.

On defense were the Ponies, the first kid on the team would stand erect against the door and was called the pillar. The rest of the team would bend over and lock their arms around each other waist high, with their head hunched below the ribcage. This chain of humanity took up the whole sidewalk, from wall to street. The other team, the offense, the riders, would one at a time dash from across the street, leap high into the air and land as close to the pillar as possible with as much downward force as they could muster without falling off. This would continue until all the riders had done the same.

Once accomplished the pony's would yell three times Johnny Ride the Pony while all the time, the riders would be jumping up and down and shaking the line. The object of the game was to collapse the pony line. If the objective couldn't be accomplished we would switch sides.

While playing one evening and my team being the riders, I was chosen to be the first to go. We were playing some kids from 10th

Avenue that we had beaten in the past and saw no reason for a different outcome.

I reared back and pushed off a wall behind me and ran toward my target at full speed. I began my leap upon the horse, and was at the acme of my run, when the chain and pillar disbanded, leaving me to crash into the metal door. As I sat there stunned the kids from 10th Ave. ran down the block laughing their ass'es off. Whenever reminiscing about that night my friends and I would laugh. It still makes me smile to this day.

On occasions, when there was a sporting event going on at the Garden. We would stand out at the main entrance and ask the people going in if they had any extra tickets. If we weren't able to score any, we would put into effect Plan B. We'd go around the corner to one of the side doors that were used to exit the Garden and jimmy it open with a butter knife. There was always the possibility of us being spotted by security. And in the event that happened, we would either make a mad dash inside, or try an exit door on the opposite side of the building.

We'd go to **Basketball** and **Hockey Playoffs,** and **Big Time Boxing Matches**. We'd see the **Horse Show**, the **Westminster Dog Show**, **The Camping Show**, and many other events that this marvelous venue made available. My personal favorite though was **Ringling Bros, Barnum and Bailey Circus**.

We would help unload the New York Rangers equipment bus, and in return we might receive passes to a practice or a signed puck. And if we were really lucky, once in a while, we'd get a cracked stick from one of the players. We never tried to steal anything because it would ruin it for all the kids in the neighborhood, and If we spotted a kid even thinking about it, we would threaten him with a beating. And if a really big guy tried to steal, we'd blow the whistle. It wasn't being a rat; it was the self- preservation of our territory. These were just a few of the things we did to break up the monotony of hanging out on the block.

CHAPTER TWENTY NINE

Day Old Bread and the Special Rye

On a crisp spring morning the smell of fresh baked bread would hang in the air and spread throughout the neighborhood. It was from Fields Bakery, located on 47th St. and 11th Avenue. It supplied fresh bread, cakes and pies to many of the restaurants and schools throughout Manhattan. They also had a retail store between 10th and 11th where they sold day old bread. Jim bought his bread there all the time it sold for a quarter a loaf retail.

That was not necessarily a great deal, except a Fields loaf was double the size of a normal one, so he would send me off to the store to pick one up. It never lasted very long, because, besides the four of us Jim was also feeding Mary and her brood.

As little as he gave us, his own kids, he always seemed to be complaining about money, always crying the blues about how much he was spending. Jesus Christ it wasn't that he was spending a lot of money on clothes for us, (he bought me none) and Maggie would subsidize him for the girls as often as possible. I was earning my own money selling papers and bought my own clothes. I always had enough pocket money to buy pizza or maybe a baloney sandwich at the Deli for myself. Every so often I would take the little ones with me to get pizza or to the local candy store for an egg cream. I later found out that Jim was gambling again, another of his past addictions that had helped to ruin his life once before.

My Father loved his rye bread, he would cook up this concoction he called the German U-boat. I'd go to the Deli and pick up a quarter pound of liverwurst and half a pound of German potato salad. He would take one slice of rye, slop some hot mustard on it, take half the liverwurst, put it on the bread, then place the potato salad on top until it was spilling over the side. Jim was only half done. Another slice of bread acted like a blanket over the potato salad, and a platform for what came next. The next thing was a thick slice of raw onion, a heaping tablespoon of Horseradish and another piece of bread. VOILA! Jim's **German U-** BOAT had been built. Jim also loved his sardine sandwiches with raw onion and pickled beets on toasted rye. His cuisine left me gaging, every time I watched him eat.

Sometimes on Saturday mornings, a few of us would head on down to the Fields Bakery loading docks. They would be awaiting the delivery trucks so they could load them up with the many different breads, cakes and pies that were to be delivered to all the upscale restaurants in the area. There were racks of fresh baked goods sitting on the dock still warm from the ovens, just cooling in the early morning air. The smells from the dock were alluring.

When the coast was clear, we would climb up onto the dock and grab a couple of whatever was quickly accessible, then tear ass out of there as fast as possible. There was nothing better than fresh baked apple or cherry pie. If we were spotted, the bakery personnel would chase us away, but they never ran after us because we only took what we could carry and never caused any damage.

CHAPTER THIRTY

Pee You - Kidney Stew

I had very little to do with Dirty Mary, she wasn't there to look after me. Her purpose was to take care of my sisters and be there for Jim. She would clean the house, cook, and do the laundry (none satisfactory). She had no bearing on me though, She was not my Mother and no matter what she thought, she wasn't going to tell me what I could or couldn't do.

Jim tried to delegate some sort of authority to her regarding certain situations, and most of the time it wouldn't bother me. Like when he had her escort me to school, to make sure I was attending. Maybe it was one of those days that I didn't feel like attending school, (which was just about every day) I would be out the back door and down the street before she left the building. The only class I ever went to at J.H.S 17 was Art. The teachers name was Mr. Lyons and everybody thought he was cool, his charismatic demeanor attractive.

D-Mary was a horrible cook. Most of the meals she made I put in the category of barely digestible. But the first time I experienced her preparing Kidney Stew for dinner, was the first of the many times I drew the proverbial line in the sand.

The stench rising from the pot was horrendous, as if someone was boiling piss. And as dinner rolled around I knew that there would be some controversy regarding my partaking of this family meal. There was no frigging way I was eating that crap. And as I sat down for dinner I immediately let it be known that I invoked my right to not poison myself with that shit. So I politely told her that I'd just have some rice with butter.

Mary acted as if she didn't hear me and placed a plate of stew in front of me, knowing full well I didn't want that crap. Now I was beginning to get annoyed. So before the shit hit the fan, I politely declined for the second time, and I pushed the plate back into the middle of the table. She pushed the plate back in my spot and gave me a disdainful glare. Once again I stated, but this time with fervor: "I do not want any of your Fucking Stew! Don't you get it?"

Mary complained to my Father that she had toiled all day in the kitchen and it showed a lack of respect to not eat what was prepared. Jim turned to me and said: She worked hard to make dinner for us and you should at least try it. So I reached my fork over to the plate, tapped the gravy from the dish, tasted it and replied: no thank you.

Mary decided to challenge me, boisterously stating that I was going to eat dinner, as it was prepared or else. "Or else what!" I replied angrily. Or else your father will punish you. I looked her dead in the eyes and told her, "I don't care if I get punished. My father can hang me upside down, blindfold me, and beat me with a stick. I'M NOT EATING THIS GARBAGE!"

Jim told me to calm down, that he didn't want screaming in front of the little ones. I said: "Dad I'm not going to eat her stew, I tried telling her nicely, but she doesn't get it." Jim said to me, OK. She continued to blather on about me not eating what she prepared, salting her words with bits of profanity until I finally blurted out the words: "Pee You to your Kidney stew." So D-M proceeded to remove my plate, tossing it into the sink and breaking the dish in the process.

It terrified the hell out of the little ones. So I jumped up and told her to stop scaring my little sisters. Then I asked them if they liked the stew, and when they both replied, yuck! I said to them: "C'mon I'm taking you both for pizza." Once again Mary turned towards Jim for some sort of moral support, and when he gave none, she stormed out of the apartment and went downstairs.

My Father didn't speak a word, but the grin on his face let me know that he approved. He was proud of me for standing up for myself. Bloods thicker than water, and my outburst assured him that I would protect my little sisters at all cost.

I spoke to my Father that night about my concerns for the way she had been treating the little ones. I let him know how she's always yelling at them. "I see it in their faces I said, she has them terrified. They think that she's going to hit them the way she does to her own kids.

I let him also know right then and there that if she started treating them like that, I would step in to protect them, I also told him that I wasn't going to tolerate her verbally abusing them any more. I said: "Haven't they been through enough in their young lives?" I thought to myself, they've been abandoned, physically abused, maybe sexually abused, and put away into an orphanage. "Wasn't that enough" They should have been the first to be removed from the orphanage, not the last. They were more defenseless than Katey and myself and needed their Mother's love and protection more than we did.

I became further estranged from Maggie over the next few years. Jim at least had an excuse. He became an indigent alcoholic. I never thought Maggie had an excuse. In my eyes a Mother never leaves her children to fend for them selves, it should be naturally ingrained to protect your kids no matter the circumstance. And being that both my parents failed to do so, I would do my best to not let my little sisters down.

I sat down and had a long talk with Megan and Maeve. I told them that they were not at fault for what happened to their family. I told them that I would be there to look after them. The little ones shared with me that Dirty Mary would constantly yell at them and had even slapped them on occasion. Then she threatened them with retribution if they complained to Jim. Over the next few years there were quite a few confrontations between D.M. and myself. They were mostly regarding the treatment of my little sisters. Most of the clashes with Mary escalated into screaming matches. One even resulted in a physical altercation.

She and I were standing toe- to- toe one day yelling at the top of our lungs at each other when she made the mistake of slapping me and scratching my face. I stared directly at her with a shit-eating grin, showing her that she couldn't hurt me. Then I said to her that if she ever raised her hand to me again I would beat the crap out of her. She tried to slap me again. I blocked her hand, grabbed her by the hair and slapped her so hard on the side of her face that finger marks appeared on her cheek almost immediately. She ran out of the house crying, and went downstairs to her Mother's apartment.

I was so pent up with emotion that I began to cry. A rage inside of me gathered such force it exploded out upon this woman. As far back as I can remember, I would hold things in, try to restrain myself, but somewhere during my life a psycho/physical malfunction manifested itself in my body causing me to lose control.

For instance, if someone would hurt me mentally or physically, I would be overcome with the fear of confrontation and back away. Then my stomach would begin to ache, my throat would close, and my mouth would dry up until I could no longer hold it in. Then boom! I would see this white light and go on the attack. All my fear would dissipate. Harms way no longer mattered. I had to alleviate this pain in my body. Emotionally drained after one of these episodes, sometimes I would start crying. Then feel like a pussy.

When Jim came home I made sure that I was there first to relay the story, to let him know what had happened. He brought me and D.M. together, admonished us both and suggested that we get along for everyone's sake. We apologized to each other in front of Jim, but I knew that this was not over, that somewhere down the line she would fuck with me.

I was going to butt heads again with this miscreant I felt it in my heart. But the funny thing was, ever since that confrontation I was never again, to be reprimanded by her. In fact Mary became my ally whenever problems arose between my Fathert and I. There were times that I even defended her honor on the street.

When some of the kids teased her children by calling her Dirty Mary, I stepped in to protect them and ask their tormentors that they stop being so mean. And if they continued, I would have to start sounding on their Mothers. Many a fistfight erupted during one of these verbal battles. It didn't matter whether you loved or hated your Mother it was a sign of disrespect. I learned early in my life that children were a brutally cruel bunch and quick to pick on the most vulnerable.

CHAPTER THIRTY ONE

The Dance Discomfited

I was Thirteen and a half years old and things were changing quickly, not only with the way my body was morphing, but also in the way I was starting to think. Pubic hair, sexual arousal, I was looking around and noticing girls for the first time. It was in a manner that attracted me to them like never before. Things were starting to get scary. What do I do? How do I act? Every day was bringing new fears and anxieties.

One Saturday I was invited to go to a dance at Sacred Heart by a friend of mine named Garry R. He was going with his older brother and assured me we would have a good time, hesitantly I agreed.

The night of the dance I was feeling very apprehensive, I didn't think my clothes were good enough. All of a sudden I was feeling very unattractive, so very out of place. Who do I talk to about how to act at the dance, about what I was feeling? I had no one to go to, no one to follow. Garry had his older brother, but my Brother Liam and I hadn't talked more than once in five years. Plus my sister Katelyn wasn't around anymore. I hadn't spoken to her since I left Maggie's.

I had so much pent up anxiety that I felt sick to my stomach. It was difficult to breathe and the tears began to well up in my eyes, all of a sudden I didn't want to go to the dance. I was having what was probably my first ever, social panic attack. Again like many times before, I questioned why this was happening to me.

I tried not to show how I felt, tried to stay calm, stay cool, and not let Gary know how frightened I was. I had gone to a few dances down in Florida at the local Elks Club when I was ten. I had even won a twist contest there. But this was different. The pressure was unbearable.

No matter how much Brylcream I used, my hair was still sticking up in the back like Alfalfa from The Little Rascals. My pant legs were too short and surely someone will ask me, 'Where's the flood". My shirt was so wrinkled it was as if I had slept in it for a month. Plus I was sweating like a pig. I was a total mess and everyone would notice it. How the hell was I going to be able to get through this?

Gary called up to my house from the street. To this point I had never let anyone actually step inside the apartment we lived in because I was so ashamed. My friends would have to ring my bell, and yell up into the hallway that they were downstairs. Or they would yell or whistle up to my window, and then I would come down.

Gary had on black chinos, black penny loafers and a nicely ironed shirt with a two-inch thin black tie. His shiny black hair was slicked back perfectly, not one single strand out of place. I thought something was afoot, I knew Gary, he wasn't the type to dress up and look like he did. He was like me. Up until now we only cared about one thing, hanging out together and having fun.

So here I was, on my way to a dance that was causing me so much angst I thought I might vomit. The walk to the dance afforded me a moment of solace, to take some deep breaths and try to regain my composure. But it didn't last very long because within minutes we were rounding 51st street, just steps from entering the dance.

The party was in the basement of Sacred Heart Church, the one affiliated with the school. We arrived at the head of stairs that led down into the basement where the dance was taking place. I stopped at the top frozen in place. I was again sweating profusely and felt sick to my stomach. I could swear that I was beginning to get more ugly by the second, and my clothes were getting rattier. And when I rubbed my head to check on my cowlick, it felt like a fan, fully spread out. Then Gary nudged me and said: "C'mon lets go."

As we descended the stairs my heart began pounding like a drum. I was imagining in my head that everyone would look at me, and start laughing. I hated the way I was dressed, my gangly physical appearance, everything about me was wrong, and I felt like such a retard. Even before we opened the door to the basement I could hear the music playing. It was the Four Seasons singing their hit: Sherry.

Just as I grabbed the door handle it flew open and a bunch of older guys came barreling past me laughing loudly. I became weak in the knees. I just knew those guys were laughing at me. I told myself that I still had time to leave and that if I ran away immediately all the anguish would disappear. Once again I felt paralyzed by my feelings.

Gary brushed by me and opened the door, and immediately a blast of sound from the speakers resonated so loudly it almost knocked me down. I had never heard music so loud or that clear before. The closest I ever came to hearing music that loud were from the jukeboxes at the bars Maggie and Jim patronized.

The basement was dimly lit but not too dark, and as I scanned the room I noticed that there were a few other kids about my age. But the vast majority seemed to be more or less sixteen and older. There was also a smattering of adults that were there as chaperones. Some of the adults were actually the Brothers from the school.

Gary spotted his brother and began walking towards him. I was no more than a step behind at all times. I wasn't going to let myself become separated from him, It was bad enough that my legs felt like they were made of rubber, to be alone by myself might have caused a heart attack.

I stayed close to Gary for the rest of the night and somehow made it through this hellish event by hugging my back to the wall, and not looking anyone in the eye. I was even frightened to approach people that were familiar to me, fearing that they might notice how uncomfortable I was. This whole night was more than I could tolerate, this scene was definitely not for me.

I've always had these feelings as far back as I could remember, afraid people would not like me, not want me around, find me out and deem me too stupid and ugly a human being to befriend. I had so much shame entrenched deep inside of me that even when showered with accolades my insecurities erased any such notions, I was damaged goods and I knew it. But there would come a time way down the road, these thoughts could be put into a temporary remission.

Ten O'clock, the dance was over and the older guys that didn't have a girl needing to be walked hom, decided to hang out in the schoolyard across the street. Gary's brother being one of them, allowed us to tail along. Still reeling from the dance, I hesitantly followed.

A short time later some of the older guys decided to purchase some alcohol and began passing the hat. As I always had cash on me from selling papers I enthusiastically dug into my pocket and pulled out the five-dollar bill I had neatly folded in my pocket. The older guys applauded my generosity. They patted me on the back and invited me whole heartily into their circle.

This was a turning point in my life, a break from the noises in my head, the self-loathing, the dark secrets I always carried around, the insecurity of adolescence magnified a hundred fold by the harsh judgments I rained down upon myself. But alcohol would change all of that.

A half hour later, two cases of beer and a few pints of liquor appeared on the scene. Everyone seemed to perk up a bit and become more boisterous and cheerful. The festivity was about to commence and I would be a part of it all. One of the older guys that went to purchase the beer made sure that I was the first to be given a can, and as he placed it in my hand he told me, "Enjoy it Kid"!

CHAPTER THIRTY TWO

The Affects Of Alcohols First Encounter

I had tasted beer before from the occasional sips taken from Maggie's glass at the Bar or the Kitchen Table. I remember that I enjoyed its bitter taste and the way the suds would tickle my nose as I bent the glass towards my mouth.

When at the bar I would ask Maggie if I could take a sip of her beer. Most of the time she'd say okay. But even if she declined, someone next to her would say, "Oh C'mon let him have a taste!" and she would usually give in. I would take my sip, spin around on the bar stool, and then sneak another sip when she wasn't paying attention.

Thinking back, these were only some of my earliest recollections of putting alcohol into my body. I might have been four or five years old the first time I tasted beer, I'm not 100% sure. But over the next few months whenever it was available I'd drink. This pattern continued and I genuinely began to be fond of its effect on me. I felt grown up, I felt at ease. There was usually gaiety surrounding the gatherings when people drank, at least in the beginning there was.

But I also remember the times when I was little and living at home and things went totally awry. A fight of some sort would break out and the cops would be called, and someone would be carted off to jail. Most a time it was my old man that was being hauled away. He had been taken to jail on quite a few occasions, almost always in a violent manner.

Sometimes it was the Bellvue Hospital Psychiatric Center to dry out and recover from the beatings sustained while resisting arrest. He had his nose broken too many times to mention and had lost all his front teeth from his encounters with the nightstick. It was quite traumatic to see your father being handcuffed and dragged out of the house and down the stairs. We younger ones would be upset and crying and begging the police to not take our Daddy away and to stop hurting him.

My Fathers alcoholism was of the worst kind. When he drank he lost jobs, and spent whatever money he made, not one bit concerned whether his family had a place to live or food on the table. And as I began to drink my beers the night of the dance I swore I would never drink the way he did.

I kicked in a few more dollars for the second trip to the store to purchase more beer. I had just finished my second one and was feeling real nice. I wasn't so apprehensive I was feeling more comfortable about myself, not so self- conscious, particularly of the things I worried about earlier that evening. I was having a great time, talking shit, getting loud and fitting in.

As the night wore on I kept on having another, then another, and by the time I started on my fifth beer, strange things started to happen. The conversations were becoming unclear, speaking became more difficult and I was beginning to feel dizzy. My stomach was churning and I started to become slightly nauseous. I didn't want to let on that I was feeling sick so I began to sip my beer a little slower than before. I vaguely remember someone asking me if I was okay and replying with a slur, "sure! Give me another." As I began drinking my next beer the urge to vomit overcame me and I stumbled towards the fence. I grabbed hold with both hands and spewed the contents of my stomach all over my shoes.

The guys were laughing and making fun of me, but at the same time congratulating me on my induction into the drinking club. I felt a little better after throwing up and continued finishing my last couple of beers. A few of hours later I decided to stagger home, as it had become extremely late. The Sun was starting to rise and I needed to get home before my Father got up. I didn't want to hear any shit. I remember waking up the next day, my head still spinning from the night before and thinking to myself, "Wow! I had a great time, I can't wait to do it again".

CHAPTER THIRTY THREE

In Preperation Of A Date

One of the older guys where I began hanging out at had taken a liking to me in the following weeks. He became like a big brother and I looked up to him. His name was Robert Dooley, but everyone called him Bobby D. But if anything my earliest experiences taught me, it was to be extremely cautious, to not get too close to people, because you will only get hurt.

Bobby was popular and dating one of the prettiest girls in the neighborhood. And it just so happened she had a younger sister my age. So Bobby decided to ask his girlfriend to fix me up with her little sister. Those were cutesy little things that they did in those days. But it made me sick when I was first approached with this venture. I not only had zero experience in these matters, I was extremely self-conscious. But I had no other choice but to agree to this pubescent liaison. Because in my mind, if I didn't agree maybe Bobby would think I was a queer.

So the day came, it was a week later and I was about to go out on my first date. The time leading up to this unwilling tryst was nerve wracking. I hadn't any decent clothes to wear, I needed a haircut, and my sneakers looked they were picked from out of a garbage can. I was definitely not the poster boy for Teen Idol.

I sold papers all that week with great fervor and by Saturday had a decent amount of money saved up. So that morning before the date I went on shopping spree and bought a new pair of chinos, a white long sleeve shirt and a brand new pair of PF Flyers. I stopped at the local barbershop for the customary coif of my time and doused with a pungent smelling goop, so the crisp part on the side of my head and the crest of a wave in the front would stay smart looking.

Looking in the mirror in front of me, I was aghast at the sight of my huge forehead, I maneuvered the crest of hair as far down as far as I could without disturbing it too much. And while taking a shower late that afternoon, something I had done irregularly at that age. I was noticing something that bothered me very little before this day. How the hell did I get such a massive amount of dirt and crud under my fingernails?

I did my best to wash the debris away, where before I would just bite my nails as low as they would go, to the point where blood was drawn. Then I would dig the rest of the dirt out with my teeth. Ah the personal hygiene of a fourteen year old boy.

I was supposed to meet Bobby at 7PM in the schoolyard, so at about 6 o'clock I began to get dressed. As I slid on the chinos the first thing I noticed was that they seemed way too large. They were not form fit like the older guys wore, they were not only too loose at the waist they were extremely baggy in the ass and long. If I didn't know any better I would have thought they belonged to Jim. Now is when it struck me. Maybe I should have tried them on before I left the store.

As I was unwrapping the shirt I began praying with all my might, "Please God let it fit." And to my amazement it wasn't half bad. Yeah it was a little tight, but I could get away with it. The pants were another story they definitely were out. Even if I kept the shirt- tail on the outside, it would still look like I shit in my pants.

I began scrambling through my drawer looking for the only two pairs of pants that I owned, hoping they would be better than the ones I had just bought.

I found them! They were lying at the bottom of the drawer. They looked pretty wrinkled, but seemed relatively clean. And as I slid these tight jeans on, the wrinkles all but disappeared. Only one slight problem, there was a mustard stain above the knee. No problem, I'd rectify that with a little spit.

Upon noticing that I hadn't bought new socks with my sneakers and knew there weren't any in my drawer, I thought the logical thing to do would be to just put on the ones I had taken off before I showered.

It must be that a fourteen year old boy's olfactory organs are genetically retarded, oblivious to BO, dirty feet odor and the like. A glob of Jims's hair cream, followed by a quick combing and I was ready to run.

Down the stairs and out the door I nervously went, every step bringing me closer to my first teenage tryst. My legs seemed to be getting heavier by the minute, my breathing was becoming more laborious and my mouth lost all its moisture. And even though it was not warm out I began to perspire profusely. It was happening again.

I knew that I was going to be harassed incessantly by the group hanging out at the schoolyard. I'd seen it before and it could be brutal. Hopefully Bobby would already be there and I wouldn't have to wait too long.

I stopped at the candy store on 51st and 10th to buy some gum so I could get some spit back into my mouth. I grabbed a handful of Bazooka gum and popped a couple into my mouth, and instantly the dryness disappeared. For a moment there I thought I would swallow my tongue. Back outside and in the street I hesitantly walked up to 52nd street. I stopped right before 52nd to gather some courage, took one very deep breath and turned the corner. This was the proverbial moment of truth.

I bopped my way towards the schoolyard, I tried my best to not show how scared I was. But no sooner did the guy's hanging out notice me, the razzing started. It's pretty shitty how people can find every little defect or quirk about you, and callously tease you unmercifly. And emit so much verbal venom that the person targeted might cry. I'd noticed it throughout my whole life but I just didn't know why they did it.

One guy yelled: "Hey Alfalfa!" while pointing to my head." Another howled: "Where's the flood?" pointing to my pants that seemed a little bit too short. "Who dressed you? Clarabelle?" As my embarrassment hit a crescendo and my face began turning beet red, all I was able to muster up was, "Fuck You! Your Mother!

The kid came over towards me, put me in a headlock and started raining noogies down on my head. The problem hanging out with older kids was, you always took the brunt of physical abuse, and as this punk was no different. He began putting more pressure on my neck, I was barely able to get out the words, I'm sorry! Get the fuck off me! You started it!"

When he let me go I began swinging wildly at him. This asshole really had me pissed. The other guys were all laughing which made me angrier and more determined to catch this jerk with at least one punch in the face. But he was much bigger than me and held me at bay. Just then Bobby showed up and told them to leave me alone.

"Bobby! You got a cigarette?" I asked. And he pulled out a brand new pack of Camels. As was custom during those days, he began smacking the pack on the back of his hand to compress the tobacco in the cigarettes. He twirled the top of the cellophane off, smacked the pack on his index finger, and out came a cigarette. I grabbed it and put it to my lips. Within a second Bobby had whipped out his Zippo lighter, and in two moves, brushing the lighter across his leg, the flame appeared. Bobby was the coolest guy I knew.

By now I had been smoking for four years and was totally addicted. My Sister Katey got me started so I couldn't tell on her. I would steal cigarettes out of Jim's pack when he was sleeping. I would also try bumming a smoke once in a while from either a stranger or one of the older kid's in the neighborhood. And when I was selling papers

I would pick up cigarette butts off the street. Most of the time by the bus stops, because people would throw away half a cigarette or more before stepping on the bus. I picked them off the street without hesitation.

I usually had a book of matches on me, but sometimes if I didn't I would have to ask one of the adults walking down the street. "Hey Mister! You got a light?" Some would look at me quizzically and keep walking. Some would stop and look at me, all five foot five and 100 pounds and say: "Get lost kid! Your too young to smoke, or it'l stunt your growth. But needing that fix, I would zealously continue searching until someone would gave me a light, or I found a book of matches on the ground with one or two matches left in it.

CHAPTER THIRTY FOUR

The Missed Kiss

Bobby shouted. "Whose got a beer?" And before you could say a word, about six guys tried to place one in his hand. He grabbed two cans, handed one to me and said: "Bottoms up Kiddo!" I've got a special night planned for you. A few beers and a couple of smokes later Bobby said to me, "It's time to go Buddy, are you ready for this?" And trying with all my manly might to get it out, I squeaked Yeah I guess so!

I placed three bazookas in my mouth and began to chew feverishly. Bobby knew that I was feeling very anxious. He said don't worry Buddy, you look fine." "It's going to be a piece of cake." Those words of encouragement lasted about the time it took to walk up the block to his girl's building, and then I was scared shitless again.

Bobby and I walked into the vestibule of the building. Then He rang the bell in three consecutive motions. That was the signal to let her know that we were here. As the buzzer rang to let us inside the hallway, Bobby put his hand gently on the back of my neck, and led me inside. I noticed I was losing flavor from my gum pretty fast, and as I went to put another piece in it wouldn't go. I had put too much gum in my mouth since I left the store and I couldn't accommodate another piece. I thought about tryingto swallow it but it would have choked me to death. So I quickly took it out with two fingers, put that hand behind my back, and dropped it on the floor near the radiator. Then I put two new pieces in my mouth.

Suddenly I heard the sound of footsteps. Tap, tap, tap, coming down the flight of stairs, Then the normal sound of someone walking. And then once again a tap, tap, tap. The sound echoed as each flight was being descended. Then at the top of the stairway Bobby's girl appeared. She was as pretty as any of the teen heartthrobs of that time. Whether it be the girl from Rebel without a Cause, Gidget, Annette Funicello or any of the many teen starlets from television or the movies, "She was so fine."

I noticed the appearance of a figure slightly silhouetted behind her and I inquisitively tried to get a peek. But before I did Bobby's girlfriend reached behind her back and began gently pulling this person from behind. It was her younger sister. And as I stared up into the light at the top of the stairs, there stood a younger version of Bobby's girl, a very pretty girl dressed almost identical to her big sister. The tight contoured jeans that descended down her legs and stopped just above the ankle. The pink fitted button down shirt that vee'd towards the bottom, that was worn outside just enough to hide the zipper of her jeans. And the white canvas sneakers, worn with no socks to showing off the beauty of the female ankle.

As I was watching this pretty girl walking down the stairs, It began to sink in just how lovely she really was, and all I could to do was step back in awe. My mind began racing, It was telling me to get the hell out of there, that this girl is in no way going to like you. She will get a closer look at you and throw up. And then bitterly argue with her sister for trying to set her up with such an ogre.

Bobby must have noticed that I was freaking out, so he placed his hand on my shoulders, bent down and whispered: "Don't worry it's going to be ok." He could see the look of terror on my face, and my body shaking. But when he put his hand on me, it succeeded in calming me down. In that moment I was able to catch my breath. But that wouldn't last too long because as I experienced each new phase of this encounter I would again become petrified.

As she got closer her face captivated me, her skin was pale like a ceramic doll. She had freckles on her face perfectly aligned from her nose to her cheeks, and light auburn hair pulled back tightly into a ponytail. In my eyes she was already crowned Little Miss America. Though there was little to see in the way of breasts, it really didn't matter, I wouldn't know what to do with them anyway. She had an appealing figure, a striking prettiness that added fuel to the fire of my anxiety. But once we exited into the cool air of the street, the sweat from my insecurities began to dry up and I was able to gain some semblance of composure.

Bobby suggested we head up Broadway towards the Penny Arcade. Immediately my adrenal glands pumped out enough epinephrine that I felt my feet leave the ground. I loved that place, and when selling papers, there would seldom be the night that I wouldn't stop in for at least a little while.

Skee-ball and the eclectic maneuvers it took to master the game. A flinch of the arm, or a blink of the eye and Bam! game ruined. The multitude of **Pinball Machines,** and the many genres they displayed. Anything from outer space adventures to the baseball game. The bells and whistles that resonated there the tickets that were earned to redeem prizes that held worth only to a child. **Chinese Handcuffs**, **Plastic Yo - yo's, Penny Candy** etc. Merchandise that if purchased directly from the manufacturer would surely cost one, one hundredth of what you would spend to win one. **The Mechanical Gunslinger** that challenged all that came his way, always with the same lame excuse of having got a little dust in his eye, if you beat him to the draw. **Fortune Telling Machines** and **Tests of Strength**. There were a million reasons to love the place.

As we entered this palace of entertainment Bobby huddled with me to check out our finances and form a plan of retreat. We wanted to make sure that we had enough money left over to stop at the soda shop later. As we split up I grabbed my date by the hand and I led her around this menagerie of fun and excitement.

First we played **Ski-Ball**, and being the coy young girl, she allowed me to show off my diverse experience with the game. Standing behind her petite frame, I explained to her how to deliver the ball to the side, just so, that it would carrom back, rolling towards the middle and go up the ramp and into the fifty point slot.

She picked up the ball and gingerly tossed it towards the target. The ball never made it up the ramp. It just rolled lazily back towards us. She turned shyly around towards me, and exclaimed, "I'm not really good at this!"

I took her arm gently, then placed the ball in her throwing hand. I pointed her towards the target placing my left hand on her left hip, and making sure that I was standing as far away from her backside as possible. With my own hand shaking from this first erotic experience, I gently squeezed her a little closer.

With my right hand together with hers, we rolled the wooden orb towards its target. The ball rolled up the ramp and landed into the thirty-point slot. We turned and looked at each other with enthusiasm. I noticed a poignant smile radiating from her ceramic like complexion. Her freckles danced about her face, she was so very pretty.

The excitement relaxed me somewhat, it allowed me to enjoy the moment. The evening was going well, but after about an hour Bobby suggested we walk up to Central Park. So as fast as we could, we headed north on Broadway towards Columbus Circle. By this time I had begun to feel more comfortable holding my date's hand.

I remember clearly how soft her hands felt in mine. The sweat from my hands was now dry now, as I became more at ease of the situation. We race ahead about a half a block and stopped. We shyly turned towards each other and smiled. I pointed out to her some of the local interests, as I had been in this area a thousand times while selling papers. She seemed impressed with my knowledge of the area.

When we reached Columbus Circle, we decided not to enter the park there. It was always crowded with winos, junkies and crazy homeless people. You couldn't enter that way without being harassed in some manner so we made a right turn and headed towards Central Park East. We wanted to see the horse drawn carriages anyway and the beautiful entrance to the Plaza Hotel.

I would sometimes enter the Plaza on the 56th Street side when selling papers, to sit and count my money. There was no way I could get in through main entrance there would be too much action...

The doormen dressed in full regalia, looking like generals in an army, hailing cabs or waiving for the limos that were standing by. Then unloading the luggage from the trunks, passing them on to the bellhops that were eagerly waiting. They would also pass on to the chauffeurs and cabbies luggage to be loaded as guests were departing. These men were the official greeter's and the last person the guests would engage with. They were the true ambassadors for this magnificent hotel.

There were a multitude of bellhops scurrying in and about, making sure the patrons, the super-rich and famous got to their rooms without a hitch, and like the doormen one of the last persons the guests would interact.

On the 56th street side lobby, as you entered, there were these two throne-like chairs that I would plop down on. Then I'd dump all of my change onto the thick, carpeted floor to be counted. I needed to see how much I had made up to this point. If I hadn't reached my goal I would continue up to 6th Avenue (Avenue of the Americas), and work my way downtown.

This part of the route had only one sure thing, the gorgeous coat check girl that worked in the bar near the corner of 7th Avenue. She gave me a hug and a dollar every night, and would occasionaly ask me if I would like to be adopted by her. On most nights she was my last sale.

Bobby the girls and I came to a halt on 59th and Central Park East across from the Plaza to pet the Carriage Horses. There were probably ten lined up along the curb, with drivers perched up high upon their tufted seats, waiting for their next fare. Then they would jump down and swing open the door to the carriage, making sure the passengers were securely seated. Then hop back up on their seats, grab the reins and take off. As they entered the park, all you could hear was the clip-clop of the horse's shoes. At this time of night the drive was very dark and romantic.

Strolling along and holding hands, always with our chaperones a few steps behind, I decided to talk to my date. I asked where she attended school, which was actually a fixed question posed to break the ice. I knew that 99% of the Irish Catholic girls in the neighborhood went to Sacred Heart. And so she quizically responded, "I go to Sacred Heart Stupid!"

I could tell that her response was not meant to be mean or malicious. It was said in a coy manner, a manner that spoke, C'mon don't tease me, you know were I go to school! She told me: "I've seen you in the Public School yard across the street many times when I got out of classes." I didn't want to tell her that I despised going to Catholic School, I had too many bad memories of places like that.

Her voice was so soft it made me feel kind of warm inside. She spoke about school, and I listened Intently even though it was boring. And then she talked about her family. It was the typical Irish Catholic family of those days. She was one of seven children three younger sisters, two older brothers and an older sister (Bobby's girl). Seven seemed to be the magic number appropriate for that era. I guess there was nothing else to do back then as a couple except procreate. She described her parents to me. Her Father was a strict disciplinarian but a loving man. Her Mom was the quintessential housewife and caretaker.

Walking along the path leading to the zoo you couldn't help but notice there were plenty of people out and about. They were sitting on the benches that lined both sides of the path, just socializing and enjoying the night air. It was a different time back then the park was safe haven, not a place to be feared once the sun went down.

We reached the entrance of the zoo and we patiently waited for our chaperones. It seemed they were taking quite a bit more time lately what with their stopping every two minutes to make out. Didn't they realize how uncomfortable it was making us? That every time we looked behind and saw them kissing, we'd turn back toward towards each other, our shyness forcing us to blush. I'd be dumbfounded on what to do or say at that moment, my hands would be shaking from embarrassment, but with a touch of excitement blended in.

"Damn it!" I started sweating and my mouth was drying up again. So I reached into my pocket, pulled out some gum and asked my date if she would like some. She nodded yes. Could it be that she shared the same nervous feelings as me? Seeing her sister kissing a boy that way, wasn't it only natural for us to feel embarrassed? I was sure she felt that way also.

Once our chaperones caught up to us, we were given the nod to continue walking. The tension that we were feeling the moment before seemed to dissipate, we both welcomed the nod enthusiastically.

We were at the seal pool for about half an hour playing around when Bobby let me know that we should be heading back to the neighborhood, as it was getting late. As uncomfortable as I had felt with this girl at times, I was hoping that the experience would last. I was kind of glad this part of my evening was coming to an end. It had been too stressful pretending as if I had known what I was doing.

During the walk home I was beginning to feel a little apprehensive again, I knew that I was expected to perform some sort of goodnight ritual, but it all escaped me. "Was I supposed to shake her hand? Was I supposed give her a hug goodnight?" "Holy shit! What was I expected to do?" I wished I could have disappeared.

All of a sudden it was if we were running a race. We were no more than three blocks from our destination. "Slow down! I screamed inside my head." I felt the panic creeping in and I thought I was going to shit my pants. So to ease my desperation I slinked backwards and gave Bobby an elbow, a signal that I needed to talk to him.

I whispered, "What do I do when we get back Bobby? " He assured me everything would be ok, that I should just follow his lead. "Go back and hold her hand, but this time squeeze it just a little. Just relax and be yourself." Be myself! "What the hell did that mean by that?" Oh! I should just be this retard that has never kissed a girl, and is so afraid he thinks he is about to cry, is that the be yourself he's talking about, I thought sarcastically. It was easy for him to say.

We rounded the corner and reached our destination. My date and I looked sheepishly at each as we entered the hallway. It was as if we were going to the gallows and there would be no pardon forthcoming. There was nothing we could do.

Bobby and his girl had entered first and immediately started walking towards the back of the hallway and under the stairwell. This was where couples went to say goodnight and to make out one more time before the evening was over.

I was standing at the front of the stairs and looked over towards my date. Her eyes were so compelling, staring down at the floor and then back up towards me. She flirtatiously beckoned me toward the back of the stairs. So I grabbed her by the hand and gently nudged her that way.

I was expected to kiss this girl. This was going to be my rite of passage. Everything regarding my manhood up to this point in my life depended on this one moment. All I had to do was lean over and press my lips against hers. It seemed simple enough.

As I made my move I noticed immediately that something was very wrong. I had misjudged my distance and began to fall off balance. As much as I tried to regain my equilibrium it was too late. My left hand instinctively rose up to break my fall, and without malice, it landed squarely on her breast. If that wasn't bad enough, my body had crashed into hers and sent her backwards toward the wall, where she proceeded to bang her head.

The next thing I heard was, "Hey! What are you doing?" And as I pushed off the wall with my free hand to stand up straight, I immediately unleashed a salvo of the most sincere apologies I had ever expressed in my life "I'm sorry! I didn't mean it! I just lost my balance. It was an accident!" "Please forgive me"

Bobby's girlfriend hearing the exclamation of disapproval from her sister immediately came over to us and asked what was going on. I was still reeling in shock from the moment and not able to respond. I just stared at her with this dumb blank look. Much to my surprise as well as a deep sense of relief, this wonderful young lady explained to her sister the truth that we had lost our balance, and fell against the wall.

Bobby was standing behind his girlfriend and began laughing uncontrollably, while I stood speechless and totally embarrassed. I had had enough of this kissing stuff for the evening. I asked to be dismissed without prejudice.

I guess all parties involved thought better of prolonging the evening and decided to part ways. And as I apologized once more to my date, she just smiled, shook her head and leaned in and kissed me on the cheek. For a moment a warm feeling came over me and all seemed fine. Fine that is until I left the protective confines of the hallway.

Almost immediately Bobby began teasing me unmerciful. Laughing hysterically, he put me in a headlock and gently knuckled the top of my head. "You were trying to get to second base on the first date Huh!" "No way I emphatically replied." He came back with: "C'mon don't lie to me. I saw what you did!" "You tried to cop a feel and got caught. Admit it!" "No Bobby I swear I didn't!" And as he let go of my head he said: "Don't worry, I'm only kidding, let's go down to the schoolyard."

After drinking a few beers, I had all but forgotten what had just transpired. But somehow over the next couple of days guys found out and would not let it go. They were constantly riding me, making me the brunt of the joke every day, until I walked away, hiding my tears of embarrassment. It got so bad I decided not to hang around with this crew any more and began staying a little further downtown, closer to home. It would be almost a year later before I would attempt to kiss a girl again.

CHAPTER THIRTY FIVE

49th Street Rerun

Back on the block, it was as if I'd never left. It was the same group of potential juvenile delinquents, hanging out with each other, looking for anything to do that might distract them from the dysfunction that was their life.

What would we do now? Rockefeller Plaza? Forty Deuce to sneak in the movies? Nah! We decided to go up to Tar Beach on 49th St between 8th and 9th Ave. There were about a dozen Brownstone Buildings connected to each other that afforded us a huge area to run around on. And if you wanted go even farther you could jump the 4 ft. gap from the building closest to 9th Ave. From there you were able to travel all the way around to 48th Street.

There must have been about nine pigeon coops on these buildings, and we played around each of them. There was this kid Charlie that hung out with us. He was a real fucking sadist. This maniac would grab a pigeon and nail its wings against the roof entrance wall. Then he 'd stand back and throw his knife at it. When he would start his sick shit, it was time for me to leave. I never trusted that kid anyway. He was this puny little shit that would act like a psycho so that no one would mess with him. I wasn't afraid of this jerk, but I always had in the back of my mind to keep a sharp eye on him.

On the days we went up on the roofs to play tag, we would start on the easternmost one that sat flush up against the Belvedere Hotel, a transient operation that accommodated businessmen on small expense accounts, or people that might have had something to do with the venue happening at Madison Square Garden. It also quartered the occasional local prostitute who needed a room for half hour, which was great for the manager, because it was money off the books.

On this particular roof there was a shack built, but abandoned by its owner due to robberies and vandalism. So it was taken over by the kid's in the neighborhood. We would hang out in it on rainy days or days that we just felt like sitting around smoking and talking shit.

This one particular day I was the first one to enter. Right away I could make out the silhouettes of three figures leaning against the back wall. When my eyes adjusted for the darkness I noticed who they were. They were three older guys from the neighborhood that we would see around once in a while.

Looking more closely I noticed two of them had small paper bags against their face, while the other was sitting there bent over at his waist. It was as if he was sleeping. There was a pungent odor that filled the air. It was the familiar smell of airplane glue, and they were sniffing it.

We all entered the shed and sat against the opposite wall. We were there to plan some fun and to decide what we were going to do with our day. All of a sudden one of the guys passed the bag to one of my crew. He said to him, put the bag over your face and breathe through your nose. The kid lifted the bag up, placed it over his face and began to breathe.

The bag collapsed, and then filled up again. Over and over for about fifteen seconds. Then he stopped, fell to his side and placed the bag gently upon his lap. He stayed like that for about a minute then began to try and sit up straight. "Wow he said: I was having this weird dream and my brain was feeling numb." Like hitting your funny bone, only it was your brain feeling numb. Cmon! Try it!"

One of the guys that had been sniffing before pulled out about five more tubes of glue and two fresh paper bags. He told us to pour the complete contents of the tubes at the bottom of the bag and then put it tightly around our face, and breathe through our nose.

When the bag got to me I never hesitated. I took it, put it over my face and began to inhale through my nose. Again and again I breathed in this toxic substance. My brain began humming, as if I it were a motor running on electricity. The buzzing got louder and then I went into a dream state, gliding through the air, high up above anywhere I had ever been before. I had been rendered unconscious by this noxious substance and it was killing brain cells by the millions with every breath I took. Then I woke, still euphoric, and I repeated it again. This was just the beginning for me. And though I rarely sniffed glue, when I did, it was done with fervor.

CHAPTER THIRTY SIX

The Thrill Of Sugar Hill

M emorial Day was just about a week away. Summer was upon me with nothing to do but get into mischief. I was at the age that the things I did before weren't giving me the same kick, and I knew that if I stayed with the bunch I was hanging out with I would find myself getting into some real trouble.

I had been selling papers on occasion to earn some money, which was more than most of the kids running in my circle were doing. I had even found a new enterprise that a couple of my buddies and I could share in.

Every Saturday morning we would go to 51st and 9th to clean car windows. It was long before the bums in the city took over the trade, or so it seemed. 51st was a main street for traffic heading west. It wasn't as congested as the regular thoroughfares most commuters used to head that way. It was a little off the beaten track.

Tenth Avenue became Amsterdam north of 59th St.. It was the main hub for Manhattanites heading north, as was the West Side Highway. The latter allowed direct accessibility to the George Washington Bridge the Holland and Mid-town Tunnels, which connected New York and New Jersey. All in all it was an ideal spot for our latest initiative.

Our tools of the trade consisted of a few rags made from old t-shirts (there were no paper towels back then) and a bottle of window cleaner. When the cars stopped for the traffic light we would spring into action. A few sprays from the bottle to the windshield, a vigorous rubbing with the rags, and "Voila!" A coin would be passed through the driver's side window.

That was the plan, but it didn't always work that way. There were times a potential customer would wave one of us away, but we would ignore it and make believe we didn't see them. You never knew what to expect, Some people might even give you a quarter, to not touch their car.

Then you had the nasty cheap bastards that rolled down the window and started yelling or even threatening you. They were the ones who's windshield we would spit on. But you had to be ready, because some knuckleheads would put the car in park, and chase you. Or they might circle around the block and try to come up behind you. But I had eyes in the back of my head. I could sense trouble.

All in all, it became a successful way to make a few dollars for the day. And even though it was an honest way to make money, I always felt that it was like begging, and so it was shameful to me. I began to have the same feelings selling papers, and would be horrified if someone from the neighborhood saw me.

As luck would have it, I received a call from my Sister Katey. She had gotten married about six months prior and was expecting her first child. Her husband Vinnie, who was also called Buddy by his friends, had a Mother that was married to a chef. And at Vinnie's request, they agreed to hire me to work with them at this resort in New Hampshire for the summer. I thought: "This won't be so bad," "I could save all my money and go home with my pockets full." Besides it would be a break for me, I was looking to get away from the people I'd been hanging out with anyway. And Buddy's Step-Dad was not only a Chef he was the Head Chef. His Mother also happened to be the Program Director. I thought to myself, "Man! Have I got it made."

It was a first-class resort that boasted a championship golf course, horseback riding and a large lake for boating. It was also noted for its fine cuisine. I was told that I would be the Chef's Helper, assisting in the preparation of meals. I knew nothing about preparing food. I could probably have poisoned someone just boiling water. But I would be able to save all the money I made because I wouldn't have to pay for food or lodging. I'd only need to spend a few dollars on necessities like, candy, toiletries, and of course cigarettes. I might not have been a daily bather by now, but I definitely had become a daily smoker.

All in all it was the right move to make. And on the plus side, I'd be getting away from Jim and his constant ball breaking. His constant barrage of insults about everything I was doing wrong. Getting away from all the bullshit would be a reprieve. The next day I went to the Port Authority Terminal and boarded my ride to my summer job.

What seemed like a never-ending trip finally brought me to the small hamlet of Sugar Hill New Hampshire: Upon exiting the bus, I noticed this handsome middle-aged woman that looked to be waiting for someone. She was perfectly groomed and impeccably dressed. And being that she was the only person there, she had to be the person that was there to scoop me up and take me to my final destination.

She came over and introduced herself as Buddy's mom, and helped me load my small bag into an old woodie station wagon. The car was emblazoned with the hotels logo on the side of it and could seat seven people comfortably. She told me to sit in the front seat next to her and then we left. I wasn't much for small talk so it was a pretty quiet ride. Fifteen minutes later we were pulling off the main thoroughfare and onto a small country road that ran up and around a steep hill.

Once we came to the crest of the road, there in all its pure beauty was my first the view of the hotel. I became totally enthralled by what I was seeing. It was a vista, right off of a picture postcard, an enormous old-fashioned clapboard inn.

There were eight huge dormers protruding out from atop its regal front entrance. Pillars mounted carefully along the front porch carried the weight of the dormers and jutting roof. The hotel sat amongst the Green Mountains of New Hampshire, a panoramic view like nothing I had ever seen in my life. I was hypnotized.

Broad manicured lawns extended completely around the premises. There were dozens of cottages outside the main house that were carefully set about the property as to not disturb the privacy of one another. These cottages were set aside, for guests of distinction and wealth. Large weeping willows bordered the extensive cobblestone driveway that stretched about an eighth of a mile long from the main road. Semi-circled, it allowed for a constant stream of traffic.

Upon the porch were two massive oak doors that loomed at the entranceway of this, the main house. Captivated by the enormity of everything, I hadn't noticed I was standing in the driveway. The beep of a horn at my back startled me. It was a imousine, and I had been blocking it from pulling in to the entrance. I waved apologetically while backing up onto the porch.

All of a sudden one of oak doors flew open and two bellboys dressed in full regalia excused themselves, while almost running me over. One of them was pulling from behind a cart to load baggage on, and as soon as the trunk of the limo was opened, he pounced on the suitcases. The other bellboy stood at attention grasping the handle of the passenger door. And as soon as it began opening he gently tugged, signaling the person inside that it was being taken care of. Then there would be the salutations welcoming the guests, with wishes for them to have a wonderful vacation. It was all done with such precision. It impressed me very much.

Massive oak trees, hundreds of years old were carefully positioned throughout the boundaries of this classic Inn, and offered up shade to the many cottages throughout the property, a reprieve from the heat of the long summer days. A championship golf course, horseback riding, and other exclusive amenities were at the disposal to the guests of this five star resort. Sunset Hill House was grand in stature and could cater up to anywhere from four to five hundred persons at any time.

Vinnie's mother walked me over to introduce me to the Chef, and to give me a Grand Tour of the kitchen. As soon as the pleasantries of the handshake were finished, I was escorted around and introduced as his helper, whatever that was going to be. This is when my tour of the kitchen began.

There must have been fifty people working in and about the kitchen at all times. There were other Chef's besides my boss the Executive Chef. There was the Pastry Chef, the Sous Chef, the PantryChef, etc. There were Specialty Cooks, Short Order Cooks, and Line Cooks. There were Assistant Cooks, Cooks Helpers, Salad Men and Bakers. These were kitchen workers everywhere.

You had servers that loaded the entrees onto the plates with the precision of a surgeon. Portions exactly the same, to a tee. Placed artisticly pleasing to the eye. The plates were then placed upon a sill atop the order checks that had been written out with the table # and dinner requests. Once a tables order was complete, the plates would then be loaded on a tray and delivered by the Waiter or Waitress that had taken the order.

Drink orders were brought to the bar, filled, picked up and returned ASAP. There were Busboys that cleared the tables as soon as the guests finished eating, and delivered them to the Dishwashers. This was the gist of the environment that I would be around. Waiters, Waitresses and Busboys were constantly running in and out between two huge swinging doors, one for entering and the other exiting. Large trays were balanced perfectly atop of one hand with up to four entrees at a time and not missing a beat. The place was a continual Bee Hive of activity.

The first few days were like any other time I'd traveled somewhere. Nervous and edgy, I was cautious around the people I was meeting for the first time. Being cordial was second nature to me, so people were usually affable in return. I could also put up this façade of being some tough kid from Hell's Kitchen, and present the air that if you messed with me there was going to be serious consequences. Even though I was scared shit.

The first week was tumultuous. I was trying to understand what it was I should be doing. I'd ask my boss and he'd send me to the Head Cook who in turn would send me to one of the Specialty Cooks who would say to me, "Why don't you take a break and come back in an hour or so." So off I would go to walk around the grounds and waste some time. It suddenly dawned on me that no one needed or wanted my help, I was placed here as a favor to Vinnie, and the little I got in the way the better it was for everyone.

Eventually I began hanging out with the Dishwashers. At least they let me help out. And besides they were a little closer to my age. I even stopped eating at the Chef's table and began eating with the regular resort workers who had their own dining room. The array of food wasn't as first-rate as at the Chef's Table, but the good company made up for it.

In my second week at the resort I was getting to know some of the guys pretty well. We would hang out in one another's rooms and play cards (I was mostly just a spectator), or we would go to the laundry area where there was also a pool table to bide the time. As the days passed by, my anxiety level began to diminish. I became much more at ease with everyone.

It was always difficult in the beginning for me when meeting new people. I would walk around with what might be construed as a chip on my shoulder. There was always this feeling out period that kept me at arms length from the people I'd meet for the first time. My fear of being around strangers, and of being the new kid on the block, dogged me., My fear of being judged inept, ugly and unwanted kept me self isolated. On top of all that, being the youngest one around didn't help much either. Some of these things still hinder me to this day.

One day during my second week, there was a buzz going around that there would be a dance in the workers dining room come Friday, a social event that was sorely needed. It broke up the monotony of the long work schedule. Without these social events I would imagine the routine of the job might drive people insane, especially young people.

I was invited to the first of these bashes by one of the younger guys I had made friends with, and even though I was somewhat apprehensive I cordially accepted.

As Friday rolled around the anticipation alone was enough to make my heart start palpitating and my mind to race. I really didn't have much of an ensemble to choose from, and panic began to seep in as I realized how ill prepared I was for such a communal experience. What was I going to do?

Finally one of the older guy's saw me freaking out and came to my rescue with a shirt that had been too small for him. Some soap and water for my sneakers, a shower and even some aftershave made me feel somewhat relieved. Brylcream borrowed from my buddy, along with his assurance that I looked good had me raring to go.

I arrived to the party a little late. People had already been drinking and pairing off. ***See You InSeptember*** by the Tokens was playing on the record player and the dancing to its melody had the middle of the room cluttered. People really seemed to be enjoying themselves. But I was shaky and nervous, my palms were sweating, I felt so out of place. As always I was unable to feel normal in a social situation. My world would grow very small, and I'd feel as if I was under a microscope. Fearful that everyone would find me out and see what a piece of shit I really was.

I figured I'd have a couple of beers, hang out for a while and then go back to my room. "But then I got tapped on the shoulder," it was one of the guys that stayed in the same quarters as me. He knew I had an infatuation with this girl I had seen around and introduced me to her. She had shoulder length blonde hair, and though she seemed to be a tad on the chubby side, she was voluptuous.

She seemed to be intoxicated, and was wavering back and forth. And when she spoke she was slurring her words a bit. She asked if I was the boy from New York, and when I replied, "Yes I am!" She grabbed my arm and said C'mon let's get the heck out of here. And off we went outside into the summer night.

There was a full moon out, and not a cloud in the sky, so it would be easy to navigate our way around the grounds. We worked our way to a secluded area of the golf course and sat down on the grass next to one of the oak trees that were scattered along its borders. I was feeling very nervous. I had never been in this position before with an older girl, or with any girl for that matter. I wasn't sure what to do.

She took hold of my shirt laid back down onto the grass and gently pulled me towards her. Our lips met together, and all of a sudden I was passionately kissing a girl for the first time.

After making out for a while, which was sufficient for me, she suddenly grabbed my hand and placed it on her breast. These were unchartered waters I was getting into, and I was feeling a little intimidated. But with my adolescent sexual genesis activated, I began to get more aroused. I knew what was happening, I'd felt it before.

The first time was about a year ago while I was showering. My penis began to harden and I got a tingling sensation as I was soaping up my body. A hot flash came over me, and a euphoric sensation had me touching it again and again. And after a few seconds, I climaxed.

The first timed it happed I panicked and felt remorseful, I thought something was wrong with me, I felt I had done something sinful. "Thanks Jim" for preparing me to be a man.

So here I was, with this experienced young woman, just going along with the program and taking her lead. After about half an hour of kissing she suggested we go back to my room and hang out. The walk back was a haze of what ifs and what do I do, I began to tremble at the thought that this could be the day I lose my virginity.

The walk back to my room was extremely sensual. I had an erection that felt as though it would bust out of my pants. My heartrate was excelerating by the second and I was breathing heavily. My anticipation was arousing.

As I opened the door to my room and turned on the light, the bed seemed even bigger than I had remembered. It took up at least eighty percent of the room. There was just a small chest against the opposite wall for my clothes. It felt Carollesque, as if I was in Wonderland and I was this small creature stepping into a room of gigantic proportion. It definitely was not a suite at the Waldorf, but was sure to suffice. Besides, I was there for only one thing, to finally break my cherry with an experienced woman.

I offered her a spot on the bed and slid up beside her to continue making out and feeling her up. My one hand was trying to reach behind her. I was fumbling to open her bra. It was an almost impossible feat for someone so inexperienced. I didn't realize I would need an engineering degree to pop it open. This was definably one of the most difficult things I had ever attempted, but I finally completed the task, the bra sprung open.

With hands that could not stop shaking I turned back around to face her and to claim the prize I worked so hard for. To see for the first time, the naked breasts of a voluptuous young woman. It's where everything began to fall apart.

After all that tenuous work, when I turned her around, she was sound asleep. "What! You've got to be kidding" I said to myself. "What do I do now?" I wasn't going to pass this up so I began shaking her and at the same time peeking at the most wonderful sight my eyes had ever beheld, the naked breasts of Aphrodite. Still she wouldn't wake up.

It seemed to me that she was just playing dead to the world, because how could anyone sleep through the bumbling chaos of me attempting to undo the clasp of her bra. I was to learn many years later about blackouts while drinking, and what could happen under the heavy influence of alcohol. But I was intent on continuing my adventure, learning about sex first hand.

I was fumbling about, attempting to take off her jeans. But once I opened the top button of her pants and pulled down her zipper, a feeling came over me that said: this was not right. How could it be right if she was not participating? So I set out to find someone with more experience than myself, which was probably every other worker at the resort.

There was this guy I knew who's room was just down the hall. His was the only one with its door open, so I figured he could help me out. When I reached the room I could see that he was lying in his bunk reading. I knocked on the doorjamb and he waved me in. He was probably somewhere in his forties or so, and surely had the experience I was seeking. I talked to him explaining my dilemma, hoping for an answer. I was sure he could help me fix this thing. He told me to wait in his room while he checked things out.

I kept peeking out of the door looking for some sort of sign that everything was okay, but nothing was happening. So a few minutes later I began walking back down the hall to see what was up. I reached the room and looked in, but no one was there, so I went outside to look for them.

I spotted the guy coming my way, so I went back inside to wait for him. As soon as he came in the door I confronted him, asking what happened. He made up some lame story, that when he reached the room he saw she was semi-conscious and after seeing her in such a vulnerable position, he helped her to get dressed and walked her back to her dorm.

I would come to know later that this pig molested her, and but for not her coming to, things could have gotten worse. I'm sure this fucking scumbag would have raped her.

It didn't take long for the story to spread, of the kid who had this girl all prepped for sex and couldn't go through with it. It was just one more debilitating incident of low self-esteem. Just more shit that I would have to deal with. And as the word spread more and more, I became the laughing stock of the resort workers, with people mumbling things and smirking as I walked by. The final straw came when I bumped into her.

She was walking with this older guy, and as they passed by they both snickered my way. I was hoping to catch her by herself and explain the situation somewhat, hoping she would forgive me and give me another chance. But I knew deep in my heart I screwed up, that I blew it. So I went off by myself, sat under one of the Oak Trees near by and cried for what seemed like an hour.

It's kind of upsetting that I was the one being disgraced and not the guy who molested her, who if given the chance surely would have raped her. That day my psyche took a direct hit. Once again my ego was shattered. I never talked to anyone about it again, until now.

CHAPTER THIRTY SEVEN

Just One-Way Out

A few days later I was doing laundry when some guys came in to shoot some pool. They asked me if I wanted to play and I nodded affirmatively. Being what recently happened I was ecstatic that someone was even talking to me. After playing for a little while a discussion just happened to pop up about what was on the other side of the wall.

The laundry room only took up half the space of the building it was located in. On the other side was a secured storage area that held a hodgepodge of items, some delicacies, some commissary. Besides **Candy, Soda, Cigarettes, Ttoiletries** and other **Dry Goods**, it stocked pantry items that needed to be under lock and key, items meant for the guests. There were cans of **Crab** and **Lobster Meat**, **Caviar** and other items of some worth.

A discussion began on how we might be able to get our hands on this merchandise, and according to my newfound friends, I was the only one who could do it. I was the only one who could fit between the gap at the top of the wall, an opening about 10 inches or so. I was the scrawniest person around and just might be able to slide myself through. The minute it was first suggested I did'nt not blink an eye, I volunteered.

Immediately one of the guy's began boosting me up towards the top. I thought to myself, "This could be my chance to redeem myself." So I grabbed hold of the top slat and somehow slithered through the opening and onto the other side. Once through the opening, it was a simple, jump down onto the floor.

Looking around my eyes grew wide when saw the assortment of contraband on the shelves. It looked like one of the delis from the neighborhood. There was everything they said and more. No one even mentioned the beer. I used cases of soda and beer to build a staircase, so I could pass the stuff over and through. As fast as I could, the first items I passed over were ten cartons of cigarettes. I made sure to not to take only one brand of smokes, I didn't want to bring on too much suspicion, just in case we were to try this again.

Then I sent some boxes of candy, a case of crab and a case of lobster. Fuck the caviar, I couldn't find it anyway. A few assorted cases of soda and beer and I was ready to get the hell out of there. I figured that was enough. Then I changed my mind, this antic was going to be a one-time thing, because as soon as it was reported they would close that gap above the wall. So I grabbed a few more cartons of smokes.

Once I was done passing over the stash, I squeezed back through the top and dropped down onto the floor. I stood up and looked around for my cronies. "Shit!" These tough guys that talked me in to doing this grabbed what they wanted and ran out as fast as their chicken ass would take them. They left me a carton of smokes and some candy, big deal. I grabbed my stuff then ran out of there as fast as I could.

That evening I was called to the Chef's office and confronted about the theft. Evidently someone had ratted me out. The Chef wanted to know who my accomplices were, but where I came from that was a no-no. If you get caught doing something you don't bring anyone else down with you. So I told him I was by myself. After the speech about being an ungratefull little shit I was on the next bus out of there.

CHAPTER THIRTY EIGHT

A New Crew

We had moved back to the East Side around this time and it just so happened to be the exact same building that I lived in when I was born, 313 East 46th Street. Jim had landed a job a while ago from Mr. John Albano, in the commercial building that abutted our apartment house. He had been gainfully employed for some years now, operating the freight elevator, and had shown himself to be dependable.

Jim's boss, whom everyone called Harry the Hat had gave him the Super's job in our building. All he had to do was sweep and mop the stairways a few times a week as needed and then make sure the garbage was taken care of. The perk was a rent-free apartment.

I was wondering since I didn't have any friends in this area, how I was going to get to see my crew. But right around the corner was the cross-town bus. It would drop me off on 49th Street and 9th avenue, exactly where I needed to be. I couldn't have asked for better. I wasn't a lazy kid, so it was only during inclement weather that I'd take the bus, otherwise I'd walk.

Upon returning to the city and giving Jim some bullshit story that I had become homesick, I noticed a change in myself. I felt a little older, a little more grown up. I figured almost having sex made me more mature than the other kids I was hanging with when I left. Not that it was a story I'd be bragging about, being that I had failed miserably to accomplish my goal. But the crowd I left behind seemed like little kids to me.

So in between selling papers, I began to once again make a geographic turn to find new friends. I went back down to the schoolyard on 52nd and 10th to see who was still hanging out, when I bumped into Garry R. Garry was my own age and we had hung out together a while ago. He told me that he had been hanging out on 48th and 9th with a bunch of new guys. So I tagged along to check things out and see if I'd get along.

The core of this group consisted of kids from different ethnicities. There was Billy the Greek, Bruno the Pollack and Georgie the Puerto Rican. Gary was Italian and Irish, but preferred to only recognize his Italian heritage. Me, I was just another a poor Mick. Only Georgie, Billy and Bruno spoke more than one language. The rest of us were third and fourth generation totally Americanized. "This crowd fit me like a glove".

We all went to Junior HighSchool 17, and I had seen most of them around. But I was going to have to change schools again because of moving to the East Side. By this time I was a lot more age appropriate for Junior High School, I was even bordering on being one of the much older students in my class. It would become my fourth year in the 7th grade. I had been in six schools since I left St. Johns. Between bouncing around at the drop of the hat with Maggie, and with my records never keeping up with me, I became lost in the educational system.

While at PS 17 there was only one class I attended, it was my Art Class, It was taught by a Mr. Lyons. We all thought Mr. Lyons was a pretty cool guy. He'd invite some of us over to his apartment on the East Side to hang out and drink. I didn't know at the time, but would find out soon enough, that he was gay. Not just gay but a child predator, and was abusing this kid Georgie from our crowd.

In those days we weren't educated enough to realize that being a child molester wasn't the same as being gay. To us they were all just Faggots. But knowing he was having sex with Georgie seemed sick. I figured as long as he didn't mess with me, I found it an okay place to hang out. Looking back on all the degenerates we encountered, I think, "What was it about our neighborhood. Why were there so many child predators in our area? Also, what was it that attracted them to me"?

Could it have been that I exuded some sort of familiarity of the atypical child of sexual abuse. Was I the kid to be easily befriended, to be approached in such a manner. Were these people abused themselves as children"? Even if that was the case, it was still not an excuse to repeat it on other unsuspecting kids. I often thought about these things, but had never spoken aloud about them. These things were taboo to speak of ever." In my mind if you were molested and someone found out, you were labeled a queer. You would be susceptible to unbearable ridicule. It was all so confusing to me.

Running with this new crowd I once again removed the façade of my morality. I didn't understand it, and it was unfair to burden myself with such tripe. It allowed me to feel as though I fit in somewhere, that there were kid's just like me, tough as shit on the outside and willing to do almost any stupid thing on a dare. But inside running scared, hoping that the deep dark secrets we held inside would never be found out. I myself was going to the grave with mine. What would people think of a damaged piece of meat like me? I was afraid of being found out and cast aside.

Gary and I were feeling kind of uncomfortable with the Georgie's the Billy's and Bruno's. They weren't doing anything positive. They were being retarded by the environment and were not growing emotionaly. So we looked around, and right under our noses, in the schoolyard of P.S. 17 we found the people we would be with, right up until we reached adulthood.

One particular day this new kid showed up on the scene. His

name was Mark but his friends called him Pee Wee. He was born in New York but raised in the Virgin Islands, and had just returned to the States with his mother. Pee Wee was to become my best friend and ally. A brother couldn't have beencloser.

I first met him while hanging out and playing this game called 1-2-3- Mum-freeze. It was a macho kind of game and only the toughest kids would participate. It entailed a lot of punching and getting punched back. Pee Wee showed he could take it and dish it out pretty good too, and I respected him for that. So it became Gary, Pee Wee and Myself, as inseparable as friends could be.

Gary was the pretty boy and a girl magnet, but didn't have the balls when something jumped off, but he had a charismatic way about himself that drew people closer to him. He was funny and good-natured, and a perfect fit to our group. Pee Wee was the opposite. Though he was good looking and girls wanted to be around him, he wasn't afraid to use his fists.

We went ice-skating one day at Rockefeller Center and I was skating a bit aggressively. It got to the point that I had to be warned numerous times by the staff to take it easy. Finally I was asked to leave the ice by one of the attendants. I brushed the guy off and continued skating in an erratic way. I was being an asshole.

As I came speeding around a corner, one of the attendants stepped out in front of me and brought me down on the ice. As I struggled with this guy two more came skating over to join the fracas. I continued to try and fight them off but it became too difficult.

Out of nowhere I see Pee Wee speeding from the opposite side of the rink, and just before he reaches us, he leaps high in the air. In what seemed slow motion, I see Pee Wee, crash down and knock these guys off of me like a bowling ball hitting a ten pin. The attendants threatened to call the cops so we took off and went back to the block. It was a story that would be often reminisced.

Myself, I was just so damn insecure that I would do almost anything to impress you. I had so much self- loathing, always feeling ugly and unworthy of any ones affection. But this liaison I had forged with these two guys made my life manageable. And though we were a contingent of a larger crowd in the neighborhood we three always stuck together.

CHAPTER THIRTY NINE

We Never Stood A Chance, A B. S. Excuse

I had begun drinking on a semi regular basis by now and hanging out until all hours of the night, looking for something to do to relieve my pent up energy. My friends and I might run rampant through the Times Square area and break into one the many movie theaters that were strewn along the 42nd street strip.

We might pounce on some unsuspecting vendor, and steal some those soft hot pretzels they sold. Or we would run amok through the Port Authority Bus Terminal, sliding down the escalators without taking into consideration the danger to others. We would sneak on the R train, an elevated line of the NYC subway system and take it to my old haunting grounds in Astoria. There we would confiscate a couple of bicycles bring them back to the city to sell.

This one time, we were leaving Astoria to return to Manhattan without any swag, On the way back I was looking out the window of the subway car contemplating the evening ahead, when upon leaving this one station I spotted a brand new 10 speed bike. It was sitting eye level with me from the second floor window of this two-story building we were passing by, Bingo! There it was.

I let friends know what I saw and told them I would be getting off the next stop to grab it. They broke out in a boisterous laughter. "Who the hell is going to break into a house to steal a bike," one of them said. I turned and confidently replied, "Me Shit-Head!" "I dare you" he retorted. Now normally I was not the one to volunteer for such an insane idea, but all you had to say was I dare you in a crowd and I was in.

We got off the train at the next stop and walked back to where I spotted the bike. I was starting to feel that nervous energy in the pit of my stomach. I had been dared and if I didn't follow through I would be subject to an unrelenting barrage of derogatory banter, so I had to at least make it look like an attempt was made.

While my pals stayed at a safe distance, a few houses back and across the street, I entered the vestibule of the building. I remember it being eerily silent for a second. I began hearing the good voice in my head saying, "I think you are making a big mistake." No sooner did that inner voice finish warning me, the bad inner voice whispered to me, "it's a piece of cake, you can do it." So I climbed the stairs and stood in front of the door to the apartment. I put my ear to the door to listen, but it was difficult. It was a congested area with a lot of outside sounds, like car horns, trains going by, and kids running around playing.

I knocked firmly on the door with a plan already thought out. If someone answered I would inquire if a certain made up person lived there, wherein the reply would be no and I would be on my way. But there was no reply, so I checked to see if the door was unlocked. No such luck. Much to my own amazement, I reared back and slammed my foot against the door splitting the jamb and having the door fly open.

My heart was beating out of my chest. I stopped to listen if there was any movement about in the hallway. Nothing stirred, so I entered the residence only to hear a radio playing. Immediately I had this faint feeling and my mouth dried up instantly. So I called out, is anyone home? No answer, so I said it again, and again no answer. I grabbed the bike and hoisted it on my shoulder and walked swiftly out of the apartment and down the stairs.

I was in a state of limbo now. It was too late to turn back and I couldn't be sure if someone would be waiting for me outside. I walked out into the bright sunlight and prayed no one would be waiting, tugging at my shirt and asking me what fuck I was doing with his bicycle.

I spotted my friends across the street, so I jumped on the bike. I drove by them nonchalantly, gave them the finger and sped off. Needless to say, that for the next month or so I was considered the craziest bastard in the neighborhood. They would be talking about that caper for a long time.

I really didn't comprehend the kind of trouble I could have been in and what crimes I might have been charged with. All that mattered was being dared to do something, and doing it. Many times in the past if I had done things an adult disapproved of, and I told the truth about it. They would preach to me, citing that most famous and dumbest old adage. "If someone told you to jump off a bridge, would you?"

CHAPTER FORTY

The Wise Ass Kid

O n one of the many occasions we ran through the Port Authority Bus Station, terrorizing the people there. The four of us were rounded up and brought to the Police Station within the terminal. As usual my disrespectful behavior got me into even more trouble with the cops. I began ranting, "why are you keeping us here? What's the charge you're holding us on?" The detective looked towards me and said, you are all being held for skylarking. I began shouting, "Skylarking! What the hell is skylarking? You can't hold us."

I should have known better and stayed quiet. This was just another big mouth dumb shit statement I couldn't control myself from blurting out. I looked around seeking support from my buddies, but all I got were blank stares. But now it was too late.

The detectives eyes bulged wide, his face turned red and I knew right then I had screwed up big time. He ran over towards me grabbed me by the back of my shirt and proceeded to kick my ass, and I mean literally. One, two, three straight kicks to my butt, and a slap across the back of the head shut me right up. After an hour later, and one insincere apology given, we were excused and told that next time we would go to jail. On the way back to the block my friends couldn't stop laughing at me while yelling, "Police brutality! Police brutality!" I joined in the banter, laughing all the way back to the block.

CHAPTER FORTY ONE

That Damn Horse Show

The Horse show was in town at Madison Square Garden. The large parking lot located on west side of the arena was empty of cars.' They were replaced by about twenty tents that were erected to house the horses at the show. The first full day they were done setting up the tents we made plans to snoop around the area. Maybe we could make a few bucks doing some chores, or go to the store for one of the workers. We had done the same when the Dog Show came to town.

Somehow word got around and about fifty kids from the area, including my guys appeared on the scene. We were kids that would usually not hang out together. We were all different ages, we all hung out on different blocks. We were just a bunch of bored kids from the area looking for something different to do.

We all arrived at the parking lot around the same time, and like a swarm of locusts were looking to ravage anything in sight, each group of us trying to best the other.

It started with running in and out of he tents, but soon progressed to climbing upon and playing on the tops of the tents. Kids were clambering up to the peaks and sliding down towards the edges, then back up again. Occasionally someone would slide too far down and fall off, but that was just part of the fun.

After about ten minutes a slew of workers came pouring out from the side doors of the Garden and began surrounding the tents. Kids were jostling for positions to make their escape. And one by one, two by two, they poured off the edges of the tents. Most of the staff just let them go, but a few uniformed guards seemed intent on our capture. Gary and I remained two of about eight kids left on our tent and were waiting for the perfect moment to jump down. Up one side down the other, all the way left all the way right, we just couldn't shake these guys. Then all of a sudden one kid slid down our side and disappeared into thin air.

The tent had finally succumbed to all the horseplay and tore from the crest of the roof to the bottom edging. And before I knew it, it was just Gary and myself, with the tents perimeter completely surrounded. Every God damned kid made it off except us. I actually had a good chance earlier, but I didn't want to leave Gary stranded by his self. "You don't abandon your friends." But after a few more attempts at escaping I came to the realization that we were trapped and captured.

I slid down to the edge so I could lower myself down to the pavement. I had my legs dangling over ready to jump down, when I was grabbed by my pant leg and yanked off, falling and almost cracking my head on the ground. All of a sudden I was lifted up off my feet by these two enormous guards. It was as if I was floating on air.

I called out to my captors to let me go, cursing up a storm and throwing around insults. Two seconds later I had had twenty arms wrestling at my clothes, they all wanted a piece of me. Gary and I were dragged through one of the side doors and placed upon a bench. We looked at each other and began cracking up. We were having a great time, and figured to be let go in a few minutes with a stern warning.

All of a sudden the hair on top of my head was grasped real hard, and in one swift move this asshole guard banged my head on the water pipe directly behind me. This was repeated two more times, and each time my skull crashed into this metal conduit I saw a white light. The sound seemed to reverberate through the stairwell. I wasn't laughing any longer.

Within ten minutes or so there was a thump on the door and in walked a cop. I said to myself, now their going to get it. I'm going to tell this police officer how these cretins assaulted me, and then they'll get theirs. I was positive that he would direct them to sincerely apologize to me for their barbaric treatment, and order them to set us free, to go about our business.

Why was it that I was always so wrong regarding my actions and their consequences? One other thing came to mind, why was it Gary didn't get the same treatment as me? "I know" It had to be those doe eyes of his that welled up with tears once he saw me getting my head banged against the pipe. This would be more fodder for my petition of discrimination that would be brought to the police officers attention. He would know how to deal with them.

To my consternation I couldn't have been more wrong. Even with my best fake tears streaming, the officer yanked me outside and asked where I lived. As soon as I told him that I resided on the East Side I was given a swift and hardy kick in the ass and told not to come around here anymore.

This hulking Irishman left his shoe imprint on my behind, along with the reality that I was always going to be the one that got smacked, the one receiving the corporal punishment, the brunt of the retaliations. What happened to that angelic face I once bore, the one that melted the hearts of everyone I met? What was it that made me the punching bag? I guess that would always be the $100,000 question. I must have been blessed the only kid with a target on his keester.

Being this gargantuan in blue was a beat cop I laid low for a few days. It gave me time enough to lick my wounds and repair my ego. Within the week I was back with the gang.

CHAPTER FORTY TWO

50 Pints And The Flying Cake

I was turning fifteen in a month and wanted to do something special. I believed that going from 14 to 15 years old would somehow magically turn me into this mature and sophisticated young man. My status had risen within the neighborhood. I actually had kids looking up to me. They heard the stories, the ones that depicted a guy that had a big set of balls, someone that would do almost anything on a dare.

They didn't know the kid that shook in his pants every time he walked out of his house, afraid that people would not accept him. That felt he would be the one shunned and spoken harshly of. The boy, that was behind the façade.

I got a job working at the Park Sheraton Hotel on the West Side. It was infamous for being the site where Albert Anastasia, the founder of Murder Incorporated was assassinated. Billy, myself, and a couple of other kids had gotten this gig passing out circulars regarding the opening of a health club at the hotel. It was one of the first establishments to advertise memberships this way. This was1966 and the only promotion I ever heard of were the TV commercials for Jack Lalaine.

There were no joggers running 10K's or marathons. The gyms you heard of were where boxers went to train. The only adults you saw on bicycles were the Delivery Men, or the occasional Good Humor Man selling ice cream. Physical activity was not high profile in New York in the 1960's. So we were used to distribute the flyers on the streets in order to enlist customers for this semi-new genre. I remember we were being paid 50 cents per hour off the books and worked the weekends and after school hours.

I had an idea and wondered, what if we could get our boss to secure a room for us at the hotel for a day. He could take it from our earnings and we would call it even. I remembered Billy the Greek had the same birth date as me and also wanted to celebrate by doing something out of the ordinary. So I ran my idea by him and he agreed.

I can't to this day figure out what this guy was thinking. How the hell was he going to rent a room for teenagers and expect things to go well? "Was he crazy or just stupid." I know one thing: after this one time I could promise you, he would never do anything like that again.

The news spread like wildfire in the neighborhood, there was going be a big party at a hotel and everyone was invited. Billy and I never said any such thing. We were going to only invite twenty or thirty of our closest friends. But once the rumor started that idea went out the window.

The catering was to be furnished by two establishments, the local bakery and liquor store. From the bakery we bought a sheet cake with the words Happy Birthday Ziggy and Billy emblazoned on the top. And from the other establishment we purchased fifty pint bottles of Gypsy Rose wine, which we ordered, well in advance. I can't remember how it started but guys started calling me Ziggy back then.

Needless to say the party turned out to be a disaster. Not for Billy and I, this was regaled as the party of the century, and laughed about for weeks. But I'm sure our former boss did not take it that way. A hundred or so drunken teens, overrunning the hotel, filling the elevators and probably scaring the shit out of the other guests. What started out to be a cool party became a debacle of the highest degree.

I remember not being able to move about, even though the bed was turned on its side to make more room, it was crushing. Somehow a large part of the sheet cake wound up on the ceiling, and some moron decided it would be fun to bust the toilet bowl with a chair. Things went bad fast.

There were a handful of kids passed out on the floor, blacked out from drinking. The noise level was deafening and you had to yell so the person you were talking to could understand what you were saying. About an hour into this shindig, security for the hotel was summoned to shut us down and throw us out. I didn't recall security entering the room because by that time I was one of the kids passed out on the floor. I learned what happened second hand, which is the curse of an alcoholic drinker. Little did I know, but I was following in Jim's footsteps. "Oh by the way", I was fired from my job at the hotel. "Really?"

CHAPTER FORTY THREE

Playing With Fire

As I stated before, we had moved to the Eastside, which meant that I would be once again attending a new school. It was Junior High School 111 on 21st Street between 1st and 2nd Avenues. My fourth Junior High and the final school I would attend.

I had been lost in the Bureaucracy that was the Board of Education. I was now spending my fourth straight year in the seventh grade, when I should have been a freshman in high school. Bouncing back and forth from Florida to New York became a severe detriment. In retrospect, it was disheartening to know that not one teacher or other faculty member ever sat me down to inquire why I was failing so miserably.

Here was another new school. Again I was the one that needed to acclimate, the one that had to meet new people. Not only that, but now I was also the oldest kid in the class. What an anomaly my education had become, four years wasted because I was not able to fit in, and had a Mother and Father that were clueless on how to help me. In my mind, It didn't fucking matter anyway.

I didn't attend school for the first three or four weeks until the postcards from P.S. 111 started to roll in. My old man was giving me a hard time, only because he had been asked to come to school regarding my truancy. So I started to show up for school. I would go to my homeroom class and check in, all the while plotting my next move, which of course meant cutting out directly after.

Some of the time in order to pass the day I would walk downtown on Second Avenue. I'd walk through Greenwhich Village then past Delancey Street. I'd stroll through Chinatown and City Hall, all the way to The Whitehall Terminal, where I would hop on the Ferry to Staten Island. The fare was a nickel at the time, but just as I did in the subway, I would jump the turnstiles and board for free. For the return trip I'd just stay on the ferry, take it back to the city, and then walk back uptown. By the time I arrived home it was after three. At that time in my life I could walk forever.

One particular day as I was leaving the school grounds I heard someone call me from behind, "Hey Joe Kenney!" And as I turned around to see who it was, there stood this tall strapping kid with long golden blonde hair. I didn't know this guy from Adam, and I was baffled on how he knew my name. It's "Danny Kowalski" he shouted out. We went to camp together. It still didn't ring a bell but it did spark my interest.

As he walked up to me he grabbed me around my neck, put me in a headlock and knuckled the top of my head. I should have known right then and there to pleasantly shake his hand, say how've you been and walk away, never speaking to him again. But I didn't.

What was it with people I met that made them think I liked to be treated that way. Was there a sign on my head I couldn't see that said: "Grab me around my head and give me noogies", I like it."

Danny seemed a personable kind of guy, until you got to know him. He was a hulking bully that no one would stand up to. They were afraid they would get their ass kicked by this Adonis of a shmuck. He was the antithesis of me. I was the a skinny little runt that had a big head, and ears that stuck out like Alfred E. Newman, so I perceived.

That very same day I met Danny he invited me to shoot some pool at a place on 23rd Street and 3rd Avenue. It was a popular place for the truants that frequented the area. I told Danny that I hadn't any money, but he insisted and told me not to worry, I didn't need any.

Now I fancied myself a decent pool player because I had been recently frequenting a pool hall on the West Side. I learned about **Straight Pool**, **Eight and Nine Ball**, **English** and **Drawback**, I was familiar with the Pool Hall vernacular. But I couldn't hold a candle to Danny. He was a hustler that made his money shooting pool against guys that thought they were pretty good. He would play like a novice until he secured a game for money and then pour it on just enough to dupe the person into thinking that he could be beaten, with a little more luck. That was his hustle

I began to hang out with Danny on a regular basis, spending most of my day at the pool hall. Then at around 3pm we'd head uptown to Kip's Bay Boys Club, where we would hang out until around five. After that I would run home to eat, and then head west to be with my friends.

One day Danny and I were hanging out at Kip's and shooting hoops, when he asked me to put on the boxing gloves with him. Being in a sane frame of mind I wholeheartedly objected. "No way!" I responded, "You'll fucking kill me". Danny assured me he would take it easy, and we would only be playfully sparring. So I put on the gloves, got laced up and raised my hands in front of my face to protect myself. As we started sparring the first thing I noticed was the reach advantage. His arms had to be 5" longer than mine when he extended his arm I'd never be able to hit him.

As we circled each other Danny threw a left jab smack between my eyes forcing my head to fly back with whiplash. He threw another jab, then a double jab, and my eyes had me seeing double. Every time I was about to reciprocate, Bang! I caught another shot to the head. He was kicking my ass.

After numerous unanswered punches, I noticed him chuckling at me. And then as my frustration grew, he began laughing out loud. This really pissed me off, so as he cackled at me some more, I lowered my head and began flailing in his direction. I must have swung a hundred times and missed. But as he continued this total emasculation of my ego, Bam! I connected directly to his jaw. He was stunned for a second but then retaliated with a left to the head and a hard hook to my abdomen.

I fell to my knees, I couldn't breathe. I had the wind knocked out of me like never before. I thought for sure I was going to vomit. I rolled on my side trying to catch my breath, and once I did I took off the gloves and threw them at his face. I told this prick not to bother me any more and to leave me the hell alone.

The next day as I was walking to school, I stopped at the local candy store. It was run by this elderly Jewish man, His nam was Irving (we called him Pops). It was the establishment many of the kids heading to school would stop at before class. I would purchase Candy and Egg Creams or or maybe a Comic Book every once in a while. But the most important item I bought was the loosey cigarette. At a nickel a pop, they were the choice for kids that had started smoking. Most kids our ages couldn't afford a whole pack by themselves, so we'd purchase loosies. Loosies were the highest profit item Irving sold, and was in the biggest demand.

As soon I entered the store I spotted Danny, but ignored him. I asked Irv for two smokes, paid him and 'started leaving without as much as one word to this jerk. "C'mon he said, don't be that way, I apologize. You caught me good and it stunned me, I just had a knee jerk reaction." Because he apologized and massaged my bruised ego, I decided to renew our acquaintanceship, but on my grounds. We entered school together and parted our ways to attend Homeroom, agreeing to meet up directly afterwards.

After Homeroom Danny and I were wasting time in the hallways waiting for the next class to begin so we could split and go to the poolhall, because in between class all the exits would be manned by teachers until the bell rang.

Once the bell rang we walked towards the west exit, it was the most inconspicuous way out. But right before we began to take the stairs to the ground floor, out of the corner of my eye I spotted a bulletin board with papers tacked on to it. I couldn't tell you what drew me towards it. Maybe it was the heightened sense of anxiety I felt when doing the wrong thing.

Then out of nowhere this asshole Danny pulls out a lighter and sets fire to the papers on the bulletin board and runs. Danny bolted for the exit howling as he ran. Stunned, I began sprinting right behind him. We flew down the stairs, and out into the street we went.

We both continued running until we crossed 2nd Avenue thinking that would be enough of a cushion to not be spotted. We hung back to see what might be going on, when all of a sudden crowds of students began pouring out from every exit of the building, there was an all-out fire drill underway. "Holy shit"! I blurted out, look at that! "Let's get the fuck out of here." So we spent the rest of the afternoon at the pool hall then parted ways.

The next morning we met up at Irv's and began discussing the previous day laughing up a storm. We hadn't ascertained the seriousness of such a reckless act. We could only see that we got away unnoticed. The day was going to be like all the others, homeroom and out the door to shoot some pool.

I was sitting at my regular desk in Home Room waiting for roll call to begin, when through the front door this very large man entered class. I saw him flash his wallet towards the teacher, turn around towards the class and ask: "Is Mr. Joseph Kenney here". All of a sudden, every head in the class turned and was staring directly at me. I felt as if the staring would burn a hole in my head, so I raised my hand and acknowledged my being there. Suddenly I could feel my face growing warm, my stomach beginning to churn. I was wondering what this person might want me for. Did something happen at home or something? He said in a very curse tone of voice, "Lets go. Follow me." And as I stood up, every eye in the room observed me as I walked out the door.

This was no ordinary visit. I sensed something was very wrong, so I asked what this might be about. When this hulking figure turned to me and said in a gruff voice: "Shut up! And come with me". He then waved me on. I knew something was really, really wrong, I just didn't know what it might be about.

As we entered the front office where the principle was, all thoughts of confusion fell immediately into place. There sat Danny on the bench that faced the hallway. All my sense of well being oozed from my body because right then I knew what I was there for.

Danny gave me that look that stare that I knew very well. It spoke to me, in a derisive kind of way, "Don't say anything. You don't know anything. Don't be a rat."

What was this code, I thought, a code that literally disallows the right course of action, one of self-preservation. Was it really necessary to implicate yourself in something you didn't do? I could understand this action being applied to my siblings at home, not wanting to get them in trouble for some stupid thing they did. But they were my blood. I was supposed to stick up for them. "But this guy" I owed him no genuine allegiance. It didn't matter though within the environment I grew up in.

From an early age I was indoctrinated and told not to be a tattletale. It was just more misguided dialogue to confuse me. And as I grew older it became the moniker, RAT FINK!. It was the Scarlet Letter, posted by the true offenders to keep anothers mouth shut. So here I was in a Catch-22 of huge proportions. This man who had whisked me out of class was a detective and he was there with his partner to get to the bottom of what occurred at school the day earlier. He ordered me into an inside office, in order to interogate me in private, his partner took Danny into another room.

The door was shut and I was told to sit down, while this man shuffled papers in front of me. He all of a sudden in a sullen tone of voice asked me; "Who set the fire"? The best answer I could come up with at that moment was: "What fire"? Whereas his open right hand, came from his right knee, and landed directly to the left side of my head.

I sat there stunned by his action and began to realize the severity of the questioning that was going on. He repeated again. "Who set the fire"? And again I said, "I don't know what you're talking about". Then whack! Another shot to the head. Then with my eyes beginning to tear I told this detective that he was not allowed to touch me. I must have heard this previously in some discussion with my know-it-all friends. But it seems no one had informed this person interrogating me, and when I once again denoted my innocence, I was snatched by my hair and my head was slammed into the wall three times.

I was beginning to panic, tears were coming down my cheeks and my heart felt like it was beating out of my chest. I didn't know what was happening in the next room. Surely Danny would explain that it was him that started the fire and I would be exonerated and released. But that wasn't going to happen. And just as my hair was pulled forward once again, with this brute prepared to strike my head against the wall, I blurted out, "it was me, it was me"! I just wanted the abuse to stop. This cop was not playing around. I couldn't reveal the true perpetrator, because echoing through my mind was the mantra, "You don't squeal on your friends no matter what".

The interview was over. I was going to be arrested for felony arson. I wasn't aware of the critical nature of this charge. To me it was only a matter of minutes when Kowalski would admit his culpability in this whole fiasco. But that never transpired and I was handcuffed, taken by my arm, marched outside and placed into the back of the Detectives car. I saw Danny when I left the office and stared him down. He bowed his head and couldn't look me in the eye. He knew this was wrong.

I was driven to the local Police Station and booked for the crime. I was asked a lot of questions regarding who was guardian for me at home. I gave all the pertinent information and was then transported to Juvenile Court on 23rd Street and 7th Avenue. I sat there for what seemed like hours. And with my head spinning like a top, I was wondering what was going to happen next.

Suddenly the detective appeared, and I was being led into a courtroom, to be brought in front of a judge. I was sure by now my Mother and Father had been notified and would have raced to the courthouse to rescue me. I had heard earlier that if no one came from my family I would be put into juvenile detention until my next hearing. I had heard stories about Juvenile Hall and wanted no part of it.

I looked behind me and scanned the room for a familiar face, but didn't see anyone I knew. My heart sank, and I began to tear up. Again my parents let me down. I was on my way to Juvenile Hall.

I didn't understand anything that was being discussed in the courtroom between the judge and what I understand now was my child advocate. They were discussing where I was to be placed when all of a sudden from the rear of the room I heard a familiar voice yell out, "I'm his sister Your Honor!"

The degree of my gratitude could not be measured in words, but it lasted only a few seconds. The prosecutor was lobbying to have me put into detention, so I figured that meant I was being locked away.

My sister Grace pleaded on my behalf and I was released into her care. Her sobbing uncontrollably had made an impression on the judge. I breathed a sigh of relief like never before.

The next few weeks had me pledging to be on my best behavior to almost anyone who would listen, My Mother, Father, Siblings and the Judge. I even petitioned God himself, even though he'd known that I was innocent. It didn't matter though I was covering all the bases.

I was sentenced by the court and given 2 yrs. probation, with a warning not to get into any trouble or I would surely be incarcerated. I felt immediately at ease not having my freedom revoked and promised myself I would not do anything wrong the rest of my natural life. Amen!

I saw my brother Liam within the following weeks. He had heard what happened and that I didn't rat. He seemed proud. I told him to tell Kowalski he was a punk for not telling the truth and hanging me out to dry.

That day I made a pledge to never ever again take the weight for something I didn't do, no matter the circumstance. I would explain it to everyone whom I might be hanging around with, that If they committed the crime and didn't take the responsibility, and put me in danger of being locked up, that I would inform the authorities post haste that it was them and I had nothing to do with it. Never again became my mantra. I would expect the same result if it applied to me.

CHAPTER FORTY FOUR

The Blinding Pants

was almost sixteen and with the Kowalski debacle well behind me, I was back where I belonged, with my true friends, the ones that wouldn't leave me in the lurch.

My friends were as dissimilar as a dog and cat. But being it was a predominantly Puerto Rican area where we were hanging out, the dress code stayed true to a certain theme. I would label it, Afro American with an, Italian Mobster flair.

Many of the Motown Groups we were listening to were sporting a certain style of clothes, like silk and wool suits and Italian knit shirts. Confusion reigned within my mind. Here I was, this Casper the ghost white kid trying to dress like the Temptations. The parties I went to resounded Latin music, as well as Salsa dancing, and though I couldn't wiggle my ass out of a wet paper bag if my life depended on it, I loved to see the Puerto Rican girls dancing, they were so fine! But I'd rarely stick around I just didn't fit in.

I myself was into soul music, like *The Temptations* and *The Four Tops*. *The Stylistics*, *The Delfonics* and *The Supremes*. *Smokey Robinson, Aretha Franklin, Sam and Dave* and *Otis Redding*. There were tons more I could mention, but I need to move on. How could you not fall in love with the music it was the birth of singing with a distinct choreography. They not only sang great, they could dance their ass off.

It was 1967 and I was turning sixteen. I was back where I belonged. Hell's Kitchen was my real home, and the kids there were my family. Pee Wee and Gary were my brothers, and were there for me no matter what. Where else was I accepted so genuinely?

The social scene was about to go through one of the most eclectic changes in history. There was going to be a movement like never before. It would permanently affect our psyches. It would render the following paragraphs moot. Easter would never again be looked at the same way.

As much as I didn't want to sell papers for fear of someone seeing meand being held up for ridicule, it was the only way I had to get money for personal needs. Easter was just around the corner, which was a time to showcase your clothes and get dressed to the Nines. So what could I do to solve my problem of having no decent wardrobe? Midnight Mass on Christmas Eve was one thing. Your wardrobe malfunctions could be concealed by coat. But not on Easter, I had a quandary to consider.

Where were my roots concerning the type of haberdasheryI should consider. I hadn't thought much about it up until now. Could it be the fact that some girls had begun to appear on the scene and were becoming a core part of our crowd? Sure, I wanted to make an impression it's just that my feelings of self-worth many times had me confused. It made me press too hard and I'd over compensate, and this time was no different. Where did I fit into this menagerie? How was I going to present myself?

There was this Puerto Rican kid named Ephrom that lived on the block we hung out on. He was a couple of years older than us and was well liked and admired, we all looked up to him. His younger brother Harry hung out with us, so Ephrom was always around. Ephrom always dressed impeccably, unless he was playing sports. He wore Italian Knit shirts, silk and wool pants and Suede Playboy's, a preferred shoe for the debonair. Not realizing what it took to be like him, I figured if I dressed like him I'd be admired the same. This meant checking out Leightons or Cy Martins, they sold the latest in the men's clothing line.

I'd been salivating at the windows, looking at the clothing and coveting it all. Even the mannequins had style. This one in particular caught my eye every night as I finished up selling my papers. It had on the most elegant black and gray Italian knit shirt, smartly buttoned up from the waist to neck. The mannequin's arms, one in the pocket and the other at its side accentuated the matching gray slacks. The sharpness of the crease from top to bottom drew your eyes down to the black alligator shoes shining in the light of the window. I wanted this outfit more than anything.

I was like the child obsessed with a toy, and wishing with all their might for Santa to bring it to them for Christmas. Promising to behave for the whole year. I was working my ass off selling the papers every day and saving the money I made. But I had two problems. I started too late to save enough money to buy everything, and I did not want under any circumstance anyone I knew, to see me selling papers. I wasn't able to interpret in my mind, the difference between being an entrepreneur (Which I truly was.) and what I perceived as being a beggar in the street. If I'd only had a mentor to inform me that what I was doing was something positive and commendable, something to receive accolades for. If I had this, I might have continued doing so.

My coffers at the time had read double zero. This meant working harder the next couple of weeks to attain my short termed goal of buying these new clothes. I had by this point shortened my paper route to exclude many of the bars on the West Side. There was the fear I could be spotted by someone I knew from the neighborhood. So by the time it came to purchasing my new outfit, I found myself on the short end of the stick.

I could afford the new knit shirt and the slacks, but the Playboys would have to wait. I could afford the knit and shoes but would have to wear an old pair of slacks. The problem with the slacks was, I didn't own a pair of slacks. All I had was a couple of old Chinos.

I could buy the pants and shoes and wear a regular dress shirt, but that wasn't going fly with me. Wearing pre-worn clothing was actually out of the question completely, due to the fact that the one or two shirts I did own were probably hanging in a closet somewhere, dirty and smelly from wearing them too often without being cleaned. My clothes became a mound of garbage, unable to ever be donned again. I was the typical teenaged slob. And besides, who would clean my things, Dirty Mary?

I had been talking to this one acquaintance about my dilemma and he suggested what sounded to me the perfect solution. He informed me that on Delancey Street the vendors sold pants that were equal in quality at only a quarter the price. So I went to Leightons and purchased that beautiful black and gray knit and my Playboys. The next day I took the bus down to Delancey to buy the pants.

The great thing about Delancey Street was that you could bounce from vendor to vendor and negotiate the best price. The proprietors hated for anyone to walk out of the store without purchasing something and would always lower the original asking price to keep you there. So I brokered the deal I needed to make, I walked away a satisfied customer. But as usual, there was one problem I hadn't foreseen.

It was Easter Sunday, and it was time to showcase my new clothing and parade around like a peacock. I took a shower, which was kind of a rarity at this juncture of my life, it just wasn't a priority, and besides the bath tub in my house was usually disgusting from not being cleaned.

I didn't want to soil my new clothes so I walked around, the tub gingerly dodging the algae that was caked against the side. Since I'd left Maggie's, I hadn't been asked to do any chores around the house, except maybe bring out the garbage once in a while. Jim never gave me a dime, so I felt no obligation to do anything. And I did as little as possible.

I put on my new clothing being extra careful, buttoning up my Italian knit shirt and making sure it looked perfect. I put on my slacks adjusting the length to my needed specification. Last but not the leastI, I checked my Playboy's to make sure not a speck of dust was on the suede. I combed my hair and sauntered out into the late morning Sun.

I grabbed the bus on 47th and rode it to 10th Avenue, right around the block from Gary's house. Upon exiting the bus I could see that there were people returning from mass at Sacred Heart Church. And as they passed by I couldn't help but notice them checking me out. They must have been thinking to themselves, Boy! That young man is sharp as a tack. I called on Gary but his Mom said he had just left, so I headed back down to 47th where I knew everyone would be. They would be hanging out at the schoolyard.

I walked along 10th Ave. to 47th Street, and as soon as I rounded the corner the sun hit me in my eyes making me wince. It had also shone directly onto my slacks. Shielding my eyes from the Sun, I looked down and saw that something was terribly wrong. It was my pants shining like a mirror, a glaring sheen that almost knocked me over. My pants were supposed to resemble gray sharkskin not some garish nightmare that resembled the chrome Christmas tree that Maggie bought a few years ago. I wanted to do an about face and run the other way.

Maybe I was making too big a deal I thought, maybe it wasn't as bad as I percieved. But as I made my way across 9th Avenue only a half of a block away, I could see some of the kids pointing in my direction. There was no mistaking what they were doing. They were laughing their asses off.

As I drew closer I could hear the jokes already barreling down in my direction, I was stunned. I had tried to be something I was not. I should have settled to dress in chinos, a regular shirt and a new pair of Converse sneakers. But no, I had to try and look like someone special. So after the brutal hazing I received, going home seemed my only option. I had been a laughing stock in front of all my friends, including some of the girls that had been coming around. And as I headed towards the East Side, I had an uncontrollable urge to cry. I mustered up all my strength to not break out in tears, but I couldn't stop it.

At this stage of my life, this disaster made my Top Ten list of things I was most ashamed about. Even throwing up in church during midnight mass because I had been drinking like a fish wasn't as bad. Sure, I was ashamed and had to face the music the next day, but that was a different type of humiliation. It became sort of, a badge of honor that guys talked warmly about. It was a goof.

There would be many times to come that I would behave tactlessly, but everyon that knew me, knew I drank to excess, that once I started drinking I couldn't stop. But I had an affable personality when sober, and would be easily forgiven.

CHAPTER FORTY FIVE

Before Things Really Got Bad

At the age of 15 besides drinking I had begun smoking pot regularly. By 16 it was Seconol's and Tuinol's. It was also the year I received official permission to smoke cigarettes in front of Jim, not that he didn't know I was smoking. I was also allowed to quit school that year. I imagine that he thought I wasn't getting anything out of it anyway. He figured he could get me a job at one of the company's where he operated the elevator. This became just another right of passage for me, but this time to failure.

The next few years were a whirlwind and a blur. The landscape of the neighborhood changed dramatically. It would become deluged with all sorts of drugs and we would be swept up in the frenzy of of it all. It wasn't only the neighborhood that was changing. We were changing just as fast.

By the time I was sixteen and a half I had a select group that I hung out with. Gary and Pee Wee were still my best friends but there had been some others that became part of our intimate social network.

By now we even had some girls as part of our make-up. The Three Isabelle's were a staple. There was Lucatoro, her cousin Pollard and

Sanchez. Gary was going steady with Polard, Pee Wee with Lucatoro. "Me", I was just good friends with them all. I was still terrified of talking to girls that way. I would stammer my words and shake inside my shoes. I couldn't gather my thoughts. But the worst thing of all was I didn't feel desirable.

So to compensate, I'd get smashed out of my mind and become the loveable buffoon. I figured that type of attention was better than nothing. It's not that I hadn't the opportunity to have a girlfriend. The Isabelle's would try to hook me up all the time. But every time I was supposed to meet the girl, I was usually falling down drunk or had taken too many pills.

I actually dated a Cuban girl named Candy for a couple of weeks. It was the first time I French Kissed a girl. She was very sexy, but crazier than I was.

Things were no better on the work front either. The boss at my first full-time job hadn't been too happy with me. I literally lived next door and was late every day. And not the five minutes late variety either, but at least a half hour or more. All I had to do was walk down three flights of stairs, open the door, turn right take three steps and I was at work.

They weren't pleased that people had to ring my bell to see if I was coming in that day. Or, that every single day I did show up, I was late. Needless to say, even with Jim's protestations that he would see to it things changed, they didn't. How on earth at the age of sixteen, and getting stoned every night and getting home in the wee hours of the morning, would I be able to rise on time and be able to function at any job. But that didn't keep Jim from finding me new work.

Of the first three places I was employed, the farthest was exactly one block away. In retrospect I think I had been resentful that I had made more money selling newspapers, than working in these minimum wage jobs that Jim got for me.

In late 1968 Gary, Pee Wee and myself had been introduced to the Filmore East. It was a venue for the popular Rock Bands as well as the up and coming groups. Up to this point the only live bands we had seen had been at the Cheetah Night Club on 52nd street and 8th Avenue. Not that it was a bad place to catch a concert, but it was more of a dance club and we had grown out of that. (Actualy, I never grew into it.)

I remember seeing **Sam and Dave and Johnny Maestro and The Brooklyn Bridge** there. But it wasn't conducive to doing psychedelics like the Filmore was. We grew our hair longer and we were dressing differently. We shopped for clothes at places like the Naked Grape, that sold used hip clothing cheap. We were fitting into this new environment without missing a beat.

The Filmorehad had hosted **The Doors** in June of that year, just prior to our first concert there. But we were able to get tickets to see **The Who** in August. We caught **Iron Butterfly, Canned Heat, Country Joe and The Fish, The Moody Blues, Jefferson Airplane** and many of the other big named bands of our time. **JimmyHendrix, Janis Joplin,** *and* **CCR**, they all played there. The list could go on and on. And we loved being part of it. **LSD, Mescaline** *or* **Psilocybin,** these were drugs we took when going to a concert.

I always had grass on me and would generously share with the other people that I got high with. It's something I did regularly with my co-workers. It made me feel important. People knew that if they wanted to get high all they had to do was seek me out. I was always down for blowing a joint.

Guys in the neighborhood were buying pounds of the stuff for a hundred bucks, bagging it up and making four hundred back. Shit! You could get 20 joints easily from a Five Dollar bag.

I was smoking a joint with this black guy from work one day, his name I don't recall. We were having a great time getting stoned and goofing on people. He said to me: This is good shit, do you think you could get me an ounce. Braggart that I was, I assured him it would be no problem. The very next day I brought him in the ounce he wanted, and he reciprocated by turning me on..

A week later while getting high with my new best buddy at work he asked if I could cop him a pound. I boasted, "Sure I can not a problem". He told me that he would front me the money and give me twenty for myself. He said he needed it before the weekend and I assured him that it would not be difficult at all.

I had every intention of coming through for this guy whenever he asked, but fell miserably short this one time. It's not that I couldn't score the stuff. It's just that when I made the purchase I figured he wouldn't miss a couple of joints from the pound, so I requisitioned some. "Big mistake!"

A few of us were hanging out at Pee Wee's the night I purchased my second pound of grass for my friend at work. I had torn a small piece from the brick to roll a couple of joints and was drinking some beers, having a great time. Then Pee Wee's brothers Buster and Rudy came in with some of their friends. I thought, who was I to be the party pooper. So I tore off a couple of more chunks and rolled about ten joints. It was only fair that I return the favor I told myself. Rudy had turned me on many times before and so without mulling the consequences we got high all night long up until about 5A.M. It's when Pee Wee's Mom would be coming home from her nursing job.

By the time I was supposed to be leaving for work there was a huge amount of pot missing from the pound. It resembled nothing like the brick I had received only hours ago. So with all of the intelligence I could muster up, the best idea I could come up with was that I just wouldn't go to work any more.

Was I fucking crazy or what! This guy was 6ft. 2 and had to be at least two hundred pounds. Or more He'd fucking kill me if I took off with his shit. But it was already too late I was screwed big time.

I quit my job immediately and layed low, staying home during the day and not answering the phone or the door. Having my little sisters checking out the front of my house, for anyone that fit his description. If the coast was clear, I would slink my way out the door and over to the neighborhood. I wish that I had never taken this guy's money because constantly looking over your shoulder is a bummer.

A couple of years later I bumped into him and was sure I was going to take a pounding, but by then I had been using heroin regularly and probably looked like death. I gave him some bullshit story that I got busted with his grass and was afraid to tell him.

CHAPTER FORTY SIX

My Girl, Talking bout My Girl

I was seventeen plus when I began my first long term and intimate relationship. She wasn't part of our crew, but she had been was from the neighborhood. Her name was Lorraine K and people knew her as Laurie. But her nickname and what she liked to be referred to was Jude.

She was the prototype hippie, long blonde hair parted in the middle, slightly tattered bellbottom jeans, Frye boots and a tiedyed shirt. She wore gold- rimmed glasses that perfectly framed her fair skinned face.

I had been passing by the apartment building she lived at and the moment I saw her I just had to say hello. I was kind of hoping to get a cordial smile or nod, but when she returned the hello it stopped me dead in my tracks. As nervous as I was to introduce myself, she was as kind in return. She had a genuine benevolence about her that made me feel relaxed, to be myself.

We talked for hours that night, and when her Grandmother finally called for her to come upstairs, while standing one step above me, she leaned over and kissed me. She gave me her phone number and told me to call her the next day. Needless to say I floated on a cloud going home that night, wishing the next day was already here. This kind of thing didn't happen to me, this wasn't my Modus Operandi. I was usually too nervous to talk to girls and needed to get loaded first.

A Breath of Distant Admiration

Like opals iridescence
Her many sides of beauty shone
A smile resounding loveliness
Like sonnets of angelic tone

Her face is comfort beckoning
A kindness rings her wave
with a demeanor of such gentleness
Like a child content at play
She brings a fondness for the day

There is an ease about her
An aura filled with tender airs
That makes her seem approachable
To share a word and know she cares
Compassion's eyes her spirit bares

Jude and I had got together the next day and every day after that for about two weeks, when she asked me a question: She said, "Joe, do you like me"? I told her: "Very much so. Why are you asking"? "It's because you haven't tried to make love to me". She actually said: You haven't tried to Ball me, which was the vernacular used in those days. Any way you put it, it was something I had dreamed about for the longest time. I was the only virgin I knew of in my group of friends. That was including the girls. I said: "Jude, I care for you very much, I was just too afraid to make a move, because I didn't want to offend you".

Meanwhile the boys were breaking my chops every day, wanting to know if I popped my cherry. I told them it was none of their business, which really let them know, not yet!

I talked to Pee Wee and told him about my dillemna. I told him that I didn't have a place to take Laurie to make it for the first time Then when he suggested I take her home to my house, I almost passed out. I laughed so hard I almost shit my pants. How was I going to take this beautiful girl to my pig-stye of a home, He concurred wholeheartedly Pee Wee was one of the few people that had ever been to my home. He knew the conditions, but he thought maybe if I brought her in the back way, she would only see the living room.

CHAPTER FORTY SEVEN

Black is Black

I had been looking to make a few dollars so I'd have money for Jude and I to go to Coney Island with my friends. I hadn't worked since I beat that guy at the job out of his money. I'd constantly worry that if I left the house in the daytime during the workweek, he'd catch me and kick my ass. Or worse, kill me. I thought I'd ask my Father for Fifty Bucks.

Jim gave me money two times a year. On my birthday and Christmas. Not a dime the rest of the year. He would loan me fifty bucks, but I would have to pay him back 60. A hundred dollars, the pay back was 120. On a hundred the payments would have to be in Thirty Dollar increments. If I couldn't make a payment, I had to give him at least Ten Bucks, which would not be deducted from the principal. That Ten Dollar payment was called a Vigorish, what might today be called a late payment fee from a bank.

Jim was a small time bookie and also collected for the local shylock. This gangster he worked for would come around every Wednesday and Friday to collect his money. My Father received a small percentage to be his lackey collection agent. I was always in debt, and my paychecks would go to pay off previous balances that I owed. So a deal was struck between Father and Son. Jim would pay for materials and I would get paid $50 to paint the living room.

Up till now the only painting I might have done in my life would have been the finger painting I did in Kindergarten. I thought a hammer was to hit someone in the head with, not a tool used for construction. What I meant was that Jim never taught me how to do anything. I don't blame him though, he probably didn't know how to himself.

I requisitioned the aid of my two best fiends Gary and Pee for this endeavor. I figured between the three of us we could pull it off. Putting our stoner heads together we made a list. First we buy two gallons of black paint, then enough tin foil to cover the ceiling. Then black linoleum that had gold veins running through it. And last but not least contact paper, resembling the stained glass windows of a church. Shortly after, I purchased a black light and some psychadelic posters. I had accomplished two things that day. I earned the $50 to go to Coney Island, and at the same time had created a very cool Head Room.

I didn't think it was time yet to expose Laurie to all of this, so other plans were made for my tryst with her. There was this kid Tommy who'd been on his own for a few years that had an apartment right around the corner from where Laurie lived. Pee Wee and I talked to him about my predicamentand, and asked if he could help me out. He said: "Sure! No problem." So with my dilemma taken care of, I made plans with Laurie for the coming Friday.

Tommy's apartment was sparsely furnished but was sufficient for Jude and I to take our relationship to the next level. The bedroom had a small table sitting in the corner. On it was a lamp with a red bulb inserted for ambiance. There was a twin size mattress on the floor, which was going to make foreplay even more difficult for me. Not that I had much experience in that area. In fact I had none.

It was Jude and I, all alone for the first time. I began trembling with anticipation and was so nervous I felt like getting up and running away. But Laurie knowing that this was unchartered territory for me was patient, gentle and understanding. When I began fumbling to undress her, she guided me and reassured me that everything was going to be just fine. The night couldn't have been more perfect, except when the boys were yelling up to the window from street. Hey Ziggy! How's it going up there? Jude took it all in stride. She was giggling, knowing that it was all in fun. She and I were now officially boyfriend and girlfriend, and life felt wonderful, at least for a while anyway.

I can understand today why my relationships with women mostly ended in sadness or with resentments and pain. The blueprint that was handed down to me by my Mother and Father reeked of disaster and was flawed beyond repair. How can love be sustained when the jealousy of a pet can produce sadistic behavior or heated arguments, and how can selfishness of the social network deprive this person, your friend and confidant, unconditional love. And when the soul sickness of addiction crosses the boundaries of principle, to drive a partner into prostitution and other immoralities, how can this be considered devotion. How sad it is to look back on.

Jude stuck by me for almost two more years, until I was incarcerated in 1970. Still I wonder to this day, if it was because of her fear of me, or did she really love me that much? I would have hoped for it to be the latter. She was a blessing unappreciated.

CHAPTER FORTY EIGHT

The- Ten-Hut! Decision

Pee Wee and I were turning eighteen, able to legally drink as well as having the right to vote. Not that we knew anything of importantance happening outside the neighborhood. Neither one of us could remember if we ever picked up a newspaper, to read that is. Politics to us was being able to negotiate a drug deal proficiently. We were just two strung out junkies stuck in the quagmire of heroin addiction, and even at our young age, we were growing tired of it all.

I wasn't born a junkie, I just happened to live in a neighborhood that became over run with heroin. It came through the streets like the plague. We were already attending the funerals of friends that overdosed or were given a hot shot of battery acid. The word of aquaintance's demise were heard almost every day, Pee Wee and I needed to do something.

The Vietnam War was on its last legs, and we had heard that if we enlisted in the Armed Forces together, we could join under the buddy system and go through basic training with each other..

Pee Wee had three brothers, Gene, Rudy and Buster. They had all served during the war and came back physically OK. We were going as the war was winding down, so we wouldn't have much to worry about? We probably couldn't tell you who the vice president of our country was, but we were sure this was the right thing to do.

Hadn't we already travelled overseas together when we ripped off Crazy Tommy, taking his drugs (acid and hash) and then absconding to St. Thomas, where we were going to become big time drug dealers; and failing miserably, coming home broke and with nothing to show from it except a few interesting stories.

We buried the acid on the beach in tin foil. And when we returned later and dug it up, we found it had disintegrated into one big pile of mush. Pee Wee had originally come from St Thomas and knew a lot of people. He wound up turning on every person he knew, until all the hash and acid was gone. Now broke and with nowhere to go, we had to return to face Crazy Tommy? It meant another stint underground until things quieted down.

One day shortly after, Pee Wee, Gary and myself had a conversation. I brought up the idea about joining the Navy. But Gary, even before I could get out a complete sentence, adamantly declined. So it was going to be just Pee Wee and myself. We were going to enlist and get out of the neighborhood, and away from the drug epidemic that poisoned it.

We went to the Armed Forces kiosk on 43rd Street and Broadway and in earnestness signed papers to enlist in the Navy. We would be leaving for basic training in June. To the Great Lakes Naval Training Center in Illinois. We had wanted to leave as soon as possible.

The following week Pee Wee and I went to the FortHamilton Army Base in Brooklyn for our preservice physical. I was worried that the doctors at the base would notice the tracks on my arms from shooting up, so I shoplifted some makeup to cover them up as best I could. Some how we passed our physicals and would be leaving in three weeks.

When I spoke to some of my family about my intentions, they were elated to see me doing something good with my life. They decided to throw me a going away party the weekend before I was to leave. Any reason for a party and a night out of drinking, you could be sure the entire clan would be there. Only Jim would be absent. By this time he was becoming sicker, his Scirrhosis of the liver and severe Emphysema kept him a recluse. He never left house, unless it was right downstairs to work.

The party was held at Shorts Bar in Astoria, the establishment Maggie might be found most evenings. She was the neighborhood barfly and a fvorite of the old men that drank there. Mom was always the life of the party, laughing and singing to the music on the jukebox, playing pool and acting suggestively around the men.

I don't remember much about that night, except people were buying me drinks left and right. Everyone was raining accolades upon me and commending me for making such a clearheaded decision. I was given many cards with cash in them. It was greatly appreciated because I would be able to go back into the city to cop some drugs and get high.

The party was in full swing but Laurie and I were getting bored. She really didn't drink much and felt uncomfortable around my family. They acted cold and aloof around her. I think she might have felt that my family blamed her for my condition, even though I had been admitted twice to the French Poly Clinic Hospital for Hepatitis C. from using a contaminated needle even before I met her. The first time I contracted it I almost died from liver failure. I'd had jaundice for more than a month when I collapsed in the street and was rushed to the emergency room. Hadn't the doctors explained to Maggie that they were treating a heroin user? I guess it was her denial for having a junkie son. So Jude made an easy target for her.

Two days before we were to leave, Pee Wee informed me that he had changed his mind. His brothers vehemently argued against him joining up.

I couldn't believe my ears. How could he let me down like that? I can't remember a day where I felt such abandonment by a friend.

I turned and stormed out of his house. And as I walked down the block towards Laurie's, I couldn't stop myself from crying. My mind was racing. How could I turn around and tell my family that I didn't want to go because Pee Wee decided not to. Hadn't they just given me a going away party? Didn't they feel relieved I was doing something positive with my life? There was no way I could back down now, no matter how bad I wanted to.

The morning I was leaving for the Navy I was to report to Whitehall Street in Manhattan to swear in. It was surreal It felt like I was having an out of body experience. Here I was, leaving home to enter the military even though I didn't want to go any longer. I felt extremely lonely riding the subway that day, I didn'tknow what to expect.

After swearing in we were handed a bus and plane ticket. We would take the bus from the Port Authority Bus Terminal to Newark Airport and take a plane on to to Chicago Illinois. They even provided us a token to get to the bus station.

As I walked west on 42 Street towards Port Authority, the feeling of running crossed my mind. I was only seven blocks from where I hung out, eight blocks to my girlfriends. But I wasn't the only person making this trek, there were five other guys from the city who also enlisted and they stayed close to me, they must have sensed I was ready to split; but it was too late, I had already been sworn in. I was officially the property of the United States Navy.

It was a long day of travelling and I was extremely tired. We had met up with about another thirty or so enlistees at Chicago's O'hare Airport. There we were met by a couple of sailors, and then escorted to an old blue scoolbus. Then we were to be transported to the base. As soo as we took off is when the bullshit started. One of the sailors screamed, "You God Damned Maggots, your ass belongs to Uncle Sam and the United States Navy now".

I wasn't ready for all this bravado bullshit and thus began the chatter in my head. It told me, I'm not going to be able to take this crap. What am I going to do about my drug habit? Boy did I make a huge mistake.

By the time I was issued my navy uniforms the following day, I was already plotting my getting out of this mess. All this screaming and shit was definitely not for me. Fucking Pee Wee!

Amid all the chaos of indoctrination we were being put through that first week, I had begun to get dope sick, withdrawing from my heroin habbit. I got up the nerve to tell one of the officers of my dilemma, that I was very sick and needed to see a doctor.

I was sent to the infirmary, it's where I told the first doctor I saw that I was going through withdrawals from heroin. I then proceeded to show him the tracks on my arms. He gave me two asprins and sent me back to my barracks.

Within a week, I attempted to escape, but was caught and returned. I was placed in the base Hospital for my heroin withdrawals and after 72 hours I was then transferred locked up and charged with AWOL. I was Facing Captains Mass, a military tribunal that would hand down my punishment.

But before Captains Mass, I was sent to a Stateside Hospital just off base and placed in a psychiatric ward. There I was monitored for the next few days. They plied me with vitamins and checked my vitals twice a day. I spoke to a psychiatrist about my drug history and my feelings regarding staying in the Navy. I told him I had made a mistake joining up in the condition I was in, and didn't think things would get any better by staying here. That was the last time I spoke to any kind of doctor. While recuperating at the Naval Hospital I met Sailors and Marines with some serious heroin addictions that just returned from Vietnam.

I empathized with their situations, and felt deep sorrow for them. Some had wanted to make the Navy a career, but were being discharged, with less than an honorable conditions They felt they were being let down, tossed in the garbage after serving their country for four years or better, depending how long they had been in the service.

They became addicted while in Vietnam, starting with the grass over there that was so powerful, most felt it had been treated with some other chemicals. Then while experimenting with heroin over there, they found they couldn't stop. Most said it better helped to deal with the war and all it's tragedies.

The moment I was returned to my company there was the immediate confrontation with the D.I. He would scream in my face and call me a fucked up junkie from New York. He was telling me that I was in for a world of shit. That's the moment when I decided to go AWOL again.

The very next day I slipped away from my company during a GI cleanup and talked my way out of the front gate. I told the guard that I lost my medical slip and needed to cross the road to the other camp, and I would be in a world of trouble for losing it. Much to my amazement, he let me pass. But before reaching the gate to the other camp you had to cross railroad tracks. That is where I decided to make my escape.

I started out by running down the tracks back towards Chicago, which was the idea main idea behind my plans for escape. I took off the blue denim shirt I was wearing and tossed it into the bushes. I then tore the arms off my T-Shirt.

In my mind, this was going to be sufficient camouflage. Now no one would know I had just escaped from the Naval Base. Looking back I can't believe how stupid I was. That no one would recognize this young kid with his head shaved walking down the railroad tracks towards Chicago.

After walking for what seemed like hours I was coming to a clearing where there was a railroad crossing. As I reached the clearing there leaning on the front of his cruiser, was a police officer from a nearby town. He said to me, " Where do you think you're going son?" Tired from walking and sweating from the insufferable heat, I replied: "I guess I'm going with you." So I got into his car and was driven to the local police precinct.

This officer was nice enough. When we got to the station he bought me a soda and a piece of candy. And while taking down my statement, he told me that I was lucky that someone from the town didn't find me because the Navy paid a Fifty Dollar bounty for every AWOL recruit they caught and they weren't afraid to use physical force. I just shrugged my shoulders and thanked the officer for the soda and candy. After taking my statement I was handcuffed and sat on a bench.

An hour or so later an MP showed up to return me to the base. As I got into the Jeep for the ride back, he said: while patting his holster, " This is a Forty Five Caliber Pistol on my hip. And if you get an idea you're going to run on me, I won't hesitate to shoot you in the back".

I thought to myself: "Who is this fucking asshole that thinks I'm about run on him". That after all day trying to get back home and only getting five stinking miles before being caught. How and where the hell would I run to, besides I was too tired and hugry and I didn'tt give a shit about anything. I knew I was in trouble, but didn't realize how deep.

I was returned to the base, but not with my company. This time I was brought to a holding area before a decision could be made on what to do with me. They called it the Indoctrination Division. It was where sailors were brought to before going to Captains Mass. Where, if I was found guilty of desertion I could be sentenced to some major time in the Brig.

At first I was locked up in a cage just outside the barracks until my papers were looked over. A couple of hours later they brought me into a dorm area where I was given the rules. If I needed to go to the bathroom which was in the front area of the dorm, I had to stop at this red line drawn on the floor and ask the watch sitting at the desk for permission to cross it to use the bathroom, two feet later I had to stop at a green line and ask the watch if I could cross it to use the bathroom. Once that permission was given and I used the head I had to ask permission to return, one line at a time.

The soldiers keeping tabs on us were Marine Corp. Most of them were allright. They were given duty there just until their papers were completed. They had served their time, and they would now be returning home. But you had the assholes that wallowed in the bullshit and treated you like a criminal. But they were few and far between. We had KP duty every day and nothing more. Working in the kitchen cleaning dishes, mopping floors, working outside picking up trash around the base, just a lot of menial work.

I was informed about three weeks into this fiasco that I woud be given a General Discharge, the Navy wanted no part of me, they weren't going to invest another minute in me. I was sent stateside again, and two days later sent home. It was thirty days exactly from the day I left Once again a failure at life I returned to the streets and resumed my heroin use.

CHAPTER FORTY NINE

Regret Is A Bitter Pill To Swallow

The Woodstock festival was only a month away and Jude wanted to go. But I had no job, no money and was already strung out. I argued the fact that it was probably going to be a bust, but the reality was I already developed a habit and had to concentrate on feeding my addiction. I gave Jude my blessings. She hooked up a ride with one of her friends and off she went to Yasgur's farm.

In the following year I was becoming more abusive towards Jude. It wasn't anything she was doing, it was all me. I had no identification with and didn't care to be around any of her friends. I had grown very resentful and jealous of her. I didn't want her to be anywhere, except with me. A typically, isolation is the first affair of business for an abuser to exact upon a partner. I was so immature that it started to wear her down. Jude knew I was shooting dope again, that I was strung out and needed money all the time. I had a full time job but it didn't pay enough to support my drug use.

I was stealing, beating people out of money or drugs, borrowing money at work and not paying it back. Finaly I wasn't even able to hold down the menial job I had. The bridges were burning fast and I was becoming a pariah to any of the decent people I knew.

Laurie had been curious about heroin for a while and asked on a few occasions to try it. She became more and more insistent until I finally caved in. At first she would only sniff it, because she was afraid of needles. But within a month or so she began skin-popping until finally she started mainlining.

At first I would have her begging on the street for spare change to help support our habits. And because she was so pretty, she could make quite a bit in only a few hours. But even then the money wouldn't go very far.

This one particular night when we had been struggling to get up enough money to buy our drugs, she brought up an idea that kind of shocked me. What if she began prostituting herself? We would be able to score enough easily to make it through the day, and then some.

Being appalled by the idea at first I let her know exactly how I felt. I said: "You are my girlfriend, the person I love. How can I let you lower yourself to become some degenerate whore like the lowlives that plied their wares on 8th Ave. "No way, I'm no pimp"! But before long she was hawking herself along the avenue.

How much lower of a human being could I become? The emotional pain of these actions drove me deeper into despair and my addiction. The first time she turned a trick she picked up this guy and brought him to that scumbag hotel on the block, the one that charged ten bucks for an hour.

I wasn't about to let her do this on her own so I went up to the room with them and sat outside the door until it was done. It's not fair to delve into the specifics. Jude was a good woman that got involved in a sick relationship.

By the spring of 1970 Jude had stopped using heroin. She had gone upstate to a friend's home to get clean and returned as healthy as I'd seen her in quite some time. She wanted me to meet the people that helped her, and for me to go upstate and get clean. After much prodding I agreed to meet her friends, and so the following weekend I boarded a bus and headed north.

I was there about two weeks and was becoming extremely restless. The people were nice enough, but were not the type of people I would normally hang out with. They were too squeaky clean for me. Growing your own food and shit and communing with Mother Nature wasn't me. I was the antithesis of them, unseemly and grungy. I liked breathing in the pollution, and I liked eating things unhealthy. So I cordially thanked my hosts and left on the next bus home.

Jude was going to stay a couple of extra weeks and meet me back in the city. It was OK by me it would give me some time to get high by myself. Even though I had detoxed off the heroin while upstate, I was using barbiturates to kick. Mentally, I wasn't able stop thinking about shooting up. And before long, I was sticking a needle in my arm again.

Laurie came home a few weeks later and told me she met this guy Jerry at the farm who lived on 55th Street and 8th Avenue. When she explained our situation to him, he invited us to stay with him. Jerry also offered to hire her to work for him. He was a professional clown and had been working as Sonny Wetson for the Wetsons hamburger chain, the second largest behind McDonalds at the time. Wetsons tried to best McDonalds by having two clowns, one male and one female. So Laurie became Wettie Wetson to his Sonny. I became very leery of this guy. I knew all he really wanted to do was get Jude into the sack.

We lived there for the next few months. Jude traveled with Jerry for grand openings in and around the metropolitan area. No overnights, I told her I didn't want her staying overnight with this guy. I didn't trust him

I Was Going Down In Flames

Jim was getting sicker and sicker, between his Emphysema and Cirrhosis of the liver. He had to quit working because he was too weak to do so. He talked his boss Harry the Hat into using me to run the freight elevator until he felt better. I would take over the graveyard shift, and this other guy would be filling in for Jim.

Needless to say I was fired within a month. I was late every day and while working would fall asleep on the job, not hearing the buzzer ring. People wound up waiting up to ten minutes, ringing the buzzer constantly before I woke to pick them up. Hanging out day and evening I got no rest, except at work.

In late October My Father was admitted to the hospital, he had taken a turn for the worse and was gravely ill. He would only last a week before he succumbed to his diseases. The combination of severe cirrhosis of the liver and emphysema was too much and he died in his sleep. Jude and I had visited him the night before, and the last words I would hear Jim say to me was "Just be a good boy". I remember how compassionate Jude was towards Jim that night, rubbing his legs and feet when he complained of numbness.

But now I was thinking about what to do to get high. Sure I felt bad my Father was so sick, but being a junkie the only one I really cared about was myself. That night I took the TV from my father's apartment to sell and buy dope. It wasn't much of a TV and I only got ten bucks for it. No one else was staying at the apartment so I crashed there that night.

My kid sister Megan went to go live with Maggie and Maeve the youngest had run away. She was 13 yrs. old and living down in the village with some guy 22 years older than her. She would become pregnant by her fourteenth birthday.

Jerry and I were not seeing eye-to-eye, he knew I didn't like him so I figured a few days away might help. I received a phone call the next day from my sister Katey that our Father had passed away. He was going to be waked in Astoria close to Marggie's.

It was kind of ironic. Here was a woman that basically didn't want to have anything to do with the man, and she was appointed to be executor of his will. Not that Jim had anything, his union benefits were just about enough to have him buried and his bank account might have had a few hundred dollars in it. Jim was always hoping to reconcile with Maggie and so she was left to facilitate his business.

I went to go see Laurie that afternoon to inform her about my Father and to maybe extract some sort of sympathy from her. I knew she was still pissed off that I went back to using dope, but she needed to put her anger aside and be there for me, self-centered as I was.

I explained to her that I had no appropriate clothing to wear to the wake. By this time any stick of decent clothing had long been sold for drugs. I literally had the clothes on my back. I also told her I needed a few dollars to get straight, so I'm not chipping in front of my family. And after begging for a while she caved in and gave me twenty bucks. She also asked Jerry if I could borrow an outfit so that I didn't show up at the wake in dirty, smelly clothing.

I would talk Jude into accompanying me to Astoria, so that I could show some semblance of normality and maybe not seem a total disgrace to my family. Laurie and I went back to Jerry's apartment so I could shower and get changed. Jerry was a somewhat larger man than me, in height and girth. His shoes were two sizes bigger than mine, so you could imagine how I looked. I wound up stuffing paper in the toe area so I didn't walk right out of them.

The pants from the suit were dragging along the ground as well as sliding down my hips. Laurie tacked the cuffs of the pants and punched an extra hole in the belt so that the pants didn't fall to the floor. I was a hundred and forty pounds soaking wet at the time. The shirt and jacket didn't fit any better. The sleeves hung down about five inches past my wrist, so that they covered my hands completely. I was an abomination.

At the wake I was a mess. Not only was I dressed like a clown I was doing a good job of acting like one also. I had people staring at me with derision. My family was appalled. After acknowledging my family and paying my respects to my Father by kneeling down in front of his coffin to pray, I sat in the first row and proceeded to sob uncontrollably.

Some members of my family came over to console me, but I think it was just to quiet me down. I was making a scene of unconscionable proportion, and they kept telling me: "You have to relax and pull yourself together." Needless to say I was finally asked to leave. I was an embarrassment to the family. And with those words of advice and the incentive of a few bucks, I was escorted to the street. I was figuratively out of sight, out of mind. My brother Liam came outside with me. He put his arm around my shoulder and walked me to the corner bar. He figured a couple of drinks would calm me down.

Liam had known the moniker of loser. Like his father, he was an alcoholic and a degenerate gambler, and usually had people looking for him to pay his debts. He had no reason to shun me. This was to be the last time I saw my family for quite a while.

I returned with Laurie to Jerry's, to give him back his clothes. She and I talked for a while. She told me that I needed to stop shooting heroin if I wanted her to stay with me. She said it was too emotionally draining waking up every day and crying because the one you love is destroying him self. She said that unless I changed she couldn't be with me any longer. Instead of listening to what she was trying to convey to me, I became angry called her a few choice words and stormed off into the night to go get high.

Later that night I returned home to Jims to catch some shuteye and to put the previous night's events behind me. I thought, "Fuck everybody, I don't need them, they can all go to hell!"

Walking up the stairs I got this feeling of trepidation and doom. It was this deep-seated feeling of being alone. As I got to the door, I reached into my pocket and took out my key. Looking up I noticed that the apartment had been padlocked shut and I wasn't going to be able to get in. I thought to myself "What the hell is going on". It was about 5 AM and I would have to wait until 8 to find out what the problem was.

I waited in the hallway for Harry the Hat, and when he arrived I was told that it was on orders from Maggie to not let me in.

I was officially out in the street. I was officially homeless. I couldn't go back to Jerry's house he despised me and told Jude that I couldn't stay there any longer. In the next two weeks my life would change dramatically.

CHAPTER FIFTY

The NACC

Two weeks on the street and with winter approaching fast, I was becoming quickly disenchanted with the position I was in. Living out in the cold was not my cup of tea. During the day I would ride the subway to get some sleep. It was also advantageous in pan handling for spare change.

The nights were frigid and lonely, and depending where I was, the Port Authority Bus Terminal, Grand Central or Penn Station. I wouldn't be able to sleep very long because the cops would come around and roust me. I hadn't any friends I could stay with and I was still angry with Jude, so I wasn't about to crawl back to her. Not that she could help me anyway.

I was living mostly on milk and Italian bread that would be delivered to Restaurants and Super Markets all over town, The deliveries began arround four A.M. The trucks would drop off milk and bread, leaving the merchandise out on the street. I'd grab a loaf of bread and a carton of milk, then find a hallway that had heat. Most of the time I wouldn't have anything else the rest of the day.

I would go back to the neighborhood on occasion where people I knew would throw me a couple of bucks or at the very least buy me something to eat. And I could also be able to pick up a couple of deuce bags, so I wouldn't be too dope sick.

Pee Wee would take care of me whenever he could, but I couldn't depend on that. So I'd break into cars to steal radios, or boost meat at the supermarkets to pay for my fixes. My family didn't want anything to do with me in this condition so I couldn't go to any of them. Things were bad.

I met this guy one day that saw my predicament and suggested to me that I should place myself in this program he heard about. It was my first time hearing anything about any sort of rehabilitation. He told me that it was a great place to go. They would send me upstate to this camp like environment. He even said that they had horseback riding up there. It all sounded pretty good to me.

That afternoon I called my sister Katelyn and told her what I was going to do and asked if I could stay the night. Katey told me that she needed to discuss it with my Brother-in law Vinnie and that I should call back later. I could hear the sadness in her voice when she spoke. She was definitely feeling bad for me. So in the meantime I went around panhandling, to try and make enough to fix up.

I called Katey back at around 6 and spoke to Vinnie. He told me that he would meet me in the city on 49th and 9th at about seven o'clock. I didn't understand, but I waited anyway.

Vinnie pulled up to the corner and I got into the car. He asked if I had eaten anything that day, I replied: Not much Vin! So he took me to a diner and bought me something to eat. It was the first hot food I had in weeks. He told me he was glad I was going to do something with myself, but he didn't want my Sister to see me the way I looked. So he told me that he would pay for me to stay at one of the local hotels. I suggested the fleabag joint on 48th Street.

I checked into the hotel and Vinnie walked me up to the room. The hotel was transient, used for prostitution and drugs, and on occasion some welfare recipients. There was no television and the bathroom was in the hallway. Voices echoed throughout the halls and because the walls were so thin you could hear some of the conversations going on.

Vinnie laid out fifteen dollars for the night and he also gave me five bucks to get something to eat the next day, he was good that way. But as soon as he left I went down to the front desk told the guy there was no way I was staying here. He told me that if I left he could only give me back ten dollars. I gladly accepted, I thought that he would have given me a much harder time. I walked up the block to Pee Wee's and told him I had fifteen bucks: I said, Let's get High!

The first thing the next morning I headed uptown. I reported to the Edgecombe Rehabilitation Center on 168th Street and Edgecombe Avenue to sign up for the facility that had horseback riding. This was going to definitely be better that living on the street, and after a relatively quick subway ride and short walk east, I was standing at the front entrance.

My heart began pounding, I was getting anxious, so I took one deep breath and I entered building. As soon as I walked through the door I immediately noticed how drab the décor was. A dim glossy green color devoid of any character.

Rows of benches lined the room, and at an old metal desk at the front of the room sat a security guard. I walked up to him and presented myself. In a gruff voice he told me to sign in and to sit down on the bench.

There were about a half dozen or so other men sitting on the benches, not one person sitting next to each other, none joining in conversation. Occasionally an office door would open and an announcement would be made. Would so and so come with me, and that person would stand up and walk into the office.

When my name was called I jumped up and walked towards the room. A tense feeling ran through my whole body, I didn't know what to expect. I sat down across from this man that had some sort of form in front of him. He introduced himself and proceeded to ask me some questions. Name! "J.P. Kenney" I replied", Address, "none", and after a few other mundane questions, we began to delve into my drug history which took up most of the time I spent with him. When we finished he told me that next I would be examined by a doctor. After being seen medically I was asked if I would like to stay in the facility during the evaluation or would I want to go home. Being I had no home to go to, I told him I would stay.

I sat back down on a bench and a few minutes later, this big burly man came out and asked me to follow him. As I passed through the door with this gargantuan one thing became crystal clear, I couldn't change my mind if I wanted to. The door slammed closed and locked. And after that moment every door we would pass through needed a key to open it. My mouth began to dry up, and I could barely breathe.

We got into an elevator and took it up to the third floor then passed through another door and into a Dorm Room type of setting. There were a lot of people milling about the main room, and as I followed this man I sensed all eyes were on me, I was new meat. I followed this guy down a hall lined with mattresses against one of the walls. He pointed to this one mattress and told me that this is where I'd be sleeping.

The mattress had only one single sheet that was stained but seemed clean enough. On top was a worn ratty blanket and pillow. I walked back to the main room to check out what was going on when this black kid pounced on me and asked: "Hey my man you got a cigarette?" I knew the situation that I might be in. and had bought two packs of smokes the night before with the money Vinnie gave me.

I had remembered one time when I got picked up for possession and was sent to the Tombs overnight, and how quickly my pack of cigarettes disappeared because I was giving so many away. I sort of figured this was the same thing, so I told the kid that I would share it with him. Boom! Another guy comes up to me and asks for a smoke. I told him: "This is the last one I'm handing out, I don't know what my situation is going to be."

So my new buddy and I walked across the room and sat on the floor near this ridiculous monstrosity they called a television. We talked for a couple hours and became friendly towards each other. He was telling me that the Rockefeller Law allowed the state to incarcerate a person proved to be an addict, and to be placed a ward of the state for three years. He said he spoke to guy's who had been in and out and they told him he was going to be locked up. He was informed that there were no places to go horseback riding. He said they told him he was in jail and better get used to it. But he also told me there was one way to get around it.

If someone in your family showed up to support you when you got in front of the judge, the judge might release you to that member of your family. I immediately sent two letters out, one to my sister Katey, the other to Jude. I told them it was imperative that someone come and represent for me, or else I was going to jail for three years.

With my letters in the mail, I went back to hanging out with my friend. I couldn't tell you my new friend's name, I don't remember. I can only explain that A: We were around the same age and B: Neither one of us cared about the color of our skin, It just wasn't that important.

We became so friendly that we ate together and goofed around all day, it broke up the monotony of our situation. Occasionally I would walk around and check out the card games that were constantly going on. I didn't know anything about the games they were playing but as I watched I began to get the gist of it. **Bid Whisk**, **Spades**, **Hearts** and **Pinochle**. I picked up the basics of how to play, and sat down at one of the tables with my buddy as a partner.

The table had these two white guys playing, and as soon as I sat, one of them said to me "Get out of here you Fuckin Mutt! You aren't playing here." When I protested the guy jumped up, got in my face and told me that if I didn't leave he'd fuck me up. He was much bigger than me and very muscular so I just walked away, wondering what the hell I did to upset him? Before long I was being focused on by most the white guy's. They continued calling me derogatory names and challenging me to fight every day.

My friend had gone home so I was feeling very alone. I had my court date coming up and was anxious to see my family and my girl. I was sure that they would be there to take me home. I really hated this place. I had given the counselor that came around every number I could think of. I wouldn't be here much longer.

It was the day of my hearing and as I went downstairs where they held court my heart began beating real fast, I was on the verge of crying. My family would know how I was being treated and would come to my rescue.

As I entered the court area I quickly scanned the room, I didn't see one familiar face. Something wasn't right somebody had to be here for me. But before I could get in one word, the hearing was over. I found out what had just occurred. Under this particular statute, I was being incarcerated and held under the jurisdiction of the Narcotic Addiction Control Commission, and I was sentenced to three years.

I thought to myself, "Three years! How the fuck can they do that?" Where's my family, where was Jude. I was escorted out of that room they called a court and went back upstairs in shock. I layed down on my mattress on the floor in the hallway, put my face in my pillow, and silently cried all afternoon.

The following day I was called into the counselors office where he explained to me that no one returned any of the phone calls that he made on my behalf, and that we needed to go over a treatment plan, and to determine which facility I would be going to. I told him any place but here. I walked out of his office feeling totally abandoned by everyone close to me.

Back upstairs I was still being harassed by the same group of guys. I still couldn't understand why. What did I do to be called a Fucking Mutt, and every time I protest someone jumps up to challenge me. I can't deal with this shit anymore!

There was this older guy that had been watching these assholes's messing with me, and came over to bend my ear. He put his arm around my neck and walked me towards his room, it kind of reminded me when Bobby from Sacred Heart put his arm around me, and would draw me closer and whisper words of wisdom, trying to teach me about life. He'd tell me that's the way it is, and theres nothing you can do about it.

The older guy asked if this was the first time I was locked up, and I replied that I had I been held over night a few times, but this had been my first time in this particular environment. He went on to explain to me that these guys who were threatening me and calling me derogatory names are treating me that way because they saw me burning behind a nigger. I was taken aback by what he said.

He went on to adamantly express, that what I had done was a big no-no. I could give a black person some of my cigarette but as soon as he put his lips on it, I couldn't take it back. You don't eat with the blacks or partner with them in a card game you need to stay with your own kind.

This was definitely not the way I wanted to live I didn't feel that way. I hated when my Father used that word, that he felt he was better than black people. Jim was not better than anyone. I never held him up as being a successful person, he wasn't. For that matter he wasn't even a successful Father. Who was he to judge other people? So in order to get along in this place, I had to act as if.

Little would I come to know that over the next three years, I would be incarcerated nearly ninety percent of the time I was sentenced to. That I would be released to aftercare time after time, serving anywhere from three to eighteen months and that I would last out on the street a maximum one month, before being locked back up. Sure I might not have been kept in a cell, but I was still locked up. I eventually began to feel more comfortable inside, than out on the street. I had become institutionalized.

CHAPTER FIFTY ONE

Escape From Edgecombe

My first bid I remained at Edgecombe because I would do the least amount of time staying there. My initial detention had to be at least one year and Edgecombe was the only facility where if you behaved, you could be released in a year. The other alternatives would have me locked up eighteen months or better.

Edgecombe was notorious for being the least favorable of all the other facilities. The food sucked and the environment was not conducive at all to rehabilitation. Shit! All you had to do was look out the window and you could see drug deals going on all day. In fact some the Hacks themselves were getting high.

Prior to starting my initial confinement I was recruited by Phoenix House. I was given the spiel about being raped by the older guys, that they liked young boys. And if I stayed where I was, it would happen to me. It worked because I made the next ferry to Hart's Island. It's where Phoenix House had their largest facility. And though they espoused you weren't locked up, you couldn't just walk away because the only way to get off of Harts Island was by ferry. And If you didn't have the proper credentitials or paperwork you weren't allowed on the boat. Hart's Island was also the location of Potter's Field where the indigents of New York City were buried.

Phoenix House was more about discussing your life's story, feeling that it, more than anything was why you used drugs. They would try to break you down, to discuss your deepest darkest secrets. They also had their own means of discipline. Depending on the infraction, they would shave your head, or have you wearing signs around your neck. You could also be put on contract, (having to scrub floors with a toothbrush).

They would set you up, blindside you by turning the attention your way during the Encounter Groups. There they would all start screaming at you, calling you a stupid fucking idiot for reasons that brought you there. They would tell you that this verbal bashing was done in the name of love. There was too much bullshit there, so I retuned to Edgecombe.

My first day back at Edgecombe was probably my worst day there. I was escorted into this room that would be where I would sleep. It had four sets of bunkbeds and a three-drawer nightstand for each person. I was making my bed when two black kids approximately my age came into the room. One of them yelled out: Who put this Honkey in my room? I don't want this white devil living with me.

He walked over to me, got very close to my face and called me Yakub and told me, "Stay out my way White Devil or you're going to die. I stared at him coldly then walked out the door. This older black guy came up to me and said: don't pay him any mind, He's a Five Percenter, Just aWanna-be Jail House Muslim.

I didn't know what the hell was going on, all I knew was I just wanted to be left alone. Eventually by my complaining, I was moved to another room. I had minimal interaction with that prick the rest of my time at Edgecomb.

I was coming up to my ninth month, and if you didn't get into any serious trouble, you could become eligible to go on a day trip to some venue or another. And being the moron I was, I went around asking some of the other inmates if there would be a chance for me to run, to split. Evidently someone brought it up to the councelor and I was put on notice.

Coming up was a trip to the Circus at Madison Square Garden and I put in for it. I had been a model inmate and they couldn't turn me down. It would go against my rehabilitation. But people had heard through the grapevine that I might have had rabbit in me and could possibly take off. So the evening of the trip one of the officers that escorted us acted like my shadow, just begging for me to try and run. But I wasn't going to be stupid I acted the perfect gentleman and created no problem.

The next trip the following month was to the Cloisters at Fort Tryon Park in Upper Manhattan.We were brought there by bus in the morning and were going to return later that afternoon. I couldn't get out of my mind thoughts that kept running through my head: "Will the opportunity to run occur" "I wonder how close they're going to be watching me?" "If I can escape maybe I could leave the State."

After about an hour of walking around pretending I was having a good time, I began to walk slower, lagging behind the group I was with. After a few more minutes it was just myself, and this older officer. I began getting butterflies in my stomach, it made me feel as if I were going to throw up. My heart was beating out of my chest.

All of a sudden I broke towards the entrance of the park! I was running down a hill and tripped, stumbling and rolling for about twenty feet. In one quick motion, I got back up at ran out of the park, straight towards the nearest subway.

I jumped the turnstile and boarded the A train downtown towards my neighborhood. The A train had a stop at Edgecombe Avenue, and I had to be carefull, a lot of the guards took the subway at this stop. So when the train entered the station I kept my head down, hoping not to be spotted. I'd have to say, the real reason I ran was because I wanted to get high, which was the first thing I accomplished. It wasn't that I missed my girlfriend; it wasn't that I missed my family; it was that I needed that dope. Once you fuck with heroin it's allways right there trying to pull you back in. Even now and away from the needle for 40+ years I think about it once in a while.

I really had nowhere to go, so within a couple of days I turned myself in. For sure I would have to take a beating. There was no way the guards were going to let me get away with making them look like saps. They were going to send the Goon Squad to kick the shit out of me. I kept saying to myself " make sure you protect your head" because these Mother Fuckers don't care where they hit and kick you.

I had seen these Gorillas work over one guy for causing problems and talking shit? They actually blinded the kid. One of these pricks kicked him on the side of his head and his eye popped out of its socket. I had thought that they were going to kill me. But I came back anyway. What actually happened was, they didn't give a shit they actually made a joke of it.

The program was losing funding and releasing people left and right. Within two weeks even I was released on my own recognizance, I just had to report to an aftercare officer once a week. Maggie found out I was being released and was expecting me. My counselor had informed her that I was being let out and if I had nowhere to go, he needed to make arrangements for me to go to a halfway house.

I guess she was feeling a little guilty and decided to try and help me out. She found me a furnished room in an apartment house in Astoria. It was $25.00 a week. The room came with a bed and closet, the use of a communal bathroom in the hall and kitchenette. That was it. I stayed there three weeks because that's all Maggie had paid for.

I had met up with Jude during my first week out and we hooked up for the night. She told me that I was looking better than she had seen in a long time. I wanted to just lay next to her, it felt so good, I'd missed her so much. But it was just going to be a one-night stand.

During the second week I met up with Pee Wee's Brother Buster, I had bumped into him and mentioned a caper I had planned. I told him I was going to need a lookout, and asked if he was interested. He agreed to come with me to Astoria that night.

There was a photo store on 30th St, off of Ditmars Blvd that I would pass every day. In the window were a couple of cameras that were left there overnight. The store was gated at night, but it was a rolling grille gate and had open grates that I would be able to reach through easily. I figured if I waited until 2AM or so, the whole block would be shut down. Then I would go up to the store, and with a hammer punch a hole in the window just big enough to snatch the two cameras.

Buster and I hung out in my room, smoked some pot, drank a couple of beers, and waited for the right time to begin our score.

We walked out into the street at 2AM exactly. Right across from my furnished room was Immaculate Conception Catholic Church. We crossed the street passing the rectory as we walked towards the corner. We turned left onto Ditmars Avenue,and looked around. Nothing looked opened the streets were dark and empty. We then walked one block to 30th Ave. and made a right. The store would be halfway down the street. But once we made the right, we were shocked by what we saw.

Not only were all the stores not closed, the street was bustling with action. There was an all night News Stand near the bottom steps of the elevated subway that had people running in and out of, buying newspapers and coffee for the ride to their jobs in the city. The diner across the street must have had thirty or forty patrons scattered about, some sitting in booths facing the street. Many of them were stopping in for coffee, or a bite to eat, after closing their favorite neighborhood bar. The area was a beehive of activitry.

Buster and I had been waiting for hours to rob this store and I wasn't about to give it up because some people were milling about. So with Buster keeping an eye out for cops on Ditmars, I walked down the block to the cameran store.

I pulled out a chisel from my waist, that I boosted from a hardware store earlier that day. It would allow me to punch a hole in the window just big enough to stick my hand through. A hammer wouldn't do the trick; I figured it would make too much noise. So standing directly in front of the window, I reached in between the grating and tapped the glass.

It didn't do anything, so I tapped again with alittle more force. Again nothing happened. The third time I really put some muscle behind it, and Bang! The whole God Damned window came crashing down.

Being so close, the sound was deafening. I was sure that it would alert the neighborhood to what was going on. And that quite possibly someone from the diner or newsstand would see me robbing the store and chase me down.

I reached in grabbed the two cameras I had my eyes on and made a mad dash towards Buster. We both then scrambled back around the corner, passing the church and back to my furnished room. Once we were safely away from the crime scene and the adrenaline calmed down we began laughing our ass off. This fiasco couldn't have gone any more wrong than we had planned, except we didn't get caught.

We waited till daylight to return to the city, even passing the crime scene, which was strewn with shattered glass. We hopped the subway to the neighborhood, and then fenced the cameras later that day.

After the three weeks in my furnished room, I went to stay with my sister Erin. I got a job at the Wetson's on Astoria Blvd making minimum wage hawking burgers. After a couple of weeks or so I had become disenchanted with my situation I started giving food away for free. Then I robbed the cash register, emptying the till and walking away. A day later I stole this piece of shit TV from my Sister's and sold it for a nickel bag.

Another time Grace hooked me up with this guy that owned a couple of hot dog wagons in the city. He supplied me with the wagon, gave me the hot dogs and soda, sauerkraut, onions and condiments and told me to go out and sell. I parked the cart on 42nd and 8th, worked all day selling out of everything, I then left the cart right there, took the money and split. Not giving a shit about anyone, my Sister or her friend.

I ran back to Edgecombe, I just couldn't deal with anything. I had no prospects I constantly felt like garbage and abhorred everything about my life. So I burned any bridge there was, back to my family. I didn't deserve them.

Due to budget cuts there was no longer a set program at Edgecombe. It became a transitional housing unit until an opening was available somewhere else and decided to opt for the Methadone Maintenance Program available at the Arthur Kill facility on Staten Island. It was a 28-day bid, and I would be high most of the time. But it would be three weeks before an opening was available. So in the meantime I was sent to the Ridge Hill Provisional Center until I was transferred to Staten Island. Of course I found a way to get into trouble in my short term there.

This was going to be my second straight year incarcerated during the Christmas Holidays, missing Thanksgiving right through to New Year's Day. The Westchester location consisted of a dozen structures that were completely self-sufficient, in that each pod in which we lived in had it's own seperate housing and dining area.

I enlisted to be a server, to clean up after each meal. It allowed me better food and larger portions. When I was off drugs and incarcerated I could eat a horse, and working in the dining area allowed me to do so.

New Years Eve was approaching it was just three weeks away, and being as impressionable as I was someone talked me into making hooch (Homemade Wine). The recipe was simple enough, bread and real fruit juice. So in an empty commercial sized plastic jar, I stuffed ten pieces of bread, poured the juice on top and closed the lid. I then hid the bottle in one of the upper cabinets.

The next morning I opened the lid and was able to smell a trace of alcohol. A few more days fermenting would be all that was needed. But of course it was not totally explained to me that the container needed to be opened twice a day to alleviate the pressure being built up inside. So near the end of the week, one morning when we entered the kitchen area it had exploded. All the contents inside the bottle were propelled from the kitchen completely across the dining room.

The whole mess area reeked of alcohol and someone was going to have to pay for this debacle. So I disclosed to the proper authorities that I was the one who should be held responsible. For my punishment I had to completely GI the area affected. Then I was placed in isolation until my transfer came through, which was only a few days later. I was now headed to the ***Arthur Kill*** facility.

Wherever I went things would never go as expected, there was always some brouhaha happening, some drama going on. So while at Arthur Kill a mass escape hardly fazed me at all. Some guy decided he wanted to leave, so he picks up his nightstand (this heavy commercial monstrocity), walks into the day room and tosses it through the window. I just sat there watching this whole thing play out in front of my eyes. It startled me for a moment. There was this big bang and then crash the whole friggin window came down. It was kind of funny though to see fifty guys jumping through the smashed window, running towards the fences, climbing up and over and disappearing into the wooded area that surrounded the facility. This was not just any window it was huge. It was floor to ceiling and about 12ft. wide

Within half an hour there were tons of cops on the scene. There were dogs brought in and a helicopter hovered above. And by the end of the day ninety percent of the escapees were returned. They all faced felony escape charges. I thought to myself: "Was it really worth it?"

I completed my 28 days of nodding out, and was being released. I was going to be recieving a daily dose of methadone, 80 milligrams. That ammount would block the sedating effect of heroin. So no matter how much I tried to use, I wouldn't feel it.

I was placed at a Halfway House in Long Island City, Queens. It would not only be the place I would be residing, it would be where I would pick up my daily dose of medication. Every morning I had to report to medical, where the nurse would administer my liquid methadone in a small plastic cup of Tang, (Immitation Orange Juice). It stopped me from using opiates allright, but I still smoked pot and drank alcohol every day.

After only two weeks I was violated. I became disenchanted with the monotony of what my life had become. So I refused to take anymore methadone and was violated. I was incarcerated, and sent to the *Iroquois Wildlife Refuge* facility in Medina, New York. It was going to be just another stop on the Merry go Round that was *The Rockefeller Program*. So I thought.

Iroquois was set smack in the middle of five thousand acres of Federal woodland and marsh. Outside its borders were nothing but farmland and dairies, so there was no need for fences around the facility, there was nowhere to go. Lord knows I tried.

Isn't it kind of bizarre that someone whom had just returned to an institution of his own free will, would upon re-incarceration, want to escape. I was a confused young man. Unbeknownst to me at the time, it was because of my inability to function in society.

The program at Iroquois was based on a point system and you needed three thousand points to be paroled to aftercare. You earned points for keeping your bunk area neat and clean. You earned points for working around the facility (maintenance or kitchen) or attending any of the vocational training programs that were available. There was the *Photo Shop, Metal Shop, Food Trade* or *Heavy Equipment Operation* classes.

A mock paycheck was handed out every Friday to all residents performing in a rehabilitative manner. If it was your first Rockefeller facility you started at zero. If you were a violator, meaning you have previously been incarcerated at one of their other facillities, you would automatically recieve 1800 points. This meant you needed only 1200 more to be released. I would only have to do what was called, a *Skid Bid,* somewhere around ninety day's. If you had zero points you were looking at anywhere from nine months to a year.

One of the things I didn't count on was, that if you were written up for any type of infraction, from insubordination to having contraband, you would have points deducted from your paycheck. So being the insubordinate little bastard that I was, I quickly dwindled away at my point total, so that within two months I was minus six thousand points and became the first person ever to be removed from their point system.

It's a good thing that the director who ran the facility took a special interest in me otherwise I'd have been on the first bus to Woodbourne Prison. She somewhat knew my story and thought that I was reachable, that I would be able to turn my life around. So she waited me out and tolerated my behavior. Don't get me wrong, she didn't let me get away anything, but she refused to transfer me.

After about seven months of lolling around and doing as minimal as I could, I started to get antsy. I put in a request for work release. I was told that if I conducted myself appropriately for one month, and did not receive one write up for insubordination, that I would be allowed work release.

I was presented with a curriculum straight from the director. I would have to pick a class that was going to afford me an education in a field that I might concider. So I chose the Photo Shop, I thought it might be fun. I would have to report to class from 9:AM -11:30AM Monday through Friday. In the afternoons I was to report to facility maintenance where from 1PM-4PM I had to do work around the premises.

If I missed one day, the work release I was striving for would be put off two days. If my living space had not been not kept as was expected, no work release for one day longer. For each breach of promise I made to the director there would be consequenses. I agreed to the terms and signed a written contract with her.

One week into my agreement, I was in the photo shop with three other guys, when one of them came up with a great idea to get high. He said someone told him: "If you mix developing fluid and grape juice it would be like tripping on LSD". And of course being slaves to our addiction we all agreed. Getting the grape juice would be easy because one of my buddies worked in the kitchen.

After dinner that evening I brought the grape juice and some paper cups to the organizer of this caper and it was planned for the next day.

The next morning in the **Photo Shop** the guy organizing this thing, brought an empty soda can and filled it with the developing fluid. We were all going to meet behind the gym after lunch. But after contemplating it for a while and talking it over with one of my other friends, I came to the conclusion that it wasn't going to be a good idea. I can't say exactly why I did'nt take part in it, but I'm glad I decided not to because, one of the guys died from liver failure and the other two went blind, one totally.

I distanced myself from the situation entirely, and when questioned denying any knowledge of the situation. After the incident all chemicals throughout the facility were kept under lock and key. Even though I would not admit to my culpability openly it did not lessen my feelings of remorse.

After behaving and fulfilling my contract with the director I was hired by, Herbert Rose Incorporated. Herbert Rose was the preeminent growers and wholesalers of all types of domestic and hybrid roses, poinsettias and mums. I would be trained in the proper technique of cutting roses as well as tending to all other related flora. This was the lowest pay scale of all the opportunities available to the residents of Iroquois. But it was supposed to be a steppingstone for me towards the job I really coveted, which was the Gypsum Mine in Oakfield. If I did well for three months I would be put on the list for the mine.

There was always an instance of a lack of judgment some protocol broken that would cause me to sabotage any opportunity someone afforded me. Any successful accomplishment would be followed by some inane action. But this one was not driven by my self-loathing. It was focused more on the affairs of the heart.

CHAPTER FIFTY TWO

A Benevolent Encounter Of The Sensual Kind

There was this girl at the job named Martha, Martie for short. I had been flirting with her every time I passed her station. She had been reciprocating the same toward me as well. She looked sort of like Jude, which made me even more attracted to her. I had taken advantage of the fact she found me intriguing, being from New York City and affiliated with a Correctional Facility. I imagined she liked the bad boy persona.

She also enjoyed the brashness I conveyed a characteristic not usually displayed by me. I was never this confident lady's man. I was the poster boy for low self-esteem and self–abhorrence.

So we devised a plan to hook up the coming Sunday. I would lie and inform the proper authority that I was asked to work overtime that day, so that it would be entered in the log and provide me transportation that day.

That Sunday morning I was dropped off at 8AM in front of the job in plenty of time to be picked up. I had it all planned perfectly Marty would pick me up at 8:30AM and drop me off at 3PM. I was going to be returning to the facility at 3:30 so I figured to be back to my place of business by 2:30.

Marty and I spent the day together acting coy and playful, the first date phenomena of attraction. It started with holding hands, then my putting an arm around her waist, then leaning in for a kiss. I felt totaly comfortable with her.

We drove around the area in her Fiat Convertible, and stopped to walk around this state forest in the area. I felt like I hadn't a care in the world the whole time we were together. We returned to the drop off spot in plenty of time, but became very engrossed with each other. Once we began passionately kissing and petting, we decided right then and there to take it to the next level. We were both worked up so much that all our logic went out the window.

There was an old barn on the premises that would be an ideal place for us to go. I would also be able to see any vehicle approaching. We entered the barn and noticed a ladder leading up to a hayloft. So we climbed up and found comfortable place to lie back and continue our tryst. Things became hot and steamy quick, we were both trembling in anticipation and before you knew it we were totally engaged. It was happening and nothing was going to change our minds.

Reminiscence

While lying in contented thought
my mind recounts the moments bliss
the night of our first passions
the tenderness of every kiss

Her skin was soft and scented
like petals of a rose in bloom
and I trembled when I touched her
her aura filled the room

As I gazed into her wanton eyes
while she laid deep in my arms

> she evoked an understanding
> that exuded lovers charms
>
> So with my senses deep in gratitude
> I reached about for one more kiss
> for she helped me come to realize
> it was a woman's touch I missed

We became so engrossed in ourselves that we forgot to notice the time. When we finished we pulled ourselves together, pationatly kissed one more time and left the barn holding each other's hands. As we came around to the front of the barn my jaw dropped at what I saw. It was "Red The Fed" leaning on the State Car that was there to take me back to Iroquois. He had this evil smirk on his face. I was busted.

I walked Marty back to her car and kissed her goodbye. I then turned and got in the car with Red. I immediately started pleading my case, trying to explain myself and possibly impart some empathy towards my situation, but he was having none of it.

CHAPTER FIFTY THREE

The Fed They Called Red And My Other Screw Ups

O f all the Hacks at Iroquois there was this one complete asshole of a human being, and he had to be the one to pick me up that Sunday. My day up until that point was perfect, it was erotic and rapturous. I couldn't have imagined a day any better. But seeing that face took the wind right out of me. It made my heart sink. And no matter how much I petitioned him, Red was going to report what he saw. He only knew one way, by the book, no leeway whatsoever.

Everybody despised Red, even his co-workers, and he loved it. He enjoyed the notoriety no matter how crass. He was a guy that loved coming to work so he could wave his authority in your face. And upon my return, he gladly entered into the Log Book that I had committed an egregious violation of the rules, which called for me to be immediately placed in the Bing until further notice.

I wound up spending two weeks in isolation while my counselor pleaded my case to the director. And after all was said and done, I had my job back and was formally introduced to Marty's family. We held a meeting in the Directors office. Marty petitioned the director on my part taking the blame for our discretion. She came to my rescue that day and I appreciated it wholeheartedly.

Marty and I dated for a couple of months until I'd worn out my welcome with her family. We were caught one day by her Mom having sex on the couch I was totally embarrassed. There was also her younger brother that I would hang out with and smoke pot. I had been getting weekend passes and spending all my time with Marty, driving her car, spending her money, smoking her dope. Even having her help me smuggle pot and wine on NewYear's Eve for the white guys at Iroqois, which almost caused a riot.

They just couldn't put shade on getting high that night, walking up to the Hack's smelling of wine, talking shit. And because I was the only person on pass that weekend, it was deduced that Mr. Kenney was the culprit. Bing! One week. They couldn't prove that it was me who dropped it off so I caught somewhat of a break.

One day I got high on the job drinking cough medicine with this other guy that worked with me, and we maliciously destroyed a section of rose bush by chopping it up with our knives. Once again Bing! One week. And I had all my privileges revoked for two months.

After complying with all the rules for the next two months I received a One Week pass and decided go back to New York, I hadn't been there in over a year. I had nowhere to go, because of all the bridges I'd burned, so I reported to that halfway house in Queens. It would give me a place to stay and I'd be able to travel at will so long as I returned to the facility by 10PM and sober.

I got into the city at around 6PM at the Port Authority Terminal and immediately went to my old neighborhood. I saw Pee Wee, and after all our salutations I asked about Jude. He had her number because when she wanted some pot she would call him. I called and recieved the okay to see her. It had been more than a year since we had seen each other and spent the night together. I guess I was hoping that it might happen again.

Walking up the stairs to the apartment at the address she gave me, my stomach began turning. On the phone she told me she was living with a cop and couldn't spend too much time with me. I knocked on the door, and when it opened and I saw her my, heart sank. Jude was more beautiful than ever and at that moment I wanted to hold her, cry, and tell her how sorry I was for everything bad I'd done to her. To tell her how much I'd missed her, how much I loved her. But as I leaned in for a friendly kiss, she backed up.

She told me that it was good to see me looking so well, and hoped all was OK. And after some small talk she reminded me it was time for me to leave. Before leaving though she asked me if I wanted some Valium and Librium, which I replied: "Sure, why not" I had at this point in my life never refused free drugs.

She brought me over to this large black garbage bag and opened it. It must have been a foot high with pills. So I grabbed two handfuls, stuffed them in my pockets, gave her a peck on the cheek and left. It would be my last time ever seeing Jude again. To this day no matter how hard I try I can't seem to picture her face.

I stopped at a liquor store, bought a pint of wine, and the next thing I remember I was waking up on the floor of a jail cell at the Manhattan House Of Detention more notably known as The Tombs. I had been arrested sometime the night before for attempted grand larceny as well as possession of a controlled substance.

After shaking out the cobwebs and realizing where I was, I prepared myself. I was going to be seeing a Legal Aid Lawyer and would be arraigned in a couple of hours. I went through my pockets to see if I had any money and to check for my ID. But when I reached into my front pocket I almost had a heart attack. I had some of the pills still left in my pocket. The cops must have missed them. So I poped them in my mouth and by the time I went to see the judge, I was feeling pretty fucking good.

After meeting with the lawyer I was led into the courtroom to be arraigned. When it was my turn I stood up and told the judge where I had been for the last year and told him how well I was doing. My actual words were: "I'm doing good Your Honor." It was 1971, and the jails were so crowded, the only people being remanded were for gun charges or worse.

The judge admonished me and told me that I had 24 hours to get my ass back to Iroquois or I would have a warrant put out for me. So I walked out of the courthouse, still high on the pills, knowing that I just caught a major break, and I took the bus back to Medina. My One Week pass lasted only about 48 hours, but it felt like a week.

The next fiasco happened when I was attending Genesee Community College in Batavia. It was just another attempt by the director of Iroqois to rehabilitate me. Right off the bat I rarely went to class, and started hanging out with some kids from town. Getting high every day I kept a small vial of urine on me in case I was drug tested. As long as I wasn't late being picked up to return to the facility no one would know the better of what I was doing. They wouldn't find out until the end of the semester.

There was this kid at Iroquois I swear looked just like Howdy Doody. He had flaming red hair and a million freckles on his face. He always had this goofy smile on and the guys would bust his balls all the time.

One day for some reason, which I can't understand to this day, I was put in charge of looking after him at school while he registered for the upcoming semester. He'd be picked up that afternoon along with the rest of us that were attending the school.

After getting him registered I brought him with me to hang out with the townies I made friends with. We were drinking and smoking pot, having a great time, when one of the girls going to the bathroom let out a scream. It wasn't a scream of fear it was a scream more of surprise.

Everyone jumped up and walked towards the bathroom. And when we looked in, Shit! There he was, the kid I was responsible for, lying on the floor of the bathroom with his pants and underwear down around his ankles, passed out. Everyone was laughing and having a good old time goofing on this kid. But I'm the one that was responsible for him. I began to panic

The first thing that went through my mind was: "What the fuck am I going to do with him"? So I got some of the boys with me to help yank his drawers and pants up, then lift him to his feet. We tried throwing water in his face, but we couldn't bring him to. He was unconscious, but breathing okay

We put him in my friend's car, drove to the college, and dumped him on the front lawn, sprawled out like a dead man. It would be half an hour before the van came to pick him up.

I knew that I was going to be in deep shit. Here I was, responsible for this kid, who after spending only a couple of hours with me, couldn't walk, reeked of alcohol and was totally fucked up. I knew it was going to be the Bing for me again, so I decided to abscond for a wehile. What the hell, it was going to be a double infraction, and if not shipped out to Woodbourne I was surely going to be put in the Bing for at least two weeks. I might as well have some fun for a few days before going back. After a week of getting stoned I had someone drive me back to Iroquois to face the consequences, which turned out to be iosolation.

I spent two weeks in solitary and then brought in front of the director for my punishment. She said: "Mr.Kenney, I have given you every resource available and you and you've managed to screw up every one. You will not be afforded any more chances. You will stay with us for three more months and then be released to aftercare. And during this time you will work in the metal shop without incurring one single write up. If for any reason you fail to abide by these rules, you will be on the next bus to Woodbourne Prison". I acted the model citizen the rest of my time at Iroquois and was released to the halfway house in Long Island City, Queens. The one I had stayed at when I had my One Week pass.

I was back in New York City with no prospects on the horizon. I had essentially cut off my family with my actions. I had committed too many offenses against them. I couldn't blame anyone but myself if they never wanted to see me again. At this point I had so much contempt for myself that it was instinctive to sabotage myself every time I was afforded a break.

As always I found a way to make a few bucks. I was copping grass for some people in the Halfway House and in turn receiving couple of dollars and some joints. I would walk up Queens Blvd. to the liquor store and buy some wine, or on occasion Tangueray, (a premixed screwdriver made with vodka and Tang.) I stayed mostly to myself, getting high and hanging out around the house. But one day I met someone that brought some interest back into in my life.

CHAPTER FIFTY FOUR

Mary Buns And Louise

I was hanging out one morning with a guy from the Halfway House. We were heading up to the boulevard to see a girl he said he'd met the week before.

We stopped by this bakery where she worked to say hello. And when we entered, standing behind the counter was this cute little blonde. He introduced me to her as Mary. And as I traded pleasantries with her we exchanged glances. I immediately felt a connection. It was in the smile she gave me that made me feel she was interested.

This kid and I left the bakery picked up some wine to get high and after a few hours went back to the house. The next morning I signed out early and headed directly to the bakery. I'm not a conceited person. God knows my esteem was always in the toilet as well as always being super shy. But I was better looking than the other guy, and she seemed more interested in me.

I walked in feeling pretty sure of myself and struck up a conversation with her. We hit it off so well that we set up a date for that afternoon when she finished work. The kid that introduced us was going to be pissed. He was trying to get with her for a while, but instead now I'm hooking up with her.

My relationship with Mary was strictly physical. We would have sex anywhere and anytime. Plus we enjoyed getting high together. It was a match made in heaven, so I thought.

I went into Astoria one day to visit Maggie. In the last two and a half years or more I might have seen her one or two times. It was close to my 21st Birthday and I had some money in the bank coming to me from my car accident at the bus station in Astoria. I had come looking for her to sign the papers with me so I could withdraw my money.

I met Maggie in front of the Astoria Federal Bank, went in, got my money, said goodbye, and left. I had received a thousand dollars as a settlement in which the lawyer recieved a third. The judge allowed my Mother to take a couple of hundred for things she said was needed for me. The rest sat in the bank for eight years gaining interest.

It seemed to me that Maggie was expecting me to hand over the money, to replace some of the things I had stolen from her the year before. But being the consummate junkie, I only thought of myself. I figured that maybe seeing me would be enough, but it was possibly the furthest thing from her mind. I said goodbye and headed back to the halfway house. But first I wanted to do a little shopping up on Steinway Street.

I wound up not shopping at all, because I stopped in a bar on my way back called The Pine Inn to have a beer or four. And while sitting there sipping my beer, in walked this girl. She was cute in a tomboy-ish way and I struck up a conversation with her. I was giving her my best lines of bullshit to try and impress her. And later when leaving, I asked if we could see each other again. So we made a date for the coming Friday night.

Now I was seeing two women at one time, something that never happened to me. I wasn't having sex with this other girl just yet I was just enjoying her company. Her name was Louise and she could always put a smile on my face with her wry sense of humor. I'm not crowing about this, but I was only with Buns for three things, sex, money, and drugs. What a scumbag I was at the time.

I was supposed to meet Buns on Queens Boulevard at 7:30 one Friday night. She was getting paid and was supposed to pick up some downs and then meet me by the bakery. I was with some kid from the halfway house and we were going to go to Astoria together later that night. I figured to get some money and some drugs from Buns, then give her some lame story and walk her home.

I stood around waiting for two hours and was becoming really pissed off. "Where was this Bitch" I thought. Then from out of nowhere two blocks away I noticed her rounding the corner. She was totally fucked up. She was bouncing back and forth from the wall of a building to one of the cars parked in the street, and from the car back to the wall. I don't know how she didn't hit the ground.

I ran towards her to keep her from hurting herself and when I reached her I grabbed her by her arms. All she could do was slur some indistinct words. I slapped her face to try and make her come around, but it had no effect on her, she just kept staggering. I made a decision right then and there to take her to the hospital, I was sure she was overdosing.

This guy I was with hailed a cab while I held her up. We poured her into the taxi and took her Elmhurst Hospital. But before we went inside I rifled through her pockets and took her drugs and money. When I think about it, even today, I feel like shit

I had turned something good into just another score. It would come back to haunt me later. There is no justification for my actions even though it had to do with my addiction. I did these things to support my habit, but it still wasn't the right thing to do. Many of them troubled me for years, especially this one in particular.

The most despicable thing I have ever done to someone still haunts me to this day. It was before the Rockefeller Program. I was on the street with nowhere to go, hungry, dirty and very depressed. I was dope sick and had no money when I bumped into this kid Mike. Mickey was this really good kid that sometimes hung out with us. His crazy brother Peludo was shooting dope and hanging out with us regulearly, That's howI knew him. Mikey was a real sweetheart.

I met up with Mike one day and he told me his Dad passed away the day before. I could see that it weighed heavily on him so I gave him a hug. Seeing my condition he invited me up to his house to shower and to have something to eat. He could see the streets were kicking the shit out of me.

After I showered Mike made me a sandwich, and then decided to take a shower himself. He had an appointment at the funeral parlor to make arrangements for his Father's wake. But while he was in the shower I noticed a suit hanging on a hook in the vestibule, and before I could really contemplate my actions, I grabbed the suit and ran out the door. I remember stopping at the corner and wanting to go back, but the action was done. There was no way to turn back. "God: Please forgive me" I murmered.

I had not seen Mary Buns for weeks. She hadn't turned up for work and none of her colleagues at the bakery had heard from her. I figured she met someone and just took off. And anyway by now I had been hanging out with Louise a lot more.

I stayed mostly by myself while at the halfway house. Things were going sort of okay. I wasn't using hard drugs very often, but had been drinking heavily. Louise didn't seem to mind too much so I continued to see her.

There was a huge turnover at the halfway house and a new group of guys were spending a lot of time hanging out there. I really didn't care for this crew, especially this one guy Tony. He was always sky high and being an asshole. I didn't hide my disdain for him, and it showed in my attitude. But I never confronted him. I figured if I ignored him he would get the message.

I ate dinner at the halfway house almost every day and would take my food tray into the TV room to eat. By now Tony was becoming more belligerent towards me in front of his clique, and always had a callous word for me. And even though it was bothering me, I didn't want a confrontation. I never was the type of guy that wanted to fight. I had to be really backed up against the wall. But Tony kept pushing and pushing until I was at that boiling point. And on this one particular evening I exploded.

He was calling me a mutt and standing in the way of my watching TV trying to provoke me, but I wouldn't bite. He then smacked my tray upwards into the air spilling my food all over the place. I jumped up and said to him: "Mother Fucker! You better stop messing with me or else you're going to regret it". And then I started walking away back towards my room.

Walking towards my room I could feel Tony right behind me. He began calling me a Punk, a Mutt, and Faggot. When I reached my bed, I felt his hand touch my shoulder. "That was it." I spun around and grabbed him by the throat with my left hand making him fall onto my bed. I knelt on his chest and kept squeezing his throat so that he could barely talk. I held my right hand in a fist over him ready to punch him square in his face. Whenever I got like this, which was rare. I'd see this white light and lose all control. I would turn into a wild animal

I somehow regained my composure, got off of Tony and ran out of the building. When I got outside tears started flowing. It was the release of all my pent up anger. I called Louise, told her what happened and asked her to meet me in the city. I remember how I felt when I saw her. It was a heavy weight lifted off of me. Someone in this world cared about me. I hadn't felt that way in a very long time, and our relationship changed from that day on.

Tony stopped bothering me for a while, because the story was going around that I stood up to him and backed him down. Guys were congratulating me. Tony actually became kind of affable after that and invited me to hang out, which I declined.

CHAPTER FIFTY FIVE

Why Ma, Why?

I t was October 30th 1972. Upon returning to the halfway house my counselor called me into his office and said a message was left for me to get in touch with my sister Katelyn. I wondered what could she want? My family and I had been estranged for quite a while and this was the first time anyone had reached out to me for some time. Something was up.

I dialed Katey's number still at a loss as to what this could be about. My Brother In-law Vinnie answered the phone and said, "Joey I've got some bad news". And before he could complete another word, I said: "My Mother's dead right"? He replied:"Yeah."

I asked him how it happened and he told me that I should talk to Katey about it. So he put her on the phone. Katey, sobbing and naturally distraught, told me that Maggie had taken too many sleeping pills and overdosed. She let me know that our Mother was going to be waked starting the next day. I acknowledged to her that I would be there and hung up.

I was feeling kind of numb. It was just two weeks ago that I saw Maggie. I had decided to stop by, say hello and introduce her to Louise. Maybe I was just trying my best to make amends for all the hurt I caused her. Still to this day I'm not a hundred percent sure why, but I felt that this was going to be the last time I saw my Mother.

I had knocked on the door and when Muggie opened it, it was with the latch on. It was her way of keeping me at bay. From behind her door she barked out the words: "What do you want!" I said: "Ma, I want you to meet Louise my girlfriend." She muttered something in the way of "hello," then told me she had to go. She then shut the door, leaving Louise dumbfounded. I never really explained much to Louise about the relationship between my Mother and myself, I hadn't yet confided in her completely. All she knew was that I lived in a halfway house in Long Island City and understood that I was there for drugs and nothing more.

The last words My Mother spoke to me were: "What do you want!" It's ironic that all I really wanted, was to reveal to her my penitence for not being a better son and to maybe renew our relationship, but it was not meant to be.

Mother's Day

Hello Mom: I whispered to a door barely ajar,
to a shadowed figure latched in loneliness.
Fatigued with life, distraught, despaired.

What do you want?
The last words spoken to a son seeking reconciliation,
to a relationship tainted in bitterness,
our fractured affair.

The facade, the one that worked so well in the past,
that repelled intruders of her space, had failed her miserably.
She was no longer the tough old gal.

Her barrier's built of resentment and shame,
from the abuses and abandonments, cemented in recurrence.
She was the repeat offender my Mom,
and I missed her deeply.

I want you to meet someone: My girl, the replacement
realizing not the neediness that would destroy this too.
My own stab at normality,morality,civility.

These were chaste ideas.
A madness concocted from a child's grief,
stirred about in a vacuum devoid of reality,
My sanctuary.

So happy Mothers Day Dear Lady,
as I think of you on this date.
Put aside for special remembrances to embrace.
I forgive you, I miss you, I love you

So here it was, another one of my parents leaving this earth too
soon. I knew she was suffering emotionally, severely depressed. She
had to be she was an alcoholic and drug addict. I don't say this to
sound malicious towards her It's just that I can relate with candor, my
own experiences of what addiction does to someone in it's throes. I
called Louise, and told her my Mother had died. I asked her to meet
me at the Pine Inn.

I walked out of ther Halfway House and up Van Dam Street to
catch the subway. I remember It was a little chilly that evening and
the ride to Astoria was somber.

Louise was already at the bar by the time I arrived. When I
entered she ran up to me, put her arms around my neck and whispered
in my ear, "I'm so sorry about your Mom." I reciprocated the hug
and thanked her for her concern. I told her that I hadn't anything to

wear to the wake and was hoping that she might be able to help out. I thought maybe she might be able to scrounge up a few bucks for me to buy something but she couldn't. She hadn't been getting along with her parents. She wasn't working or going to school so they hadn't been very happy with her. In fact she went home as little as possible because her Father became emotionally and physically abusive and her Mother didn't stand up for her.

The money I received from the accident was already gone I had spent it on pot and drinking at the bar. I had been hanging out at the Pine Inn on a regular basis and people were beginning to become familiar with me. Louise asked a friend of hers that was about my size, if he might have something for me to borrow for the wake.

It was kind of upsetting that here I was at my Mom's wake three years to the day Jim passed away and I still don't have any appropriate clothing to wear. At Jim's wake I acted up, weeping uncontrollably, feeling sorry for myself, I didn't care what my family thought. I didn't care if I was embarrassing them. I was just pitiful. I was not going to repeat that humiliating, shameful exhibition.

The clothing that I borrowed was better than anything I had owned at the time. Which was kind of easy being I only owned some old jeans, no decent shoes to speak of, or a decent shirt. "Pitifull."

When I tried on the clothing from Louise's friend I freaked out. I looked like I just stepped out of the movie Saturday Night Fever. The guy loaned me a pair of platform shoes, super big Bell Bottoms and a multi colored disco shirt. Again I was dressed like a clown.

I looked into the preverbial mirror at where I was in life at that very moment, no job, no prospects and living under the care of the State. And fearful of seeing my family, hoping that when I did, it would not become a fiasco.

I still hadn't seen my sister Erin and my Brother-in-law Hogan since I walked off with their television. I was sure He would try to start a fight with me. After I first stole the TV, I used to dream about him coming after me, it was rather disturbing.

Here I was thinking oly about myself, and not my dead Mother. I've learned over time that it's the selfishness of the addict that causes him to act so callously. But to my consternation, my family was only concerned with the goings on around them. It was I viewing myself with derision.

When I first walked into the funeral home my little sisters ran up to me and gave me a hug and a kiss. The only thing was, they weren't little anymore. Megan was eighteen and Maeve a year younger and with a little baby. My brother Liam also came over to say hello.

Kitty was there with my Aunt Gloria. Kitty was the one who had found Maggie and called the police. And with Maggie gone now, She would be going to live with Gloria upstate. She couldn't live by herself in that apartment on the West Side any longer. She needed someone to look after her. It would be the last time I saw Kitty; she died sometime after.

I acted very solemn throughout the three day's Maggie was waked, being very respectful, remaining in the background, and speaking only when spoken to. A few hours into the first day my older sisters began talking to me, asking if I was doing okay. I was on my best behavior, not acting out like I did when Jim died. I really wasn't sure how I was feeling, because I was so numb. Once the afternoon sitting was over the family was going out to eat and invited me along. I cordially declined. I told them I had to meet my girlfriend, and that we had made plans.

When I left that afternoon I called Louise to let her know that the first sitting was over and that I would be going to the bar. She told me that I should come by her house, she had talked to her parents, told them we were seeing each other and that my Mom had just passed away.

Her Mother wanted me stop by to have some dinner, But I really wasn't up to meeting anyone and asked Louise to apologize for me, and say that I would meet them another time. That evening Louise stopped by to pay her respects and I brought her around to meet everyone, she was officially introduced to my family as my girlfriend.

Guys from the halfway house also showed up, even Tony. The funny thing was, thatwhen Tony was not high he was a decent human being. It's just that he wasn't sober very often and that would cause big problems for me.

CHAPTER FIFTY SIX

Relegated To Commitment

The next few months were a blur, packed with all sorts of changes. I left the Halfway House to live with my sister Megan. She had rented an apartment in Jackson Heights, and I was staying there along with Louise.

I met Louise's family for the first time the week after Maggies funeral. They were curious for me to visit.

I had my first Italian feast that day. I thought the pasta was the meal but it was just the first course. A Roast Beef dinner replete with potatoes and vegetables followed. Last but not least a salad.

I was told by Antoinette, Louise's Mom that the salad was served last to clean your mouth. I've never forgotten that. Then to top it all off we had a choice of pastries, cake and pie.

I loved Antoinette's cooking and ate there as much as possible. She used to ask me after I ate seconds if I wanted more. And if I said no, (because I couldn't fit anymore in my stomach), she would say: "What's the matter, you don't like my food"? It was a running gag we had with each other.

I got a job with a sheet metal company, my first experience working using my hands. I had this saying I used regarding my ineptness with hand tools. I would say things like "I thought a hammer is used for bashing someones head in." or, a screwdriver was used to shimmy a door open. The only thing construcive I learned fom Jim was how to do the Jumble in the newspaper.

I still can't remember how it came about, but right around Christmas I wound up proposing to Louise. We were going to get married at City Hall but Antoinette wouldn't have it. She was going to give Louise a wedding reception and wanted her married in a church. So a date was set, we would be married in a Catholic church February 2nd 1973.

I couldn't for the world understand how someone would want to marry a person that had just overdosed in her back yard a month before, someone that she had to introduce to people by having to lift my head up off the bar passed out drunk. And worst of all, had been picked up by homicide detectives, regarding the death of a previous girlfriend. This story, as bizarre as it gets, is the truth.

Loise and I were hanging out at the Pine Inn one night when these two detectives entered the bar looking for me. They asked if I wouldn't mind coming with them to the stationhouse and answer some questions regarding Mary Buns. I replied: "Sure! I'll come".

Evidently the night I brought Mary to the hospital, she signed herself out soon after I left. And the next morning was found in a local cemetery with her jeans and panties removed. Some scumbag had left her in the cemetery passed out, and she died from an overdose of pills.

What makes this story so bizarre is that another young girl from the same neighborhood was reported missing around the same time they found Mary's body. The family of that missing girl was asked to look at a picture of the body found in the cemetery, and the Stepfather identified it as the missing girl. A month later the guy's Stepdaughter shows up with a baby, she had been in California. They had to exhume the body

The body was identified through dental records and fingerprints to be Mary. I remember telling the officers about that night and explaining to them about bringing her to the hospital. The story checked out because I actually signed papers to treat her.

Meanwhile Louise was freaking out crying, thinking they were going to take me away. I remember feeling horrible about what happened to Mary. She didn't deserve to die like that. She was a good soul.

I can't remember exactly how it happened, but my Sister Megan started dating Tony, which caused a rift between us. I left her house and through Antoinette found a basement apartment in Astoria. We needed to get one now that wew were going to be married. Antoinette paid the first month's rent and security for us.

Antoinette would pay for a lot of things. She would make sure her daughter had whatever she needed, so people didn't talk. Meaning her Sisters. Antoinettes family were always looking for some dirt.. They weren't happy that she married an Irishman, and was doubly upset that her daughter did the same.

So leading up to the wedding Louise slept at home. That's the way her Mom wanted it. Antoinette's Sisters were nothing but a bunch of Witches that had nothing better to do than talk about someone in a negative way.

Over the years Antoinette and I became very close, she became like a mother to me. In fact she became the Mother I never had. Sorry Maggie!

I wasn't too sure about my family coming to the wedding, but when I talked to them about it they seemed genuinely happy for me, and said that they would attend.

Louise and I tied the knot on February 2nd 1973. The service was at Saint Francis of Assisi Catholic Church in Astoria, and the reception was held at Ricardo's. It was a great party and everyone had a good time.

The only glitches were when my brother Liam, who was my best man cried incessantly that he spent a lot of money on the wedding, so I opened one of the envelopes given as a gift and gave him Twenty Five bucks. I couldn't understand it. I paid for his tux, I paid the priest, and I gave the tip to the limo driver. So what the hell did he pay for? Then my sister Megan's boyfriend Tony gives us a card with an IOU in it. But all in all we had a lot of fun!

December 3rd exactly ten months after our wedding the love of my life was born, a beautiful little girl we named Kirsten Marie. We had moved out of the basement right before Kirsten was born, into a one- bedroom apartment not far away from Antoinette.

I had left the sheet metal business and went to work for a company in the city, a job I had held for a little while when I lived with Jim. I had been doing fairly well, I wasn't using hard drugs, and I was paying my own rent (most of the time anyway). Antoinette had bought us a new bedroom set and also purchased a crib for her only grandchild. Louise chose her sister Mary to become Kirsten's Godmother she was always very generous towards us. Mary had arranged a baby shower for Louise that all of my sisters attended.

Me, I asked this kid I drank wiith to be the Godfather, which was his complete resume.

CHAPTER FIFTY SEVEN

In A Split Second All Can Go Wrong

My sister Megan had given birth before Kirsten was born and named her daughter Christine Marie, even though we had told her long before (once we knew we were having a girl) that we would name our daughter Kirsten Marie. It had really pissed off Louise.

I hadn't talked to my sister Megan very often since leaving her apartment. I was still miffed that she had chosen Tony over blood. But knowing her, I understood why she acted that way.

Megan was more of a wallflower, a Plain Jane. She had embraced foolhardedly, the attention Tony gave her, even though the family tried to discourage her. They had met Tony and immediately formed a very negative opinion of him.

Tony was not the social type and came across very crass, so my sisters wanted her to wait a while before she got too serious. I never cared to hang out with the guy I always felt I had to walk on eggs around him. I also didn't like his best friend Bobby. He looked like a weasel and was always whispering in Tony's ear, I didn't trust him. And the advice he gave Tony was always adverse in nature. The worst part was that Tony had this piece of shit living with them. I couldn't believe it!

I had returned from work this one particular day and decided to stop in the bar for a beer. Tony and Bobby were there, so I sat as far away from them as I could. Evidently Tony took offense to it. He walked towards me in an aggressive manner. I couldn't tell you verbatum what he said to me, but I had been sick of him fucking with me, and let him know it right then and there.

I walked out of the bar and was going home but he couldn't let it go and followed me outside. It was like the day in halfway house all over again. My blood was boiling to the point of losing it.

Tony jumped in front of me and gave me a shove. So I grabbed him and slammed him against a car. We began grappling and went to the ground each of us trying to get on top. I broke away, jumped up and noticed my pants got torn and scuffed from this melee. I was still in my dress clothes from work and it pissed me off even more. I yelled to Tony that I was going to get changed and would be right back, that then we would finish things.

I didn't want to go all the way back home so I stopped at my sister Maeve's apartment. She lived just two blocks from the bar and I knew I had some regular clothes there. Maeve was living in Maggie's old place on 35th Avenue since she died. I could change there and return quickly to the bar.

As I was dressing into my jeans and sneakers, I was ranting and raving about being tired of this Motherfucker messing with me, and as I was walking out the door, Maeve placed something in my hand. It was a switchblade knife. I don't know why, but I took it from her.

I remember walking down the street towards the bar and looking at this knife and wondering if I would use it. Was I going to need it? What about if that weasel jumped in? Is this a good idea? And before I could completely rationalize the whole situation I was outside the bar standing about five feet from Tony. He had been outside the bar waiting for me.

I was clutching the knife behind my back and when Tony noticed that I was holding something, he ripped off his belt, wrapped it around his hand with the buckle dangling, ready to swing.

There seemed to be a split second in the situation, a moment for us to restore some sanity into our thinking. But Tony swung at me and at the same time I swung my hand around instinctively towards him.

What happened next was a blur, it happened in the blink of an eye. But at the same time it seemed to be happening in slow motion.

The knife caught Tony just above his waist on his left side and went in about an inch. And as he yelled: "You stabbed me Motherfucker"! All I could think to do was drop the knife. I went into this sort of shock, feeling instant remorse. All I wanted at that moment was to go back in time ten minutes. What had I done!

I snapped back out of it to notice Tony bending down to pick up the knife, and I immediately took off. The next thing I felt was an object whizzing by my ear. Tony had chased after me and flung the knife my way, barely missing me. I continued to evade him and dashed into the only place I felt secure, the bar. People in the tavern had been watching this play out and actually tried to intervene. But when I entered, the bartender wanted no part the situation and told me to leave.

There was no way I was going back out there, and I held my ground. A second later I was floored by an object that hit me square on the back of my head. It was that fucking weasel Bobby, he hit me with a barstool. It should have been him that I stabbed; he was always in Tony's ear looking to stir the pot, to create trouble. In the next ten minutes or so things began to calm down. Tony came back in the bar to let me know that he wasn't seriously injured. I breathed a sigh of relief that I hadn't killed him.

My sister Megan was informed what transpired and had raced over to be with Tony. When she arrived she immediately went into a diatribe of profanity, cursing the day I was born, telling me that I tried to kill her man. It took a month or so for things to quiet down completely. I had stayed clear of the bar to assure myself that there would be no retaliation.

One day I received a phone call from Tony telling me that he wanted to put this thing to bed, and wanted me to come down to the bar for a beer. I obliged him with my appearance and my utmost apology for what happened. He said let bygones be bygones, as he lifted his shirt to show me the scar above his waist. I had deep regret for what had happened and was relieved that it wasn't more serious.

CHAPTER FIFTY EIGHT

Irreparable Differences

There was a lull in the animosity between Tony and myself. I was trying in earnest to befriend him even as his attitudes of aggression resurfaced. I had even gone to see him marry my sisiter, which was a complete fiasco.

He had the weasel Bobby as his best man, and both of them were nodding out on junk right at the altar during the ceremony. My older sisters were sitting in the back row mortified and amused at the same time by what was transpiring. After the service Tony's Father and Stepmothert invited Louise and I to Ricardo's for lunch, it was the same place we had our reception. I really didn't want to go, but to keep the peace we went.

The six of us sat down in the restaurant section, only to hear Tony's Old Man constantly bitching about how much lunch was costing him. The more I listened to Tony's father the more I understood why Tony was so fucked up. If I had lived around this guy as a father figure I might have killed myself from embarrassment.

He was a loud mouthed, uncouth human being that enjoyed listening to himself. He was an overbearing, classless tyrant. That had to be the reason Tony became what he was. He even made my sister walk five blocks to the church in her wedding gown, because he didn't want to lose a parking spot. PATHETIC!

Meanwhile the Weasel, this fucking animal that was Tony's best freind, would be arrested shortly after for brutally murdering his 88 year old landlady for a couple of bucks. He and his skank girlfriend stabbed this poor woman to death. I hope that both of them rot in jail.

I continued to try and be affable towards Tony, if for no other reason than to maintain my relationship with my sister, but it would be to no avail. His abhorrent actions continued to drive a wedge between us that became irrevocable, rendering me Person Non Grata at my sisters home.

Tony would continue to use narcotics over the following years, spending more time incarcerated than being at home for his children. It seemed that every time he was released on parole my sister would become pregnant, thus relegating her to a continuous life of welfare and poverty. I'm not trying to put it all on him; she needed to acknowledge her part in things.

Why would someone stay with a person like that? Someone that was never around to help take care of the children that he had helped make. Never mind impregnating a woman without so much as a thought of the consequences. I'm sure that it had something to do with the unhealthy environments that they each grew up in, but after a while it becomes a lame excuse. Even I woke up eventually to the fact that you can't blame others for the rest of your life, you have to acknowledge your own behaviors and change. It took me a long time to realize what my lifestyle was doing to my family.

I had begun using heroin again and running with this guy Sullivan from the city, not to mention stealing from my wife and removing things from our home to sell. It soon became clear that the most important thing in my life once again became a bag of dope, my family a distant second. That's what heroin does to you. I was no better than Tony, I just wasn't geting locked up on a regular basis, but that would drastically change.

CHAPTER FIFTY NINE

Still RunningThe Rat Race Of Addiction

I had a developed a little chippie shooting dope and heard through the grapvine that Tony had been up at Iroquois to get clean. It's amazing, you can't stand a person, but relate with them about drugs and all is forgiven. He had been downstate on a pass and had hatched a plan to smuggle a load of pills when he returned. He was going to pack them in a balloon, then take the balloon and put it in his rectum.

I placed a call to my old counselor at Iroqois asking for help, and arranged to go upstate for 90 days. Tony and I flew up to Buffalo N.Y. and made our way to Iroquois with balloons filled with narcotics rammed up our ass.

Louise was still naive about things and had talked Antoinette into paying for my airfare upstate, with the notion I would be getting clean. I still can't remember the first two weeks up there because I was so stoned all the time. But when the pills ran out, my desire to stay at Iroquois dissipated, I wanted out. And being I was there voluntary, they couldn't hold me. So I returned back home with a genuine aspiration to remain straight, but that lasted all but a couple of weeks.

I got a new job working local for a company that constructed displays that were to be used in the window cases of shoe stores, their biggest client being Thom McCann Shoes. I was hired as an assistant to the office manager for just above minimum wage.

Within a month I had found the local shylock and soon began borrowing cash. It put me in a position where I had to come up with money I didn't have.

The Office Manager I worked for had made the mistake of sending me to the local hardware store where the company held an open account. Besides making purchases for the company, I would go to the store, grab some tools, and put them on the company account. Then I would sell them for half of what they cost. Needless to say I wound up leaving that job shortly after. I had the heat coming down on me, so I just stopped going to work.

I owed the shylock a few hundred bucks or so. He had been one of the people that were buying tools from me, so I didn't give a shit. If he tried something, or said something, the shit woud go right back on him.

After losing my job I was again relegated to being a sneak thief, a scam artist, and neighborhood burglar. My partner Sullivan and I were doing what we could to make money, stealing shit and ripping people off from around the area. One day while looking for a score, we passed this electronics store in the area. It was a place I'd go from time to time to fence some swag I'd stolen. We cased the place and figured that it would be an easy mark. It was Sullivan, this kid named Ray and and myself. We were going to hit it that night. We'd scoop up all the calculators and take off before that cops could get there.

Ray would be at the corner on Steinway Street looking up and down, watching out for the cops. I would be standing ten feet from the door at the curb checking out Ditmars. Sullivan would be the one to shoulder the door in. The problem was the door wouldn't budge the first time he tried, so he proceeded to try and kick it in. His actions caused quite a commotion. Lights were turning on everywhere from across the street. Windows were opening and people started yelling for us to stop. All of a sudden with his last kick, the jamb cracked, the door flew open and he went inside.

The plan was to snatch as many calculators as possible as quickly as possible, then take off around the corner. We'd hide in the schoolyard until things cooled down, then go into the city and sell them.

I noticed it was taking too long. "What was the fucking problem", I was thinking, so I backed up close to the store window, peered in to see Sullivan peeling off the dollar bills scotch taped to the wall. It was atypical for many new stores to scotch tape the dollars from the stores first few sales.

I couldn't believe what I was seeing we should have already been around the corner. This asshole Sullivan had to steal the seven stinking bucks taped to the wall. He couldn't just focus on what we were there for.

I went back to my post hoping this debacle would soon be over. I yelled for Ray to get ready to run, but there was no answer. He had already split when the noise became too loud and people started yelling from their windows, he was the smart one, Pussy that he was.

Suddenly a squad car careens around the corner from Steinway and pulls up directly in front of me. The officer on the passenger side rolled down his window, and asked if I was the one that had made the call about a burglary. I looked back at him like a deer caught in headlights wide-eyed and unable to move or speak. If only I could have told him that I was waiting for the bus, I was standing directly under the sign that alluded to it.

This whole scene reminded me of an old Jackie Gleason show, where Ralph got caught in a lie and all he could say was Hummina-Huminna-Huminna. Dumbfounded to respond, it only took the cops two seconds to figure out that I had something to do with what was going on. And out came the guns and the order to get down on my knees with my hands behind my head.

At the same time, Sullivan the asshole sashays out the door with a box of calculators, directly into the arms of the local constables. If the charges weren't so serious it would have seemed comical, like a God Damned Charlie Chaplin movie.

We were transported to the 114th Precinct, where they booked us for felony burglary, and once the cops completed their paperwork we were on the next bus to the Queens House Of Detention for arraignment and a bail hearing.

Being allowed one call, I phoned Louise at home and begged and pleaded with her to ask her Mom to put up the bail. It was $2500 bond or $250 cash. Antoinette though leery had decided to post bond for me and I was released the following day with a court date set for two months later.

I was facing a 5 yr. prison term if I was convicted, so I'd have to do something drastic. Maybe I'll just not show up for court. No I thought, I would be picked up on a felony warrant. I had no means to take off to some far away place, I was too much of a malcontent, and my societal immaturity wouldn't allow it. I had to come up with another plan to work the system.

I recalled my short time at *Phoenix House* in 1970. Here was an institution with political connections and a strong reach into the criminal justice system. I had heard on numerous occasions the clout they wielded with the judges, and their ability to have people released into the custody of its program. Recovery rather than incarceration was the spiel given the courts. I voluntarily placed myself into their custody.

CHAPTER SIXTY

The Felony Or The Phoenix

The main intake center for Phoenix House was a storefront on 125th Street in Harlem. I wasted no time formulating a plan to beat my felony charge. I would develop my connection to Phoenix, which in turn would place me in their probative custody. It would be contingent on my adhering to their program.

During the intake process the first question asked is: "Are you facing any legal problems"? And as soon I disclosed my legal dilemna my examiner began to vehemently ostracize me. "You're just here to get the court off your back, so you don't go to the joint, it has nothing to do with you getting clean." What do you think we're stupid! "A lot smarter people have pulled the shit you're trying to sell us, now get the fuck out of here." Shocked by what I heard, I stood up to leave. He then said to me, "wait a minute, get your ass back here." "I want you to come back here tomorrow by 9AM, and don't be late or you're out."

The next day I arrived at 8:30 and waited for the office to open. My new found pal took down all my information then had me sit on this wooden bench. There was no word from him if I was going to be admitted, I was told to just sit there and wait, so that's what I did. He gave me a bologna sandwhich and glass of juoice around 11 O'clock, and didn't say one word to me the rest of the day.

Somewhere around 7 PM a van pulled up in front of the building. This big guy got out of the van and came inside. He gave me the once over, then walked over to the person at the desk and proceeded to talk with him. He was handed a folder, and as he turned to leave he said: "Lets go my man, you're coming with me." I humbly thanked the intake person for all he did for me and I walked outside and got into the van. About a half hour later and a borough away I reached my destination. It was the **_Phoenix House Bronx Facility_** and it was going to be my new home indefinitely, or at least until my court hearing.

We entered the place during a house meeting. They were discussing the goings on of the day. The meeting was held in the main room (a large social area filled with chairs and sofas). I walked in with my head down I felt everyones eyes in the room turn my way. It was a very uncomfortable position to be in. I then took a seat towards the rear of the room.

Everyones attention returned to the front, and the speaker at the dais. A name was called out at the meeting and this person stood up to be addressed. He was wearing this large cardboard sign around his neck and his head had been shaved. I couldn't tell what the sign said, but it looked ridiculous. The speaker said out loud to everyone in the room, that this person standing with the sign around his neck, needed everyones help. And yelled: "Are we going to help him to not kill Himself!" And the whole room loudly responded in unison: "Yes we are." Another name was shouted out causing another pperson to stand. He was wearing a diaper and holding a babies bottle. "Are we going to help this person to not kill himself!" The retort again was a resoundiong "Yes we will."

This happened about a half dozen times before the meeting adjourned to something called an encounter group. An encounter group is where the population of the house breaks up into smaller groups to confront one another about the day.

I told the guy who brought me there that I had nothing to eat all day and was very hungry. He walked up to this big black woman standing at the dais and whispered in her ear. He came back and told me to follow him. He took me to the kitchen, made me a sandwich and gave me a glass of milk. As soon as I finished I was taken to one of the rooms that had an encounter group under way.

There was a large semi-circle of men and woman sitting across from one another, and once the initial disturbance of me entering the room dissipated, the dialogue of the meeting continued. This one particular person was being questioned about an incident that happened earlier in the day between him and this other individual. What had seemed a normal conversation at the time turned into a diatribe, laced with every expletive I'd ever heard. The guy being insulted just sat there stone faced, taking this brutal verbal attack without saying one word.

A minute later he finally opened his mouth to explain his behavior, but before the second word left his lips, a salvo of insults came from every direction in the room. "Shut the fuck up!" One person said. 'You're a fucking Asshole!" Another spoke. And as this verbal assault continued all I could think was, "Boy did I ever make a mistake coming here." There's no way I'm going to let people talk that way to me without reciprocation, especially if the cause for this attack was as menial as a lapse of the tongue.

It seems someones feelings were hurt when this person flippantly made them the brunt of a joke. I thought it was a real pussy maneuver to set this guy up for such whiplashing. Boy would I ever learn quickly what all this shit was about.

I was there less than a week before I had my head shaved for using profanity towards one of my housemates and refusing to apologize. It was that or being thrown out on the street. As much as I wanted to leave, it would mean going to court without an advocate. Accomplishing one thing: Possibly a Five Year sentence in an upstate prison.

There were many times I wasn't able to conform to the strict policies of this type of therapeutic community. I know that they meant well, but I was incapable of being honest and open about my past. Which was at the core of my addictions and indiscretions. There was no way I could tell someone I had been raped and molested as a child. About the shame it caused me, a shame that could only be relieved by total oblivion.

How could I discuss my family's dysfunctional behaviors without feeling like I would be judged, how could I explain my many inhibitions that were governed by my ego, to the point of self-abhorance and antisocial behaviors. Throughout my time at Phoenix House it was displayed on a regular basis that I deplored everything going on around me.

I constantly had a shaved head and there was a time I had four signs around my neck. I was always on contract (scrubbing bathrooms and the kitchen with a toothbrush) and a smoking ban. I would be dragged from encounter group to encounter group, having people blasting me for my insolent conduct around the house. This was all done to me in the name of love of man.

The thing that made it all worthwhile though was that during these meetings, I would be allowed to smoke. I would smoke with my legs crossed, and my signs dangling from my neck. I'd have this smug look on my face that alluded to my disdain for this whole process. 'Fuck you all," I would think to myself.

After about three months my case was put on the court calendar for a hearing and it went just as I had planned. I was released into the custody of Phoenix House and would have all charges lowered contingent to my graduating its program. If I did not conform to the rules and was discharged because of my conduct, a warrant would be issued for my arrest and I would be held accountable for the original charge.

What was really a kick in the ass was that the prick that owned the electronics store store was at my hearing to make sure I was getting my just due. What a fucking hypocrite. It was okay when I was selling him stolen goods. Who was he to be sitting there with his girlfriend, and judging me, fucking asshole that he was.

I became less and less contentious over the next two months and had even worked myself off of contract. There were no signs hanging around my neck and my hair had begun to grow in very nicely. But something transpired that changed everything. It was right after my first marathon (an encounter meeting that lasts between 48 and 72 hours, using sleep deprivation as well as a psychological indoctrination to break down supposed barriers hindering a persons recovery.

I had been working handing out flyers for a local business. (Phoenix House would receive the compensation) I had without permission made a collect call to Louise to see how she and my daughter were doing. It had been almost eight months already and I had not received a visit or even a phone call from home. The staff allways told me that they were in touch with my family and everything was okay. But I needed to hear it for myself.

We used to have guilt sessions at the house to see if anyone needed to get something off his or her chest. The person running the house meeting would call out, 'is anyone is holding onto guilt today". So during this one particular meeting I raised my hand and admitted to making a phone call home. You would think I fucking murdered someone.

At the House Meeting that evening I announced in front of everyone that I had made a phone call to home while out. I was blasted for being a sneak and doing as I please. It was decided that I was to lose my hair and be put on contract once again. I fervently protested the decision on the basis of my being honest. And said I would not allow them to cut my hair anymore. That if they insisted, I was going to split. I told them that I was not a sneak, that I didn't get caught, that I was the one to admit what I did. But it was a done deal. They were taking my hair.

I stood up and walked out of the meeting with the mindset that

I was going to leave, when I was intercepted by a few of the fellas. They wanted to speak to me before I left. They reminded me of my legal situation and even told me that if I left I would shoot dope. They asked me why I was making such a big deal about my hair. Telling me that it would grow back before I knew it. I didn't want to hear it, I was leaving and there was nothing anyone could say that would change my mind.

They asked me to sit on a bench at the door for a while just to think about what I was doing, I sat down and for the next hour they paraded friends in front of me, guys and girls, to try and talk me out of leaving. I refused to listen and just kept repeating that I'm out of here.

The more I insisted I was leaving the nastier they became until they finally conceded. They gave me two tokens and wished me the best and out into the autumn night I went.

It was about midnight and it was not the best of neighborhoods to be in so I was a little nervous riding the subway downtown, but once I reached the the 59th Street station I felt relieved. I made a collect call to Louise to let her know I would be home in around an hour, and then would I explain everything to her.

It felt good to be home and sleeping next to my wife after being away for almost 8 months. It seemed I appreciated her more after being gone for so long. It was not too long ago that I had so many doubts about being married. Louise had gained some weight after having Kirsten and I had been a little embarrassed to be seen with her. But who the hell was I to feel that way, just a few months before I was this 120 lb. soaking wet junkie, with greasy brown hair and a gray complexion. The type of lowlife that steals his family's welfare checks and sells things he steals from his house. I was no fucking bargain, how dare I judge anyone especially the mother of my child.

I woke the next day in an anxious mood. I knew that a warrant would be issued for my arrest because Phoenix House would have to report my leaving, so I had to do something quickly. I made a call to someone I had known previously from the Rockefeller Program and secured a spot within their Fordham Road facility in the Bronx. I wasted no time in reporting I went there my second day home.

I was furnished a counselor and immediately told him about my legal issues so that he could contact the probation department. This was to have a hold put on the warrant until I could have a new hearing. If I could stay out of trouble and receive a stellar report from the program, I could still avoid jail time, and. that's exactly what I did.

At my hearing the judge mandated me to the Rockefeller Program and ordered that I comply and complete its itinerary. I was the model citizen while there and even helped to tutor some of the inmates taking their GED. I volunteered for anything positive and I became a genuinely model inmate. I was even allowed weekend passes after three months.

My daughter Kirsten was almost three by the time I was home for good. My first day back, Louise met me at the door with her, and when I bent down to pick her up, she ran behind her mother, afraid of me. I really couldn't blame her she didn't know who I was. I hadn't been around for over a year. She didn't even see me when I split from Phoenix she had been at her Grandmothers. Right then and there I made a decision to never use heroine again. I was home for good I was not going to be incarcerated and away from home anymore. My daughter was going to have a Father in her life.

CHAPTER SIXTY ONE

The Sternberger Corporation

The parole officer I was assigned was a decent enough guy, and must have seen something in my record that he liked. He introduced me to the manager of a National Moving Company in Long Island City, that hired men on a first come first serve basis, every morning, Monday thru Friday. Up until this point in my life I had worked strictly for minimum wage.

I would have to report to this certain area every day ready for work. The manager would appear at the hiring window at exactly 7 AM to pick guys to work that day. If you were wearing sneakers, you were sent home. If you had your hands in your pockets, you would be sent home. If you looked disinterested, you were sent home. The day I first met with the manager he schooled me on what to do and what not to do..The most important rule was never to be late, it showed a lack of respect.

Every day I was chosen to work, I worked like an animal. I watched intently how the guys loaded the 45ft. trailers, making sure the furniture was properly loaded and protected. I learned the proper way to blanket wrap the furniture so that it would not get damaged. And after about 6 months I was allocated to load one myself. But most times I just staged the furniture to be loaded on the truck.

Trucks were loaded from a manifest. Every over the road driver (long distance) would have anywhere from forty to fifty stops to make in a one week period. For each stop there was an invoice with the customers name address and items they were to receive. On each invoice was a location in the warehouse where each item was stored. So I would locate the item and stage it at the rear of the trailer to be loaded, last stop first.

I was getting picked on a regular basis because of my work ethic. All the other loaders put in a good word for me, so I stood out. There was one time that I worked twentyeight days straight, but the next morning I wasn't picked and was sent home. This was because If you worked thirty days straight, you had to be made a union member, which meant you would also receive the benefits. That would mean medical coverage for my wife, my child and myself. With a pension, as well as an annuity account.

Shaping up I was being paid the same rate as a union guy except I had no benefits. But after nine months of giving it my all, the manager worked me over thirty days straight. I was an official union member. For the first time in my life I was a functioning human being, a pillar of society. I was supporting my family, I wasn't going to jail anymore, and I was living up to my responsibility as a husband and father. My self-esteem was never higher.

There were many ups and downs to come because I was still drinking, smoking pot and snorting coke on occasion. But most of the time I was doing okay. Don't get me wrong, I definitely wasn't going to be canonized, but people noticed the change.

I still had a lot of anger deep down inside of me and it would rise to the top when I drank. I wouldn't see it coming and couldn't control it. My anger caused me to get into a lot of jams, I did things that I would never think of doing sober. I was just a nasty drunk, prone to severe antisocial, even violent behavior. I would unintentionally find trouble, which on occasion led to me getting arrested.

One Saturday while drinking with a friend on 36th street and 2nd avenue I walked around the corner to a Chinese take-out joint and ordered an egg roll. Upon paying, I thought I was short changed a quarter and began arguing with the cashier. Not long after I picked up a chair next to one of the tables and threw it through the plate glass window. This was a full floor to ceiling casement that crashed down onto the sidewalk, sending shards of glass flying in every direction. Not thinking I could have killed or seriously injured someone. There were children playing on the street near the store that could have been seriously hurt. But in that state of drunkenness I never thought about the consequences of my actions.

I went back around the corner, returning to the place I was drinking and continued as if nothing happened. Within minutes three police cars were on the scene, one driven up on the sidewalk directly in front of me. One of the cops jumped out of the car and pounced on me, while another placed me in handcuffs.

I was supposed to go with Louise the next day to pick up Kirsten who was at Girl Scout camp. We were going to have a family day, eating out and seeing the musical "Little Shop Of Horrors." But I was arrested and sent to central booking, charged with destruction of property and publc intoxication. Later that day I was transferred to the Manhattan House of Detention for arraignment.

I called Louise with my tale of woe and asked her to get money to bail me out. She in turn went crying to Antoinette once again, begging her for money to get me out of another jackpot. I missed picking up my daughter and didn't make the play because while locked up, I caught head lice from the bum I was handcuffed to, when we were transferred to the Tombs.

Many, many times my drinking caused me to make bad decisions, sometimes putting my family and others in harms way. Drink and I lose all control.

There was the time I had lost my paycheck gambling, along with my following week's pay. I was shooting dice in the locker room. I had been drinking heavily as usual and wouldn't take the advice of people telling to stop and go home. I went home with my tail between my legs and a sad story. Louise didn't want to hear it, I ate peanutbutter sandwiches evert day for lunch the following month.

One time after drinking most of the day at work I continued my drinking in a predominately African-American bar near the job. I was acting like an asshole bothering the band and trying to hit on the barmaid when some guy protested the way I was behaving, I turned to him and made a derogatory remark. Before you knew it I was fist fighting with the guy. Thank goodness I knew the manager real well, he broke up the fight and told me to go home.

Heading home on the subway I began punching out windows and shouting profanities causing general havoc on the train. People were distancing themselves from me with some actually running out of the car in fear. They wanted to get as far away from me as possible the lunatic I had become.

Two minutes later a policeman entered the car saw what I was doing and proceeded to arrest me. I spewed some racist remark toward the man, which he ignored, but when they brought me to the 114th Police Precinct in Astoria the white cops heard about my remarks and knocked the crap out of me. I also had to be brought to Astoria General Hospital to have glass removed from the knuckles on both my hands. As I began sobering up I apologized to the officer, telling him that I was not a racist, I was just a very angry person when I got drunk.

After leaving the hospital I was brought back to the station house and booked for destruction of city property and disturbing the peace. I was then transported to the Queens House of Detention again. Louise bailed me out the following morning, and from there I went directly to work. It was just another saga to tell the guys at work, while the jug of Port wine was being passed around.

It just never stopped. One time while drinking in this neighborhood bar, I went to the bathroom and there were three or four younger guys hanging out and I asked if they wanted to smoke a joint. They gladly accepted the invitation and I lit up and began passing it around. For no good reason one of them made a snide remark and I grabbed him by the shirt. Before I knew it I was on the ceramic tile floor being stomped in the head and kicked to the point, where I thought I would pass out. Somehow I was able to get up and run out of the bathroom.

I was bleeding pretty badly from my nose. "So what do I do?" I went to the bar and ordered another drink and asked the bartender for a towel and ice. I had gone to the bar with Jeff from work, this kind of scrawny guy, and John something or another (This old Irishman with a head that would tilt so much to the side, you thought it would roll off his shoulders). I wasn't about to brawl with those two. The next morning when I got up I walked into the living room where my daughter was and when she saw me she screamed. My face had been pretty well beat up my nose was broken so both eyes were blackened. I had a number of scrapes and bruises on my head and face. I scared the hell out of her.

One day after one of our morning rituals of drinking and smoking grass I had been called into the office and reprimanded by my supervisor Bobby. It had something to do with my drinking on the job. At noontime my co workers and I went to the corner bar for some liquid lunch and I was bitching about being chewed out in the morning.

I was pretty high and probably should not have continued to drink but I never knew when to stop. Dennis my supposed friend began goading me, and calling me a punk for not going back at Bobby. The other guys also joined in the fun, teasing me to no end.

I got up from my barstool and began walking back to the job to give Bobby a piece of my mind. I stormed into the office and in front of everyone I began screaming and yelling profanities, not making any sense. It was obvious to everyone in the office that I was drunk out of my mind. I reeked of alcohol and was slurring my words.

And as I stormed out of the office after this pitiful scene, I shoved the door open very hard. At the same time one of the VP's was coming in and got slammed by the door and knocked to the ground. I stopped and just stared at this man on the floor, then stepped over him and walked away without even an apology.

I went back to work and the guys were laughing their ass off, which gave me a somewhat skewed sense of bravado. Then Bobby came out to the loading platform where we were, and told me to leave the premises because I was fired.

The next day I returned to work and pleaded to Bobby to please take me back begging for forgiveness and promising not to drink on the job ever again. After a sincere and heartfelt apology to Bobby and the VP, for some reason they took me back. I was the exemplary employee for the next three months.

These stories are just scratching the surface of what I had become. For the next seven years I'd put Louise through hell. Continually getting arrested or beat up in a bar or coming home broke. It's not that I was doing these things every weekend, I was able to keep up paying the bills, supplying our family with most of the things they needed and even took small vacations twice a year.

Somehow I even got a job as a warehouse manager for an exclusive furniture manufacturer making very good money. But after one too many phone calls Louise received telling her I was in jail or in the hospital, She'd had enough. She gave me an ultimatum, stop drinking or get the hell out. She was fed up with all the bullshit my drinking and using drugs were causing.

I talked to the owner of my company Leon Rosen explaining to him that I had a problem with alcohol and needed to do something something about it. He arranged through my insurance to go to an alcoholic treatment center. While there I learned that I had a disease, and the only true means of treatment was complete abstinence. I remained sober for the next 23 years. I had gone to Alcoholics Anonymous and for the first time in my life I met people just like me, except they were staying sober and dealing with life on lifes terms. They were not using alcohol and drugs to solve their problems anymore. Though I am compelled to not mention this institution in name I must. Because through the good times and the bad that followed, I can honestly say that AA saved my life.

CHAPTER SIXTY TWO

AA All The Way

S obriety was good in the beginning all had been going well. I had made so many friends, real true friends. People that didn't want or expect anything from me, they just wanted for me to be happy and free from drugs and alcohol.

I made a meeting every day as it was suggested and had taken on a few commitments. I began by making coffee at a couple of meetings and helping to set up tables and chairs. Later on I began leading (opening up) meetings and even became treasurer for one.

After ninety days sober I was asked to speak and tell a brief story about myself, and what I had been doing to remain sober, I was scared to death. Here I was standing in front of a large group of people talking about the one thing I most wanted to keep buried forever, I had been living a lie my whole life, not wanting to be found out that I was afraid most of the time.

The catastrophic events I experienced when I was a little boy had become such an unbearable weight, that drinking and using drugs was the only option I had. But over the next few years and with the help of sponsors and confidants, I was able to find the professional help I needed to begin my healing process. It was an arduous journey that began with the acknowledgment of what is sometimes expressed as the inner child, the hurt little boy that had lived inside me.

In the beginning of my sobriety, I noticed my patience with people not in the program grew thin. I would easily blow up, sometimes over the most trivial of reasons. My anger reared its ugly head mostly at home and on the job. At the time I first got sober, I was still working for the Pace Collection Inc. as a their warehouse manager, and earning a substantial salary.

But as time went on the littlest of things that hadn't bothered me previously began to irritate me. I had no tolerance for people and would challenge everything and everyone. I was sober about four months when I was fired for acting insubordinate and hostile towards some of my co-workers. All these feelings began rising up inside of me. I became overly sensitive, and was hurt easily. My only defense at the time was to strike back, because I never gained the tools to deal with my feelings. That's why I had to seek out professional help. I still struggle sometimes. But they told me to take it easy, that it was a lifetime of work.

CHAPTER SIXTY THREE

For the Love of Nino

I was going to AA every day and really getting into the program when I met this guy Nino. We hit it off right away and began going to meetings together every day we became inseparable. If one of us was not at a meeting people noticed and would ask were the other one was. Nino ate at my house almost every day, and any time I socialized outside the meetings, like maybe going to a water park, a ball game etc. I brought Nino along.

Nino was not only an alcoholic he was also schizophrenic. But I didn't mind, he was the brother figure I never had. Nino always made me laugh, He had this habit of opening and closing his hands like a lobster when he talked and was always brutally honest.

Nino was Italian, and we became so close that we would kiss each other on the cheek when saying hello or goodnight. it was a way of expressing respect. Later on in our relationship this showing of affection would come between us.

After a couple of years Louise had become disenchanted with my sobriety. I believe she felt like an outsider, I felt like she became jealous of my new friends. I tried to include her in my life, but she would never want to participate. Even Nino noticed because Louise started acting cold towards him.

One night when I was dropping Nino off, I leaned over to kiss him on the cheek. He turned around and kissed me on my mouth. He told me he was in love with me. I immediately began to freak out. I told him I cared about him, but not in that way, and I told him never to do that again. It gave me this sick feeling, like I was being sexually assaulted again. I went home confused.

I talked to my AA sponsor about what happened, and he knowing about my past told me not to hang out with Nino for a while. So I stopped picking him up for meetings, I stopped inviting him to socialize with me. I stopped calling him, and I even stopped talking to him at meetings if we happened to go to the same one.

A couple of weeks later I noticed him at one of the meetings and when I looked at him, he seemed so very sad. He stared at me as if to say,"What did I do to you"? I felt very hurt but held my ground. A month or so passed and I hadn't seen him at the regular meetings we had gone to together.

I received a phone call shortly after telling me that Nino had jumped off of the 59th Street Bridge, he was dead. He had even laid out a suit for his wake, and had all his important papers nearby and in order. I guess he thought it would make things easier for his kids and Ex Wife. I was devastated.

Nino wasn't taking his medication properly and had slipped into a schizophrenic episode. When he was like this Nino would hear voices telling him to do things. I imagined that it seemed like jumping off the bridge was the right thing for him to do. My sense of guilt told me that if only I had been there for him he wouldn't have killed himself. For the longest time I blamed myself.

There were about two hundred people from AA at Nino's wake He was loved by everyone that knew him. But after paying their respects to his family they came to me to express condolences for my loss. They knew that I was in mourning also and they came to show me love and support. I had lost my best friend but didn't have to be alone in my sadness.

CHAPTER SIXTY FOUR

Sometimes Sobriety Is Like Patty R.

A similar thing happened with another person I was emotionally attached to. Patty R. who with his second wife Debbie had become best friends with Louise and I. We did everything together. Our families went on vacations together and we hung out together every weekend. Louise and I were even their daughter's godparents. It was good that Louise was back in my life again. But Patty eventually ruined that relationship and Debbie divorced him.

I slowly began distancing myself from Patty because he kept using drugs. I was also angry with him for spoiling the connection we had. Patty met and married for the third time, but it was a bad relationship from the start, very confrontational and cruel. It wasn't very long before he divorced again. But this time his depression got the best of him.

The last time I saw Patty alive he helped me hang shades in the new home Louise and I had purchased. He told me he was doing okay, but I knew differently. I could see in his eyes he wasn't doing well.

A few weeks later he was found in the kitchen of his home dead from an overdose. Once again I felt guilt ridden for abandoning someone. I was at the beginning of my spiritual development and I wondered why my Higher Power would put these people in my life, and then take them away, it was testing my sobriety.

I was told it was because with God I could handle these situations, and set an example for others trying to stay sober. I sometimes wish God didn't have so much confidence in me.

My Friend

I miss you in my quietness,
reflective of the times we had.
And when I think of how you left,
there are times when I get mad.

You had so much good to offer,
and of this you couldn't see.
So you let your problems drown you,
leaving all of us to grieve.

With the love that dwelt inside of you,
always shared when I was down.
You would lift me up to carry on,
and your smile would chase my frown.

My friend when you were in my life,
how we both would laugh at fear.
Now I'm going through some troubling times.
And I wish that you were here.

You would comfort me the way you did,
with your wisdom's subtle ways.
And would tell me I was your best friend,
which would always make my day.

So I'll miss you in my quietness,
and on occasions I will cry.
for my best friend is not with me,
and he never said goodbye

*Patty: I think of you often, and more than any of my friend's
I will always miss you mos*t.

CHAPTER SIXTY FIVE

Life Is Life is life.

You have to accept the lifes lessons that are given you. Here were these two wonderful men that I loved like brothers, whom were put into my life for a reason. Any time you feel such a closeness and bond with a person you need to stop for a moment, and realize how much you've been blessed. Not too many people can say that.

I had divorced Louise we hadn't been intimate in years. It was mostly my fault though. All the hurt over time drove her into the arms of another man. When I found out I thought it would kill me. I thought of ending my life every day for many months. I wasn't going to meetings since we bought the house and that was one of the reasons I felt suicidal. I was isolated and had no one to talk to. But I returned to the rooms of AA, and though the pain of abandonment felt as if I'd die, it subsided.

A year or so later I received a call from my sister Megan. Our younger sister Maeve who had contracted HIV from her womanizing husband had succumbed to her disease. It had developed into Full Blown AIDS. Her husband my Brother-inlaw had died years back.

Maeve fought the good fight, It's what she did her whole life. She was the toughest girl/woman I ever knew She backed down from no one. I remember once when she was twelve years old the cops had brought her home because she had beat the crap out of two women who were making fun of her.

If you were a female and hit her, she would just stand there with a shit-eating grin on her face, just to show you that it didn't faze her. Then bang! That person would be lying unconscious on the floor. Besides being tough, she was also a good friend, someone that could be counted on in a time of need. Maeve was generous to a fault she would give you the proverbial shirt off her back.

Louise and I drove upstate one day to visit her at a hospice for women with HIV, and she cracked jokes the whole time. When we left I told her that I'd talk to her real soon. But as always people get very busy with their life. And the call and visit did not come soon enough.

The real shity thing was, I wasn't informed until two years after her death that she had passed. My sadness was overwhelming and I cried for days, but by reminiscing the short times I spent with her, the memories of her made up for my sadness. There were many stories we would have compared and laughed about.

This book is partly dedicated to her strength in the face of the many adversities she experienced.

Mae your girls are doing so well, as are the Grandchildren you never got to see.

As a family we are not the Cleaver's and never bragged to be. As parents and grandparents, as brothers and sisters, as aunts and uncles and nieces and nephews, we cannot boast of our closeness. But in our hearts we have a love of family that conquers all adversity. We are not on the phone with each other on a daily basis, or see each other regularly. Some may not be speaking to one another another over some petty nonsense, it does'nt realy matter. But we keep each other in the memories we made, whether they were happy or sad. I truly believe we have done our best with what we were given and I wouldn't change a thing. The following prose will paint a picture of my meaning.

The Swan Inside

She was the ugliest duckling upon the lake,
never taught to swim, for goodness sake.
A fate she bore with no remorse,
being tossed aside-not her mistake.

Paddling along was all she knew,
to stay above the waters hue.
Her inner strength kept her afloat,
as well, her love of life did too.

Not one bad word you'd hear her speak,
She'd play it all with tongue in cheek.
A wry bright smile would light her face,
to chase away, what all seemed bleak

Too busy struggling throughout the day,
"So why complain" is what she'd say.
"Whining only makes it worse"
an outlook worn in times so gray

As time went by, with years assessed,
a voice within spoke: 'I've been so blessed!"
To have lived my life so full you see,
and have no regrets as I'm laid to rest

This ugly duckling that stood no chance,
at life's sometimes un-enchanted dance.

Came out the other side you see
A swan of beauty, a vision enhanced

For my beautiful Sister Maeve Parra.

In 2006 I received a phone call from Dianne, the daughter of my fathers girlfriend Mary, She informed me that my Half Sister Barbara-Anne had also contracted AIDS, and was very sick. She developed the disease by using heroin intravenously. I asked if I could talk to her, but each time I phoned I was given some lame excuse why she couldn't speak with me. When she passed I was left wondering what her life must have been like, disconnected from her family on our side. Never knowing any of the brothers and sisters she had, how sad that must have been. What could I have been able to do for her? Dirty Mary had passed years before and for a moment in my sinful mind, I was glad. She was a horrific mother that beat her children without mercy, and I wondered if she beat my sister Barbara-Anne also. I was sure I would never find out the truth.

CHAPTER SIXTY SIX

The Breaking Point

On my 55th birthday I received a call from my sister Grace with good will and salutations. As the conversation continued and the small talk reached its climax, I decided to stir the pot and bring up the subject of the molester, her ex-husband Singer. I had never discussed the matter with her, and still had reservations, even though it had been a half century ago.

As the conversation continued we reflected on the damage he had done to our family, and all the hurt he had caused. But this was only the tip of the iceberg. She told me that he also molested the children of his second wife, and that the woman did not believe ther children when they brought it to her attention.

I felt my blood pressure rise from my belly to the top of my head. Thoughts of his murder bounced back and forth within my mind. This fucking animal continued to perpetrate his malevolent and monstrous acts on other children, and was still walking the streets. I wondered how it was possible.

I also felt guilt by not bringing it out in the open years and years ago. My excuse was that I didn't want to be the one bringing the shame of it to his children, so I kept it to myself. Grace also told me that day my Mother knew about it and did nothing. It was right around the time she took off and abandoned us. She never once thought of calling the police. Her answer was to run away.

After hearing this I cut the conversation short and hung up. I didn't know how to feel. My indignation towards Maggie had subsided greatly over the years since her passing. But had reared its ugly head once again, I was devastated.

At the time, I had been out of work for about a month, recuperating from surgery. I had been assaulted on the job.

I relayed to my therapist about what my sister and I discussed, and told him I felt extremely depressed by what I heard. He recommended seeing a psychiatrist who in turn put me on medication. Then on this one particular day when I went to therapy, and upon leaving seemed to be in a pretty good frame of mind. I returned home to an empty house and began puttering around looking through the kitchen cabinets. When directly in front of me I saw bottle of Serequel that I had been prescribed to help me sleep.

Out of the blue, I grabbed the bottle and a large glass of water and began to swallow approximately twenty pills. I sat there contemplating what I had done, when a feeling of panic came over me. I didn't really want to kill myself I had too much to live for. So I called my daughter Kirsten and thank God she was home. I told her what I had done and that I could feel the medication beginning to take effect, it wouldn't be long before I was unconcious.

She told me to open the front door and wait while she called 911. When the ambulance arrived they saw that I was comatose and rushed me to the hospital where they pumped my stomach and gave me a shot of Narcon. When I finally came to, I was asked why I swallowed so much of my medication.

I told the doctor I was depressed, and that I was in chronic pain. It would become the first of my many trips to a psychiatric facility, as well as the beginning of my abusing pain medication.

Just being clean and sober is not enough in recovery; the person must live a sober lifestyle also. They have to be willing to do the right thing, no matter what the case. Whether it is the mundane Nine to Five bullshit or a crippling emotional event, you can't dwell on the negative.

In my Grand Kids who are the love of my life I see the chance of breaking this chain of dysfunction that runs rampant in my family. Their Mother will give them stability and instill in them the importance of life. Family, education, empathy for people, and respect for others and as well themselves.

Their Mother, my Daughter, takes time out of her hectic schedule to make sure they get to every extra-curricular activity available to them that will aid them in getting a quality education. As teenagers they have already achieved academic accolades in High School, as well as earning quite a few college credits along the way. I see in my daughter the things I wished my mother had shown me.

CHAPTER SIXTY SEVEN

A Synopsis

The following is a profanity-laced compilation of my life. It has allowed me to vent in a way to release the demons that have haunted me. My Book, my Prose, has allowed me to reach deep down into my soul for forgiveness of my transgressions, as well to forgive all who have ever harmed me. It is far from grammatically correct and is meant to be that way.

Synopsis of a Memoir

A textbook case espoused the psychiatrist,
unaware that I wanalyzing him.
Who was this fucking quack?
Telling me I was bound for institution life.
That these were my cards, dealt of failure,
an alcoholic Mother and Father, "So fuckin what".

Snatched off the streets and raped,
threatened with death,
by a shadow of what could be a man.

Life's worst, the molester of children.
Shouldn't happen to a six year old, right?
"Big fuckin deal"!

Again a pervert rears it's head.
This time in the name of family.
An in-law, out-law, a pig of life.
He never paid the price. "Fucking pervert"!
Got away with it all, had a fuckin ball, molested us all.
"Tough shit. Huh".

I was selling papers in bars, and bringing home the bacon.
It was more than the drunk was making.
A seven year old breadwinner.
Learning the streets, not missing a beat.
"What the fuck else did they want from me"?

Institutionalized, hurt my eyes.
Seeing a drunken father Bowery bound,
and a mother that didn't want to deal,
too busy copping a feel.
"Who gives a shit about anything"!

Removed from my family,
that was a real fuckin anomaly.
Who wouldn't feel worthless and thrown away.
Then beaten and abused,
for nothin any kid wouldn't do.
A text-book case,
"what does that jerk-off know about anything".

I was getting along, singing my orphans song.
When she made her return,
and once again I was burned.

She reeked of a mothers guilt, crying over spilt milk.
Because the scars had shown on a frail back and legs.
From the bats and straps of strangers.
She couldn't handle it and just leave shit alone.

Brought me to a strange land, isn't life grand.
To rot in isolation and failure. "Big fuckin deal".
"It's too hot in this shithouse"!

Dragged down there and left with strangers,
savages, fucking scavengers.
Had me naked in shame, and humiliating pain.
Cause I always hated my fuckin body,
big head, small dick, not slick.

An eleven year old adult, doing as I please, to appease.
Left back, left out, to drop out. It was bound to happen.
"Blow it out your ass you hypocrites"!
Textbook case, Right!

Bouncin back and forth like a fuckin rubber band.
Can't fit in, "Shit! This is a God damned sin".
Had a fight with mother.
Bitch couldn't handle the truth.
Sent me away to Dirty Mary's.
"What a plus, livin with pus."

Hells Kitchen,.How appropriate.
But for once I fit in. I had to grin.
Kids just like me, living the streets and free.
To explore, to whore, "What the fuck for!"

Runnin through the slum,
needles hangin out my arms.
Plus I drink like a fish. Ain't I a dish.
"Kill yourself Mother-Fucker", the voice kept sayin.

First love was real neat, put her on the street,
didn't miss a beat.
Jude was her name, and she knew the game
No business loving a textbook scumbag on skag.
"Love hurts"! Is what I fuckin learned.

Locked up by the state, my fate. Great!
Get him out of our sight, this child of the night.
He's a piece of shit textbook case. This is his place!

My own stupid kind, say what are you blind?
Don't be burnin behind no Darky.
What a bunch of fuckin malarkey!
They'll stick a dirty needle in their eye, to get high.
But a smoke from a black man's lips,
That'll fuckin shit'l sink ships.
Ignorant bastards!

"Fuckin Honkey! White devil!" You enslaved us for two
hundred years.
Caused my Great-grandmother tears.
"What the fuck you talking about nigger!"
Oops! "Where the fuck did that come from"?
When was that taught, this prejudiced thought?
Oh yeah! Daddy's pearls of wisdom, another gift.
History wasn't his stick-Shit!

Halfway houses my residence, my preference.
Or a lock-up no difference.
Better than the fuckin street. Can't be beat.
Three hot's and a cot, but no twat, 'What'!

Back and forth, every place they got I go.
Wouldn't you know. Must be I belong.
Been feedin into all this bull shit.

Oh! I failed to mention, the drunk is dead.
He pissed his fucking life away.
My role model, gonna miss him.

The baby maker don't wanna see me no more,
what a fuckin bore.
Just cause I robbed her house.
I was only shoutin out for attention,
"Said the quack jack."

She had her own shit, sittin in the bars, acting like a fly
Looking for a date, a mate, her fuckin fate
Killed herself and copped out.
What my life was so beautiful?
Went to her wake, it was no piece of cake.
Dressed in my usual hand me downs,
looking like the clown.

Didn't know how to act.
She didn't look real. She had no coffin appeal.
"You were too fuckin young Ma"!

Marry to get off the street, first one I meet.
Instant kid to fix everything.
This shit ain't workin.

Stick more needles in my arms.
Put em both on welfare. Take the checks too.
Rob and scheme, It's part of the dream.
Text book God damned head case in space.

Go to jail, abortion, abortion.
Keep it comin, ammo for the future.
Leave the skag, what a drag.
Drink and pill my way through the crap.
Someone gimme a fuckin map.

Slowly come around, pick my ass off the ground.
Things are lookin up, everyone says.
Who are they? What do they know.
Does my fuckin head have a window in it?

Don't they see? It's still fuckin me.
Wanna kill myself, put it all on the shelf.
It's the genetic bullshit I guess.

Get sober, dry as a hyenas ass in the Kalahari.
Don't change shit, I could really use a hit,
Except the trouble stops,
no more lock-ups, and beat- ups.

I guess it's okay, keep it in the day they say.
But there is still me, textbook asshole' "Fuck yuz all"!

Get close for what.
Headers off bridges, OD's, and death.
"Fuck this AA bullshit, I ain't gonna fit".

Scared to death my whole God damned life,
pathetic Huh!
"Fuck you if I'll show it".

The little one is grown and married now.
Where'd the time go?
How the fuck could I know, I had no one to show.
Had to go with the flow, the pace, of the textbook case.

More little ones, Grandchildren their called.
How do you handle that.
Give, give give, rid the guilt of my own spilled milk.

The spouse is doing good now. makin nice dough. but
little did I know.She hates my guts.
It ain't been right for years, too many fuckin tears.

The plan is born. Get him his house,
the dream, He'll cream.
Bring the kids along for the ride, the distraction.
He won't notice, textbook retard.

Dumb bitch left a letter layin around.
Been fuckin this guy for years, reiterating my fears.
"Dumb bitch you say"?

Thought I would die, or get fuckin high.
I wanted to fly, and say bye, Like Mommy.
But I'm still alive, I will survive, and hold face.
Cause I'm a textbook, just pleading his case.

Synopsis of a Memoir: Composed just days after learning that my mother had known about Singer and the abuses he perpetrated against her children and did nothing. I kept asking myself, what could she have been thinking? What could cause a mother to be so apathetic that she could deny her children legal recourse and possibly psychiatric counseling?

Opening up old wounds I once again returned for psychoanalysis to deal with this maelstrom I call depression I had worked hard over the years to overcome the childhood cruelties enacted against me.

I became physically injured later that year and required additional surgery. I began abusing pain medications that my physician prescribed. I struggled for years with this addiction, including being institutionalized in a psychiatric hospital on more than one occasion, until an overdose finally woke me up. I am back on depression medication and I am doing well. This has allowed me to continue and finally finish this memoir.

I owe many people thanks for their tireless help, but no one more than my daughter Kirsten, who has stood by my side throughout my struggles. She has been the rock in my life. If not for her and the love of my Grandchildren I might not have been able to endure my emotional break down. They are the main reason I continue to forge ahead. I see in my daughter a great strength of character. One I wish my own mother had. She has this tireless affection for her family. And has a ubiquitous insightfulness towards life.

So I bid farewell, ab initio, memoria, veritatem - from the beginning, within my memory, the truth.

Joseph Patrick Kenney grew up in New York City. He has one daughter and grandchildren.

Printed in the United States
By Bookmasters